The
HUMAN
RIGHTS
Handbook

The
HUMAN RIGHTS
Handbook

*A practical guide
to monitoring human rights*

Kathryn English
BA (Hons) Cardiff University
Adam Stapleton
BA (Hons) Cambridge University

Juta & Co, Ltd
1997

Published by Juta & Co, Ltd 1997

© Juta & Co, Ltd
PO Box 14373, Kenwyn 7790

Cover design by The Co-operative Workshop

First published in 1995 by The Human Rights Centre,
Essex University, United Kingdom

ISBN 0 7021 4038 4

TYPESET, PRINTED AND BOUND IN THE REPUBLIC OF SOUTH AFRICA
BY THE RUSTICA PRESS (PTY) LTD, NDABENI, WESTERN CAPE

D5073

Preface

THIS BOOK is not an original work: it draws from the scholarship and thoughts of many eminent men and women. We thank all the people we have worked with in Cambodia, Central America, England, Iraqi-Kurdistan, Malawi, Rwanda, Republic of South Africa and Turkey. Their courage and dedication were the inspiration of this book.

The authors would like to single out the following for special thanks: Daniel Alberman, Philip Astley, Kevin Bampton, John Barker, Kevin Boyle, James Hepburn, Ghanem Jawad, David Johnson, Nigel Rodley, Barbara Stapelton, Vivien Stern, and the Orange Free State Peace Secretariat for their Mediation model.

The Human Rights Handbook is only of value if it is of practical use. Any comments are welcome.
Address them, please, to the authors at:
Juta & Co, Ltd
PO Box 14373
7790 Kenwyn
Cape Town
Republic of South Africa

A journey of 10 000 miles begins with a single step

(The Venerable Maha Ghosananda)

Contents

Introduction

THE SUBJECT of 'Human Rights' raises issues that are neither simple nor clear. Human Rights are political by nature and they require political will to implement and public scrutiny to maintain. States have a duty to govern according to the rule of law and to respect the rights and freedoms of individual citizens. Citizens must also be constantly vigilant and insist on transparent and accountable government.

Whose rights come first? Whose needs are greater? Some argue that economic, social and cultural rights should come before civil and political rights; that a person's right to eat is more important than another person's freedom of expression. Others argue the other way, that civil and political rights are more important. The reality is that all rights depend on each other. Often they involve competing interests which pose problems that call for discussion and sensitivity rather than dogmatic assertion. It is helpful to keep a clear and open mind on the issues. Torture and the denial of the most basic civil and political rights and freedoms are not the result of economic under-development, but the consequence of abuses committed by individuals or groups.

This handbook is a practical guide to monitoring civil and political rights for those persons working in the field. It contains the essential human rights law texts and guidelines on working practice. It focuses on **how** to operate on the front line of human rights work in two very different contexts: how to monitor, investigate and report human rights violations in a repressive state (chapter 4); and how to monitor human rights and foster awareness in the rapidly changing climate of a State emerging into multiparty democracy (chapter 5).

The handbook sets out the groups in society which can assist human rights monitoring, and how to set up a human rights network including these groups (chapter 3). It introduces the international reporting and complaints procedures and how to use them (chapter 6).

The handbook is a guide to international *law* on human rights. As far as possible, the use of legal jargon is avoided. Before applying any law, it is useful first to know what that law means and how far it extends. Certain questions are matters of personal opinion; others are questions of law. For example, whether or not to legalize the death penalty is open to public debate; whether or not to torture someone is not – it is against the law.

Chapter 1 starts with a basic introduction to human rights and sets out some of the questions constantly asked of persons working in the field. It goes on to describe the United Nations and how it functions, before turning to basic terms and principles of international law.

In chapter 2, an introduction to the International Bill of Rights is followed by a detailed section on the International Covenant on Civil and Political Rights (ICCPR). This section is made up of Articles 1–27 of the Covenant. Each article sets out:

- the text of the article
- what it means in ordinary language
- a commentary indicating what the article means in practice and what other human rights instruments affect it, and
- questions and answers to deal with particular difficulties.

The commentary states the law as it now stands. The additional human rights texts provide greater clarity. The examples used are taken mainly from decided cases.

The Appendix contains the basic texts. The importance of knowing these texts cannot be over-emphasized. The monitor must be very sure of his/her ground. The Appendix also contains a list of the conventions each state has signed or ratified.

Vienna: The World Conference on Human Rights

In June 1993, representatives from 171 states met in Vienna, Austria, for a World Conference on Human Rights. The motto of the conference was:

Human rights: Know them, demand them, defend them.

At the end of the conference, the states' representatives agreed the Vienna Declaration and a Programme of Action. The Vienna Declaration appears throughout the Handbook (particularly Chapter 2) as the most recent reminder to states of the obligations they have voluntarily undertaken to protect the individual rights of their citizens. Even if a state has not signed or ratified any of the human rights conventions or covenants, it is at the very least *morally* bound by the Declaration signed in Vienna.

Human Rights Monitors

In repressive states, human rights work is dangerous. The state that conducts its affairs in secret does not take kindly to people trying to discover and publicize the true picture of what is really going on. Human rights monitors should always be discreet, not only for reasons of their own security, but also, more importantly, for the security of the witnesses and victims with whom they meet and talk.

The local human rights monitor working alone is exposed and without protection. Insistence is placed throughout the Handbook on setting up channels of communication – of *linking up* with other individuals, professional groups and organizations to establish a network (ch 3 and Appendix). In this way, information on the human rights situation can be communicated and the security of the monitor better safeguarded.

The work is often slow-moving: following up cases or incidents may appear to be time-consuming; evidence can be frustrating to gather; people are mistrustful and may be hostile. Patience and perseverance are essential elements in human rights work.

In a transitional state, the authorities want change but many 'in the system' may be stuck in their old ways. Often the policeman who beats up his prisoner as a matter of habit does so not because he is a brute, but because he does not know any other way; this was the way he was taught to treat prisoners. Building a culture of human rights helps to restore human dignity where it has been stripped and good sense where it has been turned upside-down. The past needs to be addressed to break the cycle of violence: those who abused the rights of others should be confronted with their actions in the interests of justice and reconciliation.

Human rights groups do not set themselves *against* authority. Rather, they challenge the authority to account publicly for its use or abuse of power. Public scrutiny is a good thing: it builds public confidence while reducing tension. A public enquiry into the police, for example, may expose unacceptable conduct: it can also draw public attention to the low levels of pay, inadequate resources and poor working conditions that a policeman is expected to put up with.

The International Bill of Rights was drawn up by hard-nosed pragmatists, not starry-eyed dreamers. It is based on enlightened self-interest, not vague altruism. Its principal aim is the avoidance of conflict by removing discrimination and inequality. Some governments are beginning to realize the benefits that flow in the longer term from practising this 'enlightened' form of self-interest. They begin to realize the benefits of peace. Repression is not just wrong – it is bad for business.

Kathryn English
Adam Stapleton
3 Temple Gardens
Temple
London

July 1996

Acronyms

UDHR	Universal Declaration of Human Rights
ICCPR	International Covenant on Civil and Political Rights
ICESCR	International Covenant on Economic, Social and Cultural Rights
OP	Optional Protocol
UNGA	United Nations General Assembly
UNSC	United Nations Security Council
ECOSOC	Economic and Social Council
CHR	Commission on Human Rights
ICJ	International Court of Justice
ILO	International Labour Organisation
ILO 169	ILO Convention no. 169
HRC	Human Rights Committee
CRD	International Convention on the Elimination of All Forms of Racial Discrimination
CT	Convention against Torture and Other Cruel and Inhuman or Degrading Treatment or Punishment
UNHCR	United Nations High Commissioner for Refugees
CR	Convention Relating to the Status of Refugees
CS	Convention Relating to the Status of Stateless Persons
NGO	Non-governmental organisation
UNHCHR	United Nations High Commissioner for Human Rights
OAU	Organisation of African Unity
OAS	Organisation of American States
CRC	Convention on the Rights of the Child
GC	Convention on the Prevention and Punishment of the Crime of Genocide
WMA	World Medical Association
LEO	Law Enforcement Officer
ICRC	International Committee of the Red Cross
IDP	Internally Displaced Person
SG	United Nations Secretary-General
APC	Association for Progressive Communication

What are human rights?

A RIGHT IS AN entitlement you own. It is a claim by you against another to the extent that by exercising your right, you do not prevent someone else from exercising theirs.

It has been said that your right to swing your arm ends where the other person's nose begins. It has also been said that one person's right is another person's duty.

A right is determined by human needs that make life fulfilling and are essential for keeping us alive – like health, it is most valued when it is lost.

A human right is an entitlement or legal claim you have – by virtue of being human – against the State.

You say a human right is a legal claim. Does that mean it is a part of law? Yes.

Which law? The international law of human rights, which is stated in the International Bill of Human Rights, is the primary source. Human rights are also protected in the constitutions and national laws of many states around the world. In addition, human rights are protected by the many Treaties, or Agreements, that governments have signed which oblige them to ensure these rights and freedoms.

Is a 'freedom' the same as a 'right'? Yes, in law they are the same. Your freedom from torture is your right not to be tortured.

Why are these laws universally recognized to be so important? The reasons are best stated in the preamble to the Universal Declaration which recognizes that

> *the inherent dignity and . . . equal and inalienable rights of all members of the human family is the foundation of freedom, justice and peace in the world and that disregard and contempt for human rights resulted in barbarous acts.*

The Preamble goes on to warn that

> . . . it is essential if man is not to be compelled to have recourse, as a last resort, to rebellion against tyranny and oppression, that human rights should be protected by the rule of law . . .

How old is this area of law?   The principles have been in existence for ages, but it was not until the end of World War II that the member states of the newly established United Nations agreed on the Universal Declaration of Human Rights and set down for the first time a list of human rights and fundamental freedoms. These were considered by the community of nations to be minimum standards by which governments should treat their citizens.

Who has these rights?   You do, I do, everyone has them: they belong to every human being. They are *universal*: male and female, rich and poor, black and white, religious and non-religious. They belong to everyone *equally*.

But what about someone who has done something terrible. Surely this person does not deserve to have any rights when s/he has shown no regard for the rights of others?   Everyone is born with the same human rights. They cannot be taken away, lost or surrendered whatever a person does or whoever that person is: they are *inalienable*. The terrible person you talk of is, before the law, just a human being. S/he is entitled to a fair trial where s/he is presumed innocent until proved guilty; if convicted, s/he is entitled to appeal and anyway to be detained in humane conditions. S/he has these rights and they must be respected.

Respect: what do you mean?   To respect the rights of another person is to value that person's humanity rather than personality. Respecting human rights involves

> a conscious effort to find our common essence beyond our apparent divisions, our temporary differences, our ideological and cultural barriers.
> (Boutros Boutros-Ghali, UN Secretary-General, in opening the World Conference on Human Rights, 1993)

Even someone who has shown no humanity to others: who has tortured, raped and murdered people? Why should I respect that person's rights?   Because s/he is still a human being. Everyone has the right to be presumed innocent until proved guilty, otherwise how do we know that s/he committed these serious crimes? Everyone has the right to a fair and public hearing before an independent and impartial tribunal and to be sentenced according to law if found guilty. This is what is meant by the 'rule of law'.

This is not enough for me: I want an eye for an eye.   Of course criminals should be brought to justice. However, the law is not about passion or emotion. It is about establishing what happened and attempting to ascertain the truth. This involves listening to each side and giving the person a chance to explain his/her actions. This can take time because the evidence is not available or the political situation does not permit it. Justice can be slow in coming.

What of these other words you use – equality, for example?

> *Equality may perhaps be a right, but no power on earth can ever turn it into a fact.* (Balzac)

Each of us is different, unique. We have various talents. You may run quicker than I; I may jump higher than you. How then can we say we are equal? We cannot.

> *Human rights teach us in a direct, straightforward manner that we are at the same time identical and different.* (Boutros Boutros-Ghali)

Human Rights law is not about establishing equality, but protecting individuals from discrimination. You should not be discriminated against simply because of who you are or what you believe in. The law applies equally to rich and poor. The migrant worker is entitled to equal pay for equal work alongside the national of the country in which s/he works. Women have the same rights as men.

But a woman's place is in the home caring for her family! In many cultures this is the traditional role of women. And if a woman wishes to be in the home that is her right. It is also her right to work outside the home if she wishes and receive equal pay for her work. It is the duty of the state to make this opportunity available.

When you talk of the duty of the state, I thought states could do what they wanted inside their own country and tell other states to mind their own business and not interfere in the affairs of others? This is what is called 'national sovereignty', which calls on states to respect each others' borders and political independence. However, there is a difference between meddling in the internal affairs of others and taking steps aimed at getting governments to observe standards of conduct to which they have committed themselves.

So when you speak of a state's duties to the individual, these are duties that the state can agree to or reject? First, states agree to certain Treaties, Covenants and Conventions (they all amount to the same thing) which set standards for the treatment by the state of its citizens and calls them to account for the efforts they make to implement these standards and answer allegations that may arise. Second, even if they do not agree to these treaties, as member states of the United Nations, they pledge under the United Nations Charter to *promote respect for, and observance of,* human rights. Third, the International Bill of Human Rights and the other human rights conventions make up a body called international human rights law. How a government treats its citizens is now the legitimate concern of the international community.

Here is what the Secretary General of the UN, Boutros Boutros-Ghali, said on opening the World Conference on Human Rights in Vienna in 1993,

It is the state that the international community should principally entrust with ensuring the protection of individuals. However, the issue of international action must be raised when states prove unworthy of this task . . . and when – far from being protectors of individuals – they become tormentors. . . . In these circumstances, the international community must take over from the states that fail to fulfil their obligations.

He closes this section of his speech by asking

. . . whether a state has the right to expect absolute respect from the international community when it is tarnishing the noble concept of sovereignty by openly putting that concept to a use that is rejected by the conscience of the world and by the law. Where sovereignty becomes the ultimate argument put forward by authoritarian regimes to support their undermining of the rights and freedoms of men, women and children, such sovereignty – and I state this as a sober truth – is already condemned by history.

So why does the international community not stop the atrocities going on all around us? The 'international community' is made up of states which have their own interests abroad and concerns at home. Generally, they do not care to entangle themselves in the affairs of other states. However, there is increasing pressure by the international community on these states to improve their human rights records. The problem is that the means are not yet available to stop other states abusing their citizens. International law has no police force, no army and no courts to enforce it.

What is the difference between a human rights violation and a criminal offence? Both involve wrongdoing. A criminal act is an act or acts done by one or more persons that is harmful to society and has been forbidden by the domestic law of the country. A human rights violation is committed by the state through its agents (the police, armed forces and anyone acting with the authority of the state) against the individual.

When an individual commits a crime, he is arrested, charged and tried in a court of law. Who tries the state, or its agents, for human rights violations? The courts.

What, a judge try the President? Of course. This is why it is important for power in the state to be divided up: the government (executive) should be separate from the parliament (legislature) which, in turn, should be separate from the courts (judiciary). So that power is not concentrated in any one person or body and everyone is subject to the law. This is a cornerstone of the democratic process.

But where this separation of powers does not exist, who tries the state? At present, there is no means of enforcing international law through a legal process. The United Nations can impose, through the General Assembly, economic sanctions on a country, but short of armed intervention in certain circumstances we shall go into later (see: p 55), there is not a great deal that can be done.

So what's the point? I'm told I have these rights but what use are they if I cannot

enforce them – if my government can abuse them with impunity? Slowly but surely governments are becoming aware of the importance of a good human rights record. A poor human rights record is highly embarrassing to governments. It is bad for the image of the country; it is bad for business. They are able to get away with it partly because people do not know what their rights are *in law*. For this reason, the motto of the World Conference in Vienna was:

Human rights: Know them, demand them, defend them.

Educating people, informing them and the outside world of what is happening makes it difficult for the state to issue credible denials or claim ignorance and may make the international community take action.

It all sounds very political. I'm not politically concerned. As someone said: *when I give food to the poor, I am called a Saint; but when I call on the government to feed its people, I am accused of seeking to subvert the authority of the state.*

    The issue of 'Human Rights' is a political issue. It concerns the relationship between the state and the individual. The International Covenant discussed in this book is called the International Covenant on Civil and Political Rights. But it is also a legal issue. Your right to life, liberty and security is your legal right not to be arbitrarily arrested, detained or 'disappeared' and killed. When you demand the government respect this or any other right, your legal right becomes a political demand.

But what of groups or individuals who use their 'rights' to bring down an elected government only to replace it with a dictatorship? Any group engaged in any activity aimed at the destruction of any of the rights and freedoms contained in the ICCPR is acting contrary to the purposes and principles of the International Bill of Human Rights and cannot use that treaty as a shield for activities that undermine the very rights it was set up to protect (see Art 5 on p 24).

But what can a state do when it is threatened from within? Must it continue to allow people freedom of expression and so on? It is at these moments that the rights of the individual are most threatened. Under the ICCPR, a state can declare a state of emergency and suspend some obligations to the extent strictly required by the demands of the situation (see: Article 4 p 22). Certain obligations can never be suspended under any circumstances. Freedom from torture, for example, is one of them.

Surely if a terrorist has planted a bomb and he is caught and refuses to disclose the location, it would be justified for the police to use torture to force 'the truth' out of him? Torture, cruel or inhuman treatment or punishment is never justified or defensible as a matter of law. Nor is it a defence to say: 'I was ordered to.'

But can't governments argue that they are forced to respond with extreme measures to extremist groups? Any emergency measures must be reflected in changes in the national law. They must contain proper safeguards to protect those caught up in the 'extremism' but who play no active part in it. These emergency measures must comply with the standards set by international law.

Some of the worst violations of human rights have been conducted in the name of some inspiring idea, like 'the State'; 'Patriotism'; 'the People'; 'the Masses'; 'the Economy' or 'the One True Faith', which have all been used, and still are used, as a disguise or veil to conceal severe state repression.

What about the atrocities committed by armed opposition groups – aren't they human rights violations too? They are in the minds of the victims and their relatives, understandably. However, human rights law is concerned with the conduct of the *state* towards the *individual*. The law is there to regulate the state in its use of power and so protect the individual from abuse. The atrocities committed against individuals by armed opposition groups in the name of a cause or political goal also violate the basic standards by which human beings live. In moral terms there is little to distinguish them; but in legal terms, they are quite separate.

Which of all these rights come first? None of them. They are all interrelated and *indivisible*. The pledge all Member States of the United Nations take to advance human rights is a pledge to promote *all* human rights, as the General Assembly has observed:

> promotion and protection of one category of rights should never exempt or excuse states from the promotion and protection of another.

But aren't 'human rights' something imposed on the rest of the world by the West? Human rights are not a western invention, nor do they encompass merely western values. They are to be found in each culture and in each of the world's great religions. Emphasis may vary from region to region and from country to country.

You say this book is only dealing with civil and political rights, rather than economic, social and cultural rights. What if I am hungry, my child needs a hospital and my husband is unemployed – am I not entitled to demand that the state recognize these rights take precedence over a student's right to voice his/her opinion about the government? It is sometimes the case that rights appear to conflict or compete with each other. It is argued by some, for example, that certain countries cannot 'afford' human rights; that they have to be restricted in the interest of boosting the economy. This is an argument for the reintroduction of slavery and not a justification for failing to implement basic international standards. The assertion that your right should take precedence over mine is unlikely to find favour with me if it is put in the form of a demand. All rights pose problems that call for discussion and thought as to their application in daily life.

What's the point? If I protest or raise my head to speak out at best I'll be ignored and at worst I'll be arrested or 'disappeared'.

> The will of the people shall be the basis of the authority of government.
>
> (UDHR 21)

Where a government ignores the will of the people and goes further and seeks to suppress the will of the people, it becomes a tyranny. As such, it loses the legitimacy by which it pretends to govern.

Yes, but who am I to challenge a government?

> *Man dies in all who keep silent in the face of tyranny.* *(Wole Soyinka)*

Yes, but why me?
> First they came for the Jews
> and I did not speak out –
> because I was not a Jew.
> Then they came for the communists
> and I did not speak out –
> because I was not a Communist.
> Then they came for the trade-unionists
> and I did not speak out –
> because I was not a trade-unionist.
> Then they came for me –
> and there was no one left to speak out for me.

> *(Pastor Martin Niemoller)*

The United Nations

What is the United Nations – how does it work? The UN was founded in 1945 at the end of World War II. It was set up to help stabilize international relations and give peace a more secure foundation. The document that created the UN is the Charter of the United Nations. It was written by the representatives of 50 nations. The Charter sets out the aims and purposes of the UN, its powers and structure. Among its purposes, Article 1(3) includes: '. . . *promoting and encouraging respect for human rights and for fundamental freedoms for all without distinction as to race, sex, language or religion'.*

Article 56 contains a pledge that binds all member states to take *joint and separate action* to achieve the purposes set forth in Article 55 *(c)*, namely

> *universal respect for, and observance of, human rights and fundamental freedoms for all without distinction . . .*

Is the Charter a treaty? Yes, under international law, it has the status of a binding multilateral treaty.

How does this affect the human rights obligations of states? They have a treaty obligation to respect and observe the human rights and fundamental freedoms catalogued in the UDHR. The pledge requires states to refrain from committing gross violations or systematic transgressions. In the *Vienna Declaration* signed in June 1993 at the end of the World Conference on Human Rights by over 170 member states, the point was made emphatically that:

> *Human rights and fundamental freedoms are the birthright of all human beings; their protection and promotion is the first responsibility of government* (Art 1)

> *Respect for human rights and fundamental freedoms without distinction of any kind is a fundamental rule of international law* (Art 15)

At the end of 1995, the UN had 185 members, nearly every State in the world.

The UN General Assembly (UNGA) The General Assembly is made up of representatives of all the member states. Each has one vote. It reaches decisions on important questions concerning, for example, international peace and security. One of its functions is to bring about the realization of human rights and fundamental freedoms for all without distinction.

Since the adoption of the UDHR in 1948, the UNGA has adopted a number of *Declarations* and *Conventions* on human rights. The UNGA has also passed many decisions, or *Resolutions*. These Resolutions reflect world opinion on major international issues.

Most items relating to human rights are referred to the Third Committee (see chapter 6 at page 142).

The UNGA meets each year between the end of September and the middle of December. It may also meet in special or emergency session at the request of the Security Council, or of a majority of the members of the UN.

The UN Security Council (UNSC) The Security Council has the primary responsibility under the Charter for maintaining international peace and security. It consists of 15 members. Five are permanent (China, France, the Russian Federation, the United Kingdom and the United States of America) and ten are elected by the UNGA for two-year terms.

Each member has one vote. Decisions require a majority of nine and the agreement of *all* five permanent members. This is known as the 'Great Power unanimity', or *veto* power.

Under the Charter, the members of the UNGA agree to accept and carry out the decisions of the Security Council.

ECOSOC The Economic and Social Council (ECOSOC) co-ordinates the economic and social work of the UN. Fifty-six members serve for three years to promote, among other things, respect for and observance of human rights and fundamental freedoms for all.

It holds two sessions a year in New York and Geneva. Other commissions have been established under the Council to assist it in its work. The Commission on Human Rights is one of these. It may consult non-governmental organizations (NGOs) to benefit from their expertise and experience.

Commission on Human Rights (CHR) The CHR is the main political body in the UN dealing with human rights issues. Its mandate, or job, is to deal with *any matter* relating to human rights.

It sets international standards by drafting treaties and preparing studies. It also undertakes special tasks assigned to it by the UNGA or ECOSOC including the investigation of human rights violations by establishing procedures, or 'mechanisms', to respond to them. To assist the CHR in its work, it has set up the Sub-Commission on Prevention of Discrimination and Protection of Minorities.

The Sub-Commission is made up of 26 independent experts elected by the CHR on the basis of regional distribution. Aside from its tasks of preventing discrimination and protecting minorities, it carries out any other functions assigned to it by the CHR. It meets for four weeks each year after pre-sessional working groups of 1–2 weeks duration. Representatives of NGOs and government observers can attend.

The Sub-Commission is notable for its independence and openness to NGOs. The CHR has created other bodies to assist it in the promotion and protection of human rights. There are groups and individuals who study and report on specific *countries*. There are also groups and individual experts who study and report on *types* of human rights abuse, such as torture and arbitrary execution (see ch 6 at p 123).

International Court of Justice (ICJ) The ICJ is the principal judicial organ of the UN. Its jurisdiction covers all questions which States may refer to it, and all matters provided for in the Charter, or treaties and conventions in force. Therefore, any dispute relating to the application, fulfilment or interpretation of a Convention can be referred to the ICJ. For example, under the Genocide Convention (see p 64), any dispute shall be submitted to the International Court of Justice at the request of any of the parties to the dispute.

The ICJ has 15 judges elected by the UNGA and UNSC. They are chosen on the basis of their qualifications, not on the basis of nationality. No two judges can be nationals of the same state. The ICJ sits in The Hague in The Netherlands.

UN Secretariat The Secretariat carries out the day-to-day administration of the organization. The head is the Secretary-General (presently, Mr Boutros Boutros-Ghali) who is appointed by the UNGA on the recommendation of the UNSC for a term of five years.

The High Commissioner for Human Rights In December 1993 the UNGA created the post of High Commissioner for Human Rights following a recommendation in the Vienna Declaration. In February 1994, Mr Jose Ayala Lasso was appointed. The High Commissioner's job is wide in scope and is to promote and protect all human rights throughout the world. The High Commissioner is also head of the Centre for Human Rights.

Centre for Human Rights   The Centre is the part of the Secretariat that provides services to UN bodies concerned with human rights, including: the UNGA and its Third Committee, ECOSOC, CHR, the Sub-Commission on Prevention of Discrimination and Protection of Minorities, Working Groups established to elaborate international standards on new subjects and the Committees set up under the various human rights Conventions. It carries out research and studies on human rights at the request of these bodies and follows up and prepares reports on the implementation of human rights. In addition, it provides advisory services and technical assistance, publishes and distributes information and material on human rights.

The International Labour Organization (ILO)   The ILO was established in 1919. In 1945 it became a part of the UN system. It is composed of governments, employers and workers. At the annual International Labour Conference, the ILO adopts Conventions and Recommendations dealing with international labour standards and a number of rights and freedoms, from freedom of association to the rights of indigenous and tribal peoples. It makes recommendations which provide guidelines for the law-makers and governments on how to implement the Conventions.

International law

International law is made up of custom and treaty law.

A Treaty is the same thing as a Convention or Covenant. It is a promise or agreement negotiated by countries amongst themselves – or via a body like the United Nations – and then adopted. When a state wishes to become a *party* to a Treaty, Convention or Covenant, it *signs* the document.

A state is not bound by the Treaty, however, until it has *ratified* it. The act of ratification legally binds the state under the terms of the Covenant, Convention or Treaty: it becomes a *state party* to the document. In the old days, ambassadors negotiated treaties far from home. They signed a treaty on behalf of their ruler and then returned with the text. The ruler would then agree it or not. This agreement would then be communicated to the other party and, at that moment, the treaty would be ratified.

Often, the period between signature and ratification amounts to a number of years; sometimes ratification does not follow from signature at all.

Why?   Some states are required by their own constitutional law to go through a certain process if an international treaty is to become domestic, or national, law. It has to be approved by parliament or congress, and this takes time. Others need to make adjustments to their own laws to meet their obligations under the new treaty and, again, this can take time. A treaty does not become law until it has been ratified. Some states do not wish to be bound by the terms of a treaty although they support its general aims, so they do not proceed to ratification.

A human rights Convention or Covenant takes up a lot of time and effort before it comes into effect. A simpler approach, called a *Declaration*, may be used, sometimes as a prelude to the drafting of a Convention. A Declaration is not a treaty: it is not signed or ratified. In theory, therefore, it is not binding in international law. It is a statement of principles. It sets out standards by which states ought to govern. *The Universal Declaration of Human Rights* (UDHR), however, has such moral weight and has been cited in so many countries' constitutions and legal cases that it is now widely agreed to be part of international customary law and so is probably binding on all states.

What is international customary law?   Customary law is law that has grown out of customs or practice. It is not written down. It is general practice that, through common use, has become accepted as law. International customary law has developed in much the same way.

The UDHR lists a number of provisions that most states would agree reflect general principles common to the major legal systems.

When does a Treaty come into force?   This is usually provided for in the treaty itself. The international human rights law treaties all came into force when ratified by the number of states specified in the treaty.

A state that wishes to become a party to a treaty after it has come into force *accedes* to it. Accession and ratification amount to the same thing. The ICCPR and ICESCR were adopted by the General Assembly in 1966. They did not come into force until 1976, with the ratification of the 35th state party.

Are treaties set in stone, or can they be amended?   Treaties can be amended like any legal document. Amendments and additions are contained in *Protocols*. The First Optional Protocol to the ICCPR additionally allows for the *individual right of petition*. Any party to the ICCPR may ratify this instrument as well.

A number of treaties have Protocols. Some have been added years after the treaty was originally drawn up to fill in gaps. Each protocol requires a separate ratification by each state.

What if a state wants to become a party to a treaty but dislikes one of its provisions?   Then it can enter a *reservation* to the treaty. In this way, a state shows that it does not wish to be bound by some specified provision. If a state enters a reservation under the ICCPR, the reservation is scrutinized to decide whether or not it is against the object and purpose of the Covenant.

> *The World Conference on Human Rights encourages states to consider*
> - *limiting the extent of any reservations they lodge to human rights instruments,*
> - *formulating any reservations as precisely and narrowly as possible,*
> - *ensuring that none is incompatible with the object and purpose of the relevant treaty, and*
> - *regularly reviewing any reservations with a view to withdrawing them.*
> *(Vienna Declaration, Art 5)*

The Human Rights Committee states in a General Comment (No 24) that it is desirable in principle that states accept the full range of obligations, because *the human rights norms are the legal expression of the essential rights that every person is entitled to as a human being.*

It goes on to state what rights may not be made the subject of reservations, namely those that represent international customary law.

Is there ever an occasion when a state party to the ICCPR can suspend its obligations under the Covenant – say, in time of civil war? Yes, in certain exceptional circumstances, a state can *derogate* from its obligations.

Under the ICCPR, when a 'public emergency which threatens the life of the nation' occurs, then the state party can suspend (or derogate from) certain obligations under the treaty (see Art 4 ICCPR at p 22).

Can the state limit or restrict human rights in any other way? Only in very limited circumstances. The UDHR allows only for those limitations that are

> *determined by law solely for the purpose of securing due recognition and respect for the rights and freedoms of others and of meeting the just requirements of morality, public order and the general welfare in a democratic society.*   *(Article 29)*

Boundaries must be set with reference to the rights and freedoms of others (see Art 19 at p 53).

Can a state party to the ICCPR change its mind and no longer consider itself bound by a covenant ratified by a former regime? Treaties usually do allow for *denunciation*, ie a formal announcement by a state party that it intends to withdraw from the treaty. They allow, for example, a state party to denounce a treaty 'at any time' by written notification to the Secretary-General. The denunciation will take effect shortly thereafter.

However, neither the ICCPR nor the ICESCR provide for denunciation.

Chapter 2

The International Bill of Rights

The Universal Declaration of Human Rights (UDHR)

THE UDHR WAS completed in 1948 by the members of the newly formed United Nations following on the end of World War II. Its aim was to set basic minimum international standards for the protection of the rights and freedoms of the individual. Its provisions are considered so fundamental and have been quoted so often in domestic and international courts and by governments all around the world, that it is widely regarded as forming part of international customary law.

The International Covenants:
- on Economic, Cultural and Social Rights: (ICESCR);
- on Civil and Political Rights: (ICCPR);
- the Optional Protocol to the ICCPR (OP).

These covenants came into force in 1976 and, together with the UDHR, they form the International Bill of Human Rights (see Appendix 2, 3, 4, 5).

The two covenants make the standards set out in the UDHR more legally specific: the language used is more formal and legalistic. A state signals its intention of being bound by their provisions when it signs one or both of them and is bound once it ratifies or accedes to the Covenants (see above at p 10). While there is overlap between the two Covenants, in the main the ICCPR deals with civil and political rights and freedoms; and the ICESCR with economic, social and cultural rights and freedoms.

The rights contained in the ICCPR must be put into force immediately after it has been ratified (*All persons SHALL be equal before the law, etc*).

The rights contained in the ICESCR can come into force more gradually (it talks of rights that are recognized and commits states parties *to take steps* towards their realization). This is because the international community recognized the varying stages of development in countries and accepted that while all should aspire to social and economic development, it would be a gradual rather than instant process.

The Optional Protocol to the ICCPR is a separate treaty and, therefore, requires separate ratification. It creates a complaint procedure for individual victims of violations.

The complaint is heard by the Human Rights Committee created by the ICCPR. Its powers and duties are set out in Articles 28–45 ICCPR (see ch 6 at page 136). The Human Rights Committee issues 'General Comments' to the UN General Assembly, ECOSOC and states parties in order to provide clarification and interpretation of the ICCPR and to assist states in its implementation. The Committee has issued General Comments on public emergencies, the right to life, torture, freedom of expression, detainees and propaganda for war, among others. These General Comments do not have the force of law, but carry enormous weight and authority.

The two Covenants apply the standards of the UDHR to create the minimum safeguards which the state party must adopt to ensure the protection of the rights and freedoms they contain. In some instances, the ICCPR goes into considerable detail as in Article 14, setting out clearly the steps that must be taken when a person is deprived of his/her liberty (see Art 14 at p 44).

Some rights and freedoms are at greater risk of abuse or infringement than others. As a result of pressure from governments and independent organizations, the UN General Assembly has proclaimed Declarations and adopted Conventions on particular rights and freedoms.

A number of treaties and Conventions have grown up to form a substantial legal framework for the world-wide protection and promotion of human rights. Freedom from torture, for example, is protected by Art 7 ICCPR and a separate international Convention (see Art 7 at p 31).

States are only bound in law by those treaties or conventions they have acceded to or ratified.

When you talk of a state being 'bound in law' what law do you mean? It depends. When a state ratifies or accedes to an international treaty, it is under an obligation to translate the provisions of that treaty or convention into its own national or domestic legislation. In the constitutions of some countries, it is an automatic process; in others, it is more complicated. Hence, the vague phrase 'bound in law' could mean national law or international law.

So what kind of law do you refer to when you talk of 'the rule of law'? The rule of law is a term that refers to a state in which people are governed according to laws that are just and fair and which apply to all people equally – and not a government decree disguised as 'law'.

The rule of law is not a western idea, nor is it linked up with any economic or social system. . . . As soon as you accept that man is governed by law and not by whims of men, it is the rule of law.
                    (Adetokunbo A Ademola, former Chief Justice of Nigeria)

How can you tell if the rule of law operates in any country? By comparing national laws with international laws, codes and guidelines. If governments pass laws that contravene the UDHR and ICCPR, whatever their justification, they are acting outside internationally recognized standards of conduct. What a government argues is 'lawful' just because it enacts legislation may turn out to be arbitrary or unlawful interference when compared with international standards.

If I think there is no rule of law operating in my country, can I go straight to an international court? No, domestic remedies must always first be exhausted. International solutions can only be sought as a last resort (see p 127). Test cases brought before the national courts makes the state argue its case. The determination of an issue by the courts strengthens the legal institutions and legitimizes (or not) the action of the state.

But what about those countries that have not signed or ratified those covenants? How can they be bound by something they have not signed? First, all members of the UN have taken a pledge to

promote universal respect for, and observance of, human rights and fundamental freedoms for all without distinction . . .
                                    (UN Charter, Art 56.)

Second, there is *customary international law* which does not require a state to sign or ratify anything. It recognizes the principles in the UDHR as representing international legal standards. It does not matter that the state concerned has not ratified the ICCPR or ICESCR. Customary international law also recognizes, for example, that slavery and genocide are crimes under international law – whether or not a state has ratified the Genocide or Slavery Conventions.

The Human Rights Committee has included the following acts practised, encouraged or condoned by a state to be breaches of international customary law:

- slavery
- torture
- arbitrary deprivation of life
- arbitrary arrest and detention
- denial of freedom of thought, conscience and religion
- presuming a person guilty until he proves his innocence
- executing pregnant women and children
- permitting the advocacy of national, racial or religious hatred
- denial of persons of marriageable age the right to marry
- denying minorities the right to enjoy their own culture, profess their own religion, or to use their own language. (*General Comment No 24*)

Since these provisions of the ICCPR represent international customary law, a state party cannot enter a reservation against any of them.

INTERNATIONAL COVENANT ON CIVIL AND POLITICAL RIGHTS

Article 1

(1) *All peoples have the right of self-determination. By virtue of that right they freely determine their political status and freely pursue their economic, social and cultural development.*

(2) *All peoples may, for their own ends, freely dispose of their natural wealth and resources without prejudice to any obligations arising out of economic co-operation, based upon the principle of mutual benefit, and international law. In no case may a people be deprived of its own means of subsistence.*

(3) *The states parties to the present Covenant, including those having responsibility for the administration of Non-Self-Governing and Trust Territories shall promote the realization of the right of self-determination, and shall respect that right, in conformity with the provisions of the Charter of the United Nations.*

- **All peoples have the right to decide their own political future.**
- **All peoples have the right to use their own natural wealth as they see fit.**

Commentary

'Self-determination' is a simple enough idea to grasp in everyday language. Unfortunately, it is not so simple in the sense it is meant here. The purpose of the right was to bring *a speedy end to colonialism* and to promote the democratic process by *having regard to the freely expressed will of the peoples concerned.* 'Peoples' is a word that has yet to find a legal definition. It seems that 'Peoples' refers to the majority rather than any ethnic group or other minority.

'Self-determination' means self-government rather than independence. The ICCPR expressly forbids any interpretation that would *dismember or impair, totally or in part, the territorial integrity or political unity of sovereign states.* The fear was that the world would divide up into many mini-states with evil consequences for global peace and the world economy.

This prohibition allows for three exceptions where people are struggling:
- against colonial rule; or
- against a racist regime; or
- against domination by an alien (foreign) power.

A group that enjoys the support of the majority of the people and comes within one of these three categories may seek and obtain international recognition as a Liberation Movement. Certain rights and duties flow from such recognition:

- States falling into one of the three categories of colonial, racist or alien domination must allow the free exercise of self-determination.
- The liberation movement is (implicitly) entitled to use armed force to secure self-determination.
- Other states are bound to assist the liberation movement (through peaceful means) and desist from providing assistance to the oppressing state.

If self-determination is denied the issue can be brought before the United Nations for enforcement through peaceful sanctions.

I am confused. Is this the case: that an armed struggle is legitimate when it is a 'liberation movement' which, in turn, must represent a struggle against (a) **colonial,** *(b)* **alien, or** *(c)* **racist domination?** Yes, it is legitimate in the eyes of the international community and therefore capable of recognition.

Then what about the armed struggle waged against an oppressive, authoritarian regime. Is that not also a liberation struggle? Not in the present legal sense, no. It may change. This subject is being intensely debated all over the world. The type of armed struggle referred to here is termed 'insurgency', or armed opposition, and while it may obtain legitimacy in the eyes of the international community through the passage of time and the occupation of territory, it does not acquire the status of a 'liberation movement'.

Right freely to dispose of national wealth This right is defined in more detail in the Charter of Economic Rights and Duties of States and includes the right of each state to:
- regulate foreign investment;
- take measures to ensure that transnational corporations comply with its laws and comply with its economic and social policies;
- expropriate or nationalize foreign property subject to providing adequate compensation.

Article 2

(1) Each state party to the present Covenant undertakes to respect and to ensure to all individuals within its territory and subject to its jurisdiction the rights recognized in the present Covenant, without distinction of any kind, such as race, colour, sex, language, religion, political or other opinion, national or social origin, property, birth or other status.

(2) Where not already provided for by existing legislative or other measures, each state party to the present Covenant undertakes to take the necessary steps, in accordance with its constitutional processes and with the provisions of the present Covenant, to adopt such legislative or other measures as may be necessary to give effect to the rights recognized in the present Covenant.

(3) Each state party to the present Covenant undertakes:

    (a) To ensure that any person whose rights or freedoms as herein recognized

are violated shall have an effective remedy, notwithstanding that the violation has been committed by persons acting in an official capacity;

(b) To ensure that any person claiming such a remedy shall have his right thereto determined by competent judicial, administrative or legislative authorities, or by any other competent authority provided for by the legal system of the state, and to develop the possibilities of judicial remedy;

(c) To ensure that the competent authorities shall enforce such remedies when granted.

- **Governments shall respect and ensure individual rights without distinction of any kind . . .**
- **by passing laws that give effect to these rights, and**
- **by providing any person whose rights have been violated with an enforceable remedy at law.**

Commentary

The rights and freedoms set out in the UDHR and ICCPR are universal: whether a person is coloured purple, speaks a strange language, professes an odd political doctrine and practices a peculiar religion or is disabled in any way s/he is entitled to these rights.

'Discrimination' is implied in any act which denies equality of treatment to certain individuals because they belong to particular groups.

Article 2 obliges a state party to:
- compare its own national laws with the ICCPR;
- pass whatever laws may be necessary to protect, or give effect to, any of the rights contained in the Covenant;
- ensure the right to claim compensation or remedy before a court for any violation of these rights;
- ensure that any compensation or remedy is enforced.

(See Arts 3 and 26 ICCPR below and how to lobby in ch 5 at p 118.)

Affirmative action is sometimes required by states *to diminish or eliminate conditions which cause or help to perpetuate discrimination* (HRC: *General Comment No. 18*). For example, in a state where a section of the community is prevented from exercising its rights under the ICCPR, the state should take specific action to correct these conditions. This may involve preferential treatment for this community as compared with the rest of the population. However, *as long as such action is needed to correct discrimination . . . it is a case of legitimate differentiation . . .* (HRC).

Other relevant information

International Convention on the Elimination of All Forms of Racial Discrimination (CERD)

> . . . *any doctrine of superiority based on racial differentiation is scientifically false, morally condemnable, socially unjust and dangerous*

and that there is no justification for racial discrimination, in theory or in practice, anywhere.   *(Preamble)*

Racial discrimination is defined in the convention as

. . . any distinction, exclusion, restriction, or preference based on race, colour, descent or national or ethnic origin which has the purpose or effect of nullifying or impairing the recognition, enjoyment or exercise, on an equal footing, of human rights and fundamental freedoms in the political, economic, social, cultural or any other field of public life.

(Art 1)

The aims of the CERD include:
- prohibiting racial discrimination by authorities and private organizations;
- making it a criminal offence to incite racial discrimination.

States parties should bring criminal proceedings against racist organizations *at the earliest moment.* They should make such organizations illegal and prosecute those who take part in them (CERD Committee *General Recommendation XV*).

The CERD lists a number of human rights that must be protected such as:
- equality before the law
- protection against violence
- just and favourable conditions of work
- the right to housing
- the right of access to any place or service used by the public

While the CERD recommends that states establish tribunals to deal with violations of its provisions, it also creates its own procedure for individual complaint (see ch 6 at p 136).

The CERD committee has said:

Law enforcement officials should receive intensive training to ensure that in the performance of their duties they respect as well as protect human dignity and maintain and uphold the human rights of all persons without distinction . . .   *(General Recommendation XIII)*

Under the CERD a state party is obliged to pass laws to outlaw any groups who advocate racial hatred – but what about their freedom of speech? Are these groups not entitled to say what they like about who they like? Some freedoms and rights are not absolute. They are subject to limitations. All rights and freedoms must be balanced with the freedoms and rights of other people. There is a line to be drawn between the exercise of free speech and incitement.

Even in societies most zealous of safeguarding the right of free speech, there are laws against defamation and sedition. Laws against incitement

> *to racial discrimination or hatred are ... no less necessary to protect*
> *public order or the rights of others.*   (Committee of Experts under CERD)

Further the advocacy of racial hatred is expressly prohibited by article 20 (see p 54.

Vienna Declaration

> *Respect for human rights and for fundamental freedoms without*
> *distinction of any kind is a fundamental rule of international human*
> *rights law ...*   (Art 15)

> *Special attention needs to be paid to ensuring non-discrimination, and*
> *the equal enjoyment of all human rights and fundamental freedoms by*
> *disabled persons, including their active participation in all aspects of*
> *society.*   (Art 22)

Article 3
The states parties to the present Covenant undertake to ensure the equal rights of men and women to the enjoyment of all civil and political rights set forth in the present Covenant.

- **Women have the same rights as men.**

Commentary
Women have long been recognized as a vulnerable group. The addition of Article 3 highlights this concern.

This provision requires not only measures of protection but also affirmative action designed to ensure the positive enjoyment of rights. This, states the HRC, cannot be done simply by enacting laws. The appointment of national bodies and greater international co-operation are required to solve the practical problems connected with the insurance of equal rights for men and women (*General Comment No 4*).

Other relevant information
The Convention on the Elimination of All Forms of Discrimination Against Women (CEDAW) provides states parties with a checklist of rights that attach to women and which any state party is bound to protect in its national law.

Under the Convention, each state party shall ensure the rights of women to
- the same employment opportunities as men;
- free choice of profession and employment; and
- equal pay for equal work;

and take the necessary measures (including legislation) to ensure that women
- are not dismissed from their work on the grounds of pregnancy;
- are granted paid maternity leave; and

- are provided with the necessary supporting social services.

In law women are identical to men, particularly in concluding contracts and administering property. In marriage, states parties are under a duty *to take all appropriate measures* to eliminate discrimination against women in marital and family relations. In common with men, women have the same right

- freely to choose a spouse and enter into marriage only with their free and full consent;
- the same rights and responsibilities during marriage and at its dissolution;
- the same rights to decide on the number and spacing of their children;
- the same personal rights as husband and wife including the right to a profession and occupation.

States parties should, therefore, take active steps to pass laws that eliminate discrimination against women.

The Committee of CEDAW has commented on specific articles of the Convention as regards violence against women. Discrimination against women, states the Committee, includes gender-based violence, that is *violence that is directed against a woman because she is a woman or that affects women disproportionately*. Gender-based violence may breach provisions of CEDAW whether or not those provisions mention violence, for example:
- the right to liberty and security of the person;
- the right to equal protection under the law;
- the right to equality in the family;
- the right to the highest standard available of physical and mental health; and
- the right to just and favourable conditions of work.

Further, discrimination is not restricted to action by, or on behalf of governments. States parties are under an obligation to take measures to eliminate discrimination against women *by any person, organization or enterprise* (Art 2e). Therefore, states that fail to take the necessary steps to prevent, or investigate and punish the acts of private individuals, are in breach of the provision. In reviewing the causes of gender-based violence, the Committee targets 'traditional attitudes' that regard women as being subordinate to men or having stereotyped roles. These attitudes *perpetuate . . . family violence and abuse, forced marriage, dowry deaths, acid attacks and female circumcision . . . and . . . contribute to the propagation of pornography and the depiction . . . of women as sexual objects, rather than as individuals*. In dealing with gender-based violence, the Committee calls on states parties to ensure that
- laws give adequate protection to all women;
- the media respect, and promote respect for women;
- education and public information programmes are introduced to help eliminate prejudices which hinder women's equality;
- preventive and punitive measures are put in place to overcome trafficking and sexual exploitation; and

- women are protected from sexual harassment and other forms of violence in the workplace. (*General Recommendation No 19*)

In cases of family violence, the Committee is specific in its recommendations, which include:
- criminal penalties where necessary;
- prohibiting any defence of 'honour' in regard to the assault or murder of a female family member; and
- providing safe refuges for victims of family violence and support services.

Vienna Declaration

The full and equal participation of women in political, civil, economic, social and cultural life, at the national, regional and international levels, and the eradication of all forms of discrimination on grounds of sex are priority objectives of the international community. (Art 18)

Article 38 stresses the importance of working towards:
- the elimination of violence against women in public and private life;
- the elimination of all forms of sexual harassment, exploitation and trafficking in women;
- the elimination of gender bias in the administration of justice;
- the eradication of any conflicts that may arise between the rights of women and the harmful effects of certain traditional or customary practices, cultural prejudices and religious extremism.

Article 4

(1) In time of public emergency which threatens the life of the nation and the existence of which is officially proclaimed, the states parties to the present Covenant may take measures derogating from their obligations under the present Covenant to the extent strictly required by the exigencies of the situation, provided that such measures are not inconsistent with their other obligations under international law and do not involve discrimination solely on the ground of race, colour, sex, language, religion or social origin.

(2) No derogation from articles 6, 7, 8 (paragraphs 1 and 2), 11, 15, 16 and 18 may be made under this provision.

(3) Any state party to the present Covenant availing itself of the right of derogation shall immediately inform the other states parties to the present Covenant, through the intermediary of the Secretary-General of the United Nations, of the provisions from which it has derogated and of the reasons by which it was actuated. A further communication shall be made, through the same intermediary, on the date on which it terminates such derogation.

When a state declares a State of Emergency it can suspend certain rights and freedoms but some rights can never be suspended, such as:

- *the right to life;*
- *the right to recognition as a person before the law;*
- *freedom of thought, conscience and religion;*
- *freedom from torture;*
- *freedom from slavery;*
- *freedom from imprisonment for debt; and*
- *freedom from retroactive penal legislation.*

Commentary

Other rights can only be suspended, or derogated from, in the following circumstances:

- there must be a public emergency which threatens the life of the nation;
- the public emergency must be officially proclaimed;
- the Secretary-General of the United Nations must be informed immediately;
- suspension of rights must be confined strictly to the demands of the situation;
- any suspension must be in accordance with international law;
- any suspension must not be based solely on grounds of discrimination.

What is a 'public emergency'? It is a calamity of such magnitude that it literally *threatens the life of the nation.* It can be a natural disaster, such as an earthquake. It can be a civil war or armed uprising. Whatever form it takes, the government must officially announce a state of public emergency and the measures it is proposing to take. Those measures must also be communicated to the UN Secretary-General with an explanation why these measures are necessary.

In a situation such as this, the government is surely justified in using extreme measures? The government may take any number of measures it considers necessary to re-establish order and security. However, these measures must apply equally to everybody and not single out one class of people for 'special treatment'. They must not go beyond the needs of the situation. The HRC has said that measures taken under a State of Emergency are of an *exceptional and temporary* nature and may only last as long as the situation requires. They must be scrutinized to see if they are *strictly required.* This highlights the importance of an independent judiciary and an entrenched bill of rights in the constitution (see ch 5 at p 117). They must also be in line with international law: for example, torture can never be justified.

I thought all rights were equal – are these non-derogable rights more important than other rights? Under the ICCPR there is no hierarchy of importance of rights. Some rights of profound importance are not included in the list of non-derogable rights. One reason for certain rights being made non-derogable is because their suspension is irrelevant to the legitimate control of the state of national emergency (for example: no imprisonment for debt – Art 11 at p 40). Another reason is that derogation may be impossible (for example: freedom of conscience – Art 18 at p 51). At the same time, some provisions are non-derogable exactly because without them there would be no rule of law. (HRC *General Comment No 24*)

Article 5

(1) Nothing in the present Covenant may be interpreted as implying for any state, group or person any right to engage in any activity or perform any act aimed at the destruction of any of the rights and freedoms recognized herein or at their limitation to a greater extent than is provided for in the present Covenant.

(2) There shall be no restriction upon or derogation from any of the fundamental human rights recognized or existing in any state party to the present Covenant pursuant to law, conventions, regulations or custom on the pretext that the present Covenant does not recognize such rights or that it recognizes them to a lesser extent.

- *Nobody can claim the right to act in a way that destroys the rights in the ICCPR.*
- *Just because a right is not listed in the ICCPR does not mean that it does not exist.*

Commentary

No government, group of people or individual person can use the ICCPR to justify acts designed to destroy the very rights the Covenant seeks to protect. No individual or group may use the provisions of the ICCPR as a *shield* for activities which will undermine those rights. The state may not use the articles as a *sword* to limit or restrict rights and freedoms beyond that which the UDHR and Covenant allow. For example, you cannot claim that you are exercising your right to free expression when, in fact, you are promoting racial hatred.

Where there is conflict between this article and the law of a state party, the provisions giving the maximum protection for the rights and freedoms of the individual should take precedence.

Article 6

(1) Every human being has the inherent right to life. This right shall be protected by law. No one shall be arbitrarily deprived of his life.

(2) In countries which have not abolished the death penalty, sentence of death may be imposed only for the most serious crimes in accordance with the law in force at the time of the commission of the crime and not contrary to the provisions of the present Covenant and to the Convention on the Prevention and Punishment of the Crime of Genocide. This penalty can only be carried out pursuant to a final judgement rendered by a competent court.

(3) When deprivation of life constitutes the crime of genocide, it is understood that nothing in this article shall authorize any state party to the present Covenant to derogate in any way from any obligation assumed under the provisions of the Convention on the Prevention and Punishment of the Crime of Genocide.

(4) Anyone sentenced to death shall have the right to seek pardon or commutation of the sentence. Amnesty, pardon or commutation of the sentence of death may be granted in all cases.

(5) Sentence of death shall not be imposed for crimes committed by persons below eighteen years of age and shall not be carried out on pregnant women.

(6) *Nothing in this article shall be invoked to delay or to prevent the abolition of capital punishment by any state party to the present Covenant.*

- **The state must protect the individual's life.**
- **When a state takes away a person's life just because it decides to do so, it acts arbitrarily.**
- **The death penalty can only apply to the most serious crimes.**

The right to life is NON-DEROGABLE and, therefore, cannot be suspended under any circumstances.

Commentary

> *The deprivation of life by the authorities of the state is a matter of the utmost gravity. Therefore, the law must strictly control and limit the circumstances in which a person may be deprived of his life by the authorities of a state.*
> (HRC *General Comment No 6*)

The action of the state must not exceed the requirements of law enforcement. The fact that an act by the authorities may be lawful under national law does not prevent it from being arbitrary under international human rights law. For example, a law that authorizes law enforcement officers to lie in wait for, and shoot to kill, armed insurgents would violate this article (see *Basic Principles on the Use of Force and Firearms by Law Enforcement Officers* (LEOs) in ch 3 at p 77 and Appendix 9). In times of emergency the state must strictly apply the rule of law to protect the innocent from suffering.

The right to life should not be too narrowly interpreted. The state is required to take positive measures including reducing infant mortality and to increase life expectancy by adopting measures to eliminate malnutrition and epidemics. Poor prison conditions that affect the health of prisoners may also fall within this provision.

Forms of state-sanctioned killing

Judicial: The death penalty Under the ICCPR, states parties are not obliged to abolish the death penalty but to limit its use and in particular, to abolish it for other than the most serious crimes.

Execution of sentence must meet the test of least possible physical and mental suffering. The HRC has held that execution by gas asphyxiation, for example, does not satisfy the test and constitutes cruel and inhuman treatment (see Art 7 below at p 28). The HRC has also stated that by definition every execution of a sentence of death may be considered to constitute cruel and inhuman treatment within the meaning of Article 7.

While the article permits imposition of the death penalty, the wording suggests that abolition is desirable. The HRC considers abolition by countries to be *progress in the enjoyment of the right to life.*

Article 6 contains procedures that must be complied with before the death penalty can be carried out. They include:

- the right to a fair hearing
- the presumption of innocence
- minimum guarantees of a defendant's right to petition or seek:
  - a review of his/her case;
  - changing a death sentence to imprisonment;
  - a pardon
- the prohibition on passing a death sentence on any person who is under 18 and/or pregnant.

It would amount to a breach of Art 6 where these procedural preconditions are not satisfied.

The UN *Safeguards guaranteeing protection of the rights of those facing the death penalty* expand on these guarantees:

- Serious crimes: mean crimes of specific intent with fatal or other extremely grave consequences.
- Persons who shall not be sentenced to death should include new mothers and people who have become insane.
- The death penalty can only be imposed when the guilt of the person is based upon clear and convincing evidence leaving no room for an alternative explanation of the facts.

The Second Optional Protocol (OP2) to the ICCPR abolishes the death penalty. A state which accedes to or ratifies OP2 undertakes to abolish the death penalty within its jurisdiction. An increasing number of countries are abolishing the death penalty. They include the following 57 countries:

Andorra	Angola	Australia	Austria
Cambodia	Cape Verde	Colombia	Costa Rica
Croatia	Czech Republic	Denmark	Dominican Republic
Ecuador	Finland	France	Germany
Greece	Guinea-Bissau	Haiti	Honduras
Hong Kong	Hungary	Iceland	Ireland
Italy	Kiribati	Liechtenstein	Luxembourg
Macedonia	Marshall Islands	Mauritius	Micronesia
Moldova	Monaco	Mozambique	Namibia
Netherlands	New Zealand	Nicaragua	Norway
Palau	Panama	Portugal	Romania
San Marino	Sao Tome & Principe	Slovak Republic	Slovenia
Solomon Islands	Spain	Sweden	Switzerland
Tuvalu	Uruguay	Vanuatu	Vatican City State
Venezuela			

Non-Judicial: Summary and arbitrary executions These killings have been defined as

- an execution in which the due process of law and in particular the minimum guarantees as set out in Art 6 (above) and Arts 14 and 15 (below) have not been respected;
- killings carried out by order of a government or with its consent or knowledge, without any judicial or legal process;
- death resulting from abuse or excessive use of force by law enforcement officials; and
- killings of civilians carried out by members of the armed or security forces, in violation of law governing the state of war or armed conflict.

These killings are also called extra-legal, or extrajudicial, executions since they take place outside the judicial process and are illegal under national and international law. Some of the victims are made to 'disappear' before they are killed.

The UNGA adopted *Principles on the Effective Prevention and Investigations of Extra-legal, Arbitrary and Summary Executions* in 1989. These Principles set out the action every government should take to prevent, investigate and punish any extra-legal execution.

Prevention
- Make it a criminal offence which no circumstances can ever justify – such as war or public emergency; and set sentences accordingly.
- Establish a clear structure of chain-of-command control to ensure that officers do not commit such an act; and that those who do order, or tolerate, such an act are held criminally responsible.
- Make it part of the training of the security forces that anyone ordered to commit such an act has a *right and a duty to refuse.*
- Guarantee protection to individuals or groups threatened with death.
- Ensure that detainees are held in recognized places of detention and that accurate information is available to their relatives, lawyers or other persons properly concerned.
- Grant independent inspectors unlimited access to all places of detention at any time.
- Co-operate with international investigations.

Investigation
- Conduct thorough, prompt and impartial investigations in all suspected cases.
- Establish procedures to carry out such inquiries including investigative offices.
- Provide these offices with the resources they need; including the authority to oblige officials (and any witness) to appear and testify.
- Establish a commission of enquiry in particularly serious cases or where the investigative offices above prove inadequate (see ch 5 at p 116).
- Ensure a thorough autopsy is carried out to establish – at the least – the identity of the deceased and the cause and manner of death (see: Appendix 6).
- Protect all those involved in the investigation from intimidation and suspend from office those implicated.

- Keep the families and legal representatives of the deceased informed at all stages of the investigation, notify them of any hearings and ensure the return of the deceased's body on completion of the investigation.
- Make public a report on the findings of the investigation and steps the government will take in response to it.

Legal Proceedings
- Ensure that those identified by the investigation as participants in such an act are brought to justice and that
    - the justification by a person that s/he was 'ordered to' is no defence;
    - superior officers/officials are responsible in the chain-of-command for the acts of those under them, if they had a *reasonable opportunity to prevent them*;
    - no blanket immunity from prosecution is granted to those involved in such acts.
- Provide *fair and adequate* compensation to the families and dependants of the deceased within a reasonable period of time.

What about death squads who act outside the 'chain-of-command' structure but have official support – what can be done about them? Pressure should be put on the government – from within and outside the country – to prohibit and disband these organizations and bring any perpetrators to justice.

Should there always be an enquiry when someone dies in custody? Yes – always. The enquiry, or inquest, must also be open to the public. An enquiry not only exposes, it also protects. An enquiry may reveal criminal acts and corrupt practices; it may also show decent professional people doing the best they can in the circumstances. An enquiry exposes the weaknesses and strengths in a system. It can show where there is need for improvement or greater government expenditure. It provides an independent and impartial insight into the workings of the security forces and makes them accountable for their actions.

Surely nuclear weapons present the greatest threat to the right to life facing mankind today? The members of the Human Rights Committee agree. The HRC is concerned that the use of nuclear weapons may be brought about not only through war but accident or error. They observe that *the very existence and gravity of this threat generates a climate of suspicion and fear between states* and go on to state that *The production, testing, possession, deployment and use of nuclear weapons should be prohibited and recognized as crimes against humanity.* They end by appealing to the international community to *rid the world of this menace.* (*General Comment No 14*)

Article 7
No-one shall be subjected to torture or to cruel, inhuman or degrading treatment or punishment. In particular, no-one shall be subjected without his free consent to medical or scientific experimentation.

- *The deliberate infliction of pain or suffering by agents of the state is a crime in international law*

This right is NON-DEROGABLE and cannot be suspended under any circumstances.

Commentary

Torture is defined as any act:

- intentionally inflicted by, or on the orders of, or with the agreement of, a public official, or person acting in an official capacity;
- causing severe pain or suffering, physical or mental, on a person, in order:
  - to obtain information or a confession
  - to punish
  - to intimidate or coerce
  - or for any other reason based on discrimination.

Torture is an aggravated, or worse, form of cruel, inhuman or degrading treatment or punishment.

Cruel Punishment A cruel punishment is one designed to inflict suffering unnecessarily. It is also a punishment which does not accord with the dignity of the human being. Its definition depends on a wide range of circumstances. For example, it includes, depriving a person

> of the use of any of his natural senses, such as sight or hearing, or of his awareness of place or the passing of time
> > (Body of Principles for the Protection of all Persons under any form of Detention or Imprisonment)

Or stripping someone of their nationality, as this

> strips the citizen of his status in the national and international political community and amounts to the total destruction of the individual's status in organized society (US Supreme Court)

Inhuman treatment or punishment The treatment or punishment must come up to a *minimum level of severity* to be inhuman. What amounts to a minimum level depends on all the circumstances of the case. Any method of interrogation that goes beyond mere question and answer puts pressure on a person, but it cannot be classed as inhuman by that fact alone. There must be something more: some act designed to cause severe mental or physical stress, such as prolonged solitary confinement or the deprivation of sleep.

Degrading treatment Treatment which grossly humiliates an individual or forces him/her to act against his/her will or conscience is degrading. The treatment need not be physical: any act which lowers a person in rank, position, reputation or character can be regarded as 'degrading treatment' if it reaches a certain level of severity.

It includes all techniques designed to arouse in people

> *. . . feelings of fear, anguish and inferiority capable of humiliating and debasing them and possibly breaking their physical or moral resistance.*
> *(European Court of Human Rights)*

It is an offence to a person's dignity and personal integrity to treat him/her as *an object in the power of the authority* rather than as a human being. (*European Court*)

The treatment need not be public: it is sufficient if a person is humiliated in his/her own eyes. For example:

> *The punishment of 'lashing' (or beating someone) not only humiliates and disgraces the offender but also degrades all others who take part in the procedure.*
> *(European Commission on Human Rights)*

The HRC has held that poor prison conditions such as over-crowding, deprivation of food and clothing, death threats and incommunicado detention, amount to a breach of Art 7.

But if a harsh punishment stops crime, isn't that better for everyone? There is no evidence that it does. The fact that a punishment may sometimes appear to be an effective deterrent does not excuse it, if it is also degrading. Any punishment that contravenes basic international standards is unacceptable and cannot be justified.

Proof There are a number of difficulties involved in proving a violation of Art 7 because:
- usually there are no witnesses; or
- the victim fears reprisals upon him/herself or members of his/her family; or
- there is reluctance by the authorities to admit breaches by their law enforcement agencies, or to implement an investigation; or
- the torture, or other cruel, inhuman or degrading treatment or punishment has left no visible marks.

For this reason, the HRC has stated that in proceedings under OPI it is for the state to disprove any allegation.

Duty of the state

> *. . . it is not sufficient for the implementation of this article to prohibit such treatment or punishment . . . states must ensure an effective protection through some machinery of control.* (HRC)

The HRC recommended a number of safeguards, including:
- no detention incommunicado;

- granting prisoners access to persons such as doctors, lawyers and family members;
- only holding prisoners in places of detention that are publicly recognized and equipped with a register that is available to persons concerned;
- making confessions or other evidence obtained through torture or other treatment contrary to Art 7, inadmissible in court;
- training and instructing law enforcement officials not to use such treatment.

The HRC rejects the use of amnesty laws in favour of offenders, commenting:

> *Amnesties are generally incompatible with the duty of states to investigate such acts; to guarantee freedom from such acts within their jurisdiction; and to ensure that they do not occur in the future. States may not deprive individuals of the right to an effective remedy.*　　(General Comment No 20)

Other relevant information
The *Convention against Torture and Other Cruel, Inhuman or Degrading Treatment or Punishment* (CT). States parties to the CT must
- make torture a criminal offence;
- arrest any torturer discovered to be within its jurisdiction and either extradite or prosecute that person; and
- compensate victims of torture.

Vienna Declaration　　The states present in Vienna solemnly stated that torture is

> *. . . one of the most atrocious violations against human dignity, the result of which destroys the dignity and impairs the capability of victims to continue their lives and their activities . . .*

The Declaration calls for the early adoption of an Optional Protocol to the CT to establish a preventive system of regular visits to places of detention. It also calls on all states to *abolish* any legislation that leads to impunity for those responsible for grave violations of human rights such as torture and to *prosecute* such violations, thereby providing a firm basis for the rule of law. (Part II, Arts 55, 60 and 61)

Article 8
(1) *No-one shall be held in slavery; slavery and the slave trade in all their forms shall be prohibited.*
(2) *No-one shall be held in servitude.*
(3) (a) *No-one shall be required to perform forced or compulsory labour;*
　　(b) *Paragraph 3(a) shall not be held to preclude, in countries where imprisonment with hard labour may be imposed as a punishment for a crime, the performance of hard labour in pursuance of a sentence to such punishment by a competent court;*

(c) For the purpose of this paragraph, the term 'forced or compulsory labour' shall not include:

   (i) Any work or service, not referred to in sub-paragraph (b) normally required of a person who is under detention in consequence of a lawful order of a court, or of a person during conditional release from such detention;

   (ii) Any service of a military character and, in countries where conscientious objection is recognised, any national service required by law of conscientious objectors;

   (iii) Any service exacted in cases of emergency or calamity threatening the life or well-being of the community;

   (iv) Any work or service which forms part of normal civil obligations.

- **Slavery is a crime under international law.**

It is a NON-DEROGABLE right and cannot be suspended under any circumstances.

Commentary

Freedom from slavery was the first 'human right' to be recognized by international law. The term 'slavery' is defined in the Slavery Convention as

> . . . the status or condition of a person over whom any or all of the powers attaching to the right of ownership are exercised.

Slave trade   In the later *Supplementary Convention on the Abolition of Slavery*, this phrase means and includes:

- all acts involved in the capture, acquisition or disposal of a person with intent to reduce him to slavery;
- all acts involved in the acquisition of a slave with a view to selling him or exchanging him;
- all acts of disposal by sale or exchange of a person acquired with a view to being sold or exchanged;
- and, in general, every act of trade or transport in slaves by whatever means of conveyance.

Even if a State has not ratified this Convention, under the *Geneva Convention on the High Seas*, States shall adopt

> . . . effective measures to prevent and punish the transport of slaves in ships. . . . Any slave taking refuge on board any ship . . . shall ipso facto (by that very fact) be free.

Servitude   The Supplementary Convention defines the following institutions and practices similar to slavery:

1. Debt bondage: A person in debt to another promises, as security for that debt, his/her personal services or the services of someone under his/her control.

2. Serfdom: Someone who is bound by law, custom or agreement to live and work on land that belongs to another and to perform some service to that other – for reward or not – and is not free to change his situation;

3. Any institution or practice whereby:
   - a woman, without the right to refuse, is promised or given in marriage on payment of money or in kind to her parents, guardian, family, or any other person or group; or
   - the husband of a woman, his family or his clan, transfers her to another person for value received or otherwise; or
   - a woman on the death of her husband is inherited by another person;
   - a child or young person under the age of 18 years is given by his/her parents or his/her guardian to another person with a view to the exploitation of the child or young person of his labour.

Forced or compulsory labour   The ILO defines this as

> . . . *all work or service which is exacted from any person under the menace of any penalty and for which the person has not offered himself voluntarily.*   (ILO 29)

Such work must be:
- against someone's will;
- oppressive or unjust or involve unavoidable hardship.

Under the ILO *Convention concerning the Abolition of Forced Labour* (ILO 105), states parties are required to suppress and not to make use of forced or compulsory labour:
- as a means of political coercion or education; or
- as a punishment for holding or expressing political views or views ideologically opposed to the established political, social or economic system;
- as a method of mobilizing and using labour for purposes of economic development;
- as a means of labour discipline;
- as a punishment for having participated in strikes;
- as a means of racial, social, national or religious discrimination.

Article 9
(1) Everyone has the right to liberty and security of person. No one shall be subject to arbitrary arrest and detention. No-one shall be deprived of his liberty except on such grounds and in accordance with such procedures as are established by law.

(2) *Anyone who is arrested shall be informed, at the time of arrest, of the reasons for his arrest and shall be promptly informed of any charges against him.*

(3) *Anyone arrested or detained on a criminal charge shall be brought promptly before a judge or other officer authorized by law to exercise judicial power and shall be entitled to trial within a reasonable time or to release. It shall not be the general rule that persons awaiting trial shall be detained in custody, but release may be subject to guarantees to appear for trial, at any other stage of the judicial proceedings, and, should occasion arise, for execution of the judgement.*

(4) *Anyone who is deprived of his liberty by arrest or detention shall be entitled to take proceedings before a court, in order that the court may decide without delay on the lawfulness of his detention and order his release if the detention is not lawful.*

(5) *Anyone who has the been the victim of unlawful arrest or detention shall have an enforceable right to compensation.*

- **No-one can be arrested or detained without a good and lawful reason.**

Commentary

Rights under Article 9 are:
- to be informed of the reason for the arrest and any charges;
- to be brought promptly before a judge;
- to be tried within a reasonable time or released;
- to be released on bail pending trial;
- to apply to court to challenge the lawfulness of detention; and
- to compensation for wrongful arrest.

The first paragraph of this article applies to all deprivations of liberty, whether in criminal cases or others such as: mental illness, vagrancy, drug addiction, educational purposes, immigration control and the like. Harassment, intimidation and threats by government officials or government agents would breach this article.

Arbitrary arrest and detention An arrest that is carried out by policemen or law enforcement officials (or other agents of the state) by methods that are not *established by law* is arbitrary. The procedure for arresting and detaining a person must be clearly set out and must conform to established principles of justice. The practice of some security forces to 'disappear' their citizens is not a practice established by law and so qualifies as arbitrary arrest and detention. *'Arbitrariness' is not to be equated with 'against the law', but must be interpreted more broadly to include elements of inappropriateness, injustice, and lack of predictability and due process of law. . . .* (HRC)

. . . shall be informed, at the time of arrest . . . When someone is arrested s/he has the right to be told immediately of the reasons for his/her arrest.

. . . shall be promptly informed of any charges . . .   The person has the right to be told within a reasonable period of time from arrest the charge(s) against him/her. This time is usually fixed by law. In cases where the accused is detained in custody, the time should be counted in days and not weeks.

. . . shall be brought promptly before a judge . . .   This period is usually fixed by law. There must be no unnecessary delay. Keeping someone incommunicado for a month without access to lawyer or family before bringing that person before a judge is not acting promptly. The importance of bringing a person promptly before a judge is that:
- the judge sits in open court;
- it is a public place;
- family and friends know where the person is;
- everyone knows what the charge(s) is (are);
- everyone can see what condition the prisoner is in;
- the process of justice can be seen to be under way.

. . . or other officer authorized by law to exercise judicial power . . .   state tribunals set up under 'emergency procedures' to dispense summary 'justice' breach this provision. The phrase *judicial power* means that a tribunal has proper judicial independence, such as a judge, or officer authorized by law and
- enjoys a degree of stability;
- is not subject to any authority in the exercise of his/her duties as a judge;
- all his/her duties guarantee an impartial attitude.

. . . entitled to trial . . .   Security measures under a state of emergency which authorize the indefinite detention of individuals without charge beyond a reasonable time are *serious violations of the right to freedom* (Inter-American Commission of Human Rights). Time limits are set down in most penal codes.

It shall not be the general rule that persons . . . shall be detained in custody
The arrested person has a qualified right to be granted his/her liberty, or to be given bail, while awaiting trial. This right is subject to exceptions where, for example, it is *reasonably* feared the person will
- fail to appear for trial; or
- commit further offences while on bail; or
- interfere with the course of justice (by intimidating witnesses or destroying evidence); or
- for the person's own safety.

Article 9(4)   Where in criminal cases a person's detention is thought to be unlawful (not established by law), then it can be challenged in court and the state must justify the reasons for a person's detention. If the state fails to satisfy the court as to the lawfulness of the person's detention, the court will order his/her release. This procedure is known as *habeas corpus.* It is an additional safeguard for the liberty of the individual to prevent arbitrary measures of detention. This right to control by a court of the legality of detention applies to non-criminal matters and all cases where the individual is detained as mentioned above.

. . . an enforceable right to compensation . . . Victims of unlawful arrest or detention have the right to go to court and demand compensation. This provision appears in the constitutions of many countries. It is another way of making the police and military accountable for their actions.

Other relevant information

The *Declaration on the Protection of All Persons from Enforced Disappearance* adopted by the UNGA in 1992 states that no state shall practice, permit or tolerate enforced disappearances. The 'disappeared' have been defined as

> *. . . people who have been taken into custody by agents of the state, yet whose whereabouts and fate are concealed and whose custody is denied.*

The preamble to the Declaration states that

> *. . . enforced disappearance undermines the deepest values of any society committed to respect for the rule of law, human rights and fundamental freedoms, and that the systematic practice of such acts is of the nature of a crime against humanity.*

The Declaration sets out the reasons why an act of enforced disappearance is *an offence to human dignity:*

- the persons involved are outside the protection of the law;
- it inflicts severe suffering on them and their families;
- it violates the rules of international law that guarantee:
  - the right to recognition before the law;
  - the right to liberty and security of the person; and
  - the freedom from torture and other cruel, inhuman or degrading treatment or punishment.

The obligations which the Declaration places on states may be set out in a 14-point Programme for the Prevention of 'Disappearances'.

1 Official condemnation The highest authorities of every country should demonstrate their total opposition to 'disappearances'. They should make clear to all members of the police, military and other security forces that 'disappearances' will not be tolerated under any circumstances.

2 Chain-of-command control Those in charge of the security forces should maintain strict chain-of-command control to ensure that officers under their command do not commit 'disappearances'. Officials with chain-of-command responsibility who order or tolerate 'disappearances' by those under their command should be held criminally responsible for these acts.

3 Information on detention and release Accurate information about the arrest of any person and about his/her place of detention, including transfers and releases, should be made available to relatives, lawyers and the courts. Prisoners should be released in a way that allows reliable verification of their release and ensures their safety.

4 Mechanism for locating and protecting prisoners Governments should at all times ensure that effective judicial remedies are available which enable relatives and lawyers to find out immediately where a prisoner is held and under what authority, to ensure his or her safety, and to obtain the release of anyone arbitrarily detained.

5 No secret detention Governments should ensure that prisoners are held only in publicly recognized places of detention. Up-to-date registers of all prisoners should be maintained in every place of detention and centrally. The information in these registers should be made available to relatives, lawyers, judges, official bodies trying to trace people who have been detained, and others with a legitimate interest. No-one should be secretly detained.

6 Authorization of arrest and detention Arrest and detention should be carried out only by officials who are authorized by law to do so. Officials carrying out an arrest should identify themselves to the person arrested and, on demand, to others witnessing the event. Governments should establish rules setting forth which officials are authorized to order an arrest or detention. Any deviation from established procedures which contributes to a 'disappearance' should be punished by appropriate sanctions.

7 Access to prisoners All prisoners should be brought before a judicial authority without delay after being taken into custody. Relatives, lawyers and doctors should have prompt and regular access to them. There should be regular, independent, unannounced and unrestricted visits of inspection to all places of detention.

8 Prohibition in law Governments should ensure that the commission of a 'disappearance' is a criminal offence. The sentence should reflect the gravity of the offence. The prohibition of 'disappearances' and the essential safeguards for their prevention must not be suspended under any circumstances, including states of war or other public emergency.

9 Individual responsibility The prohibition on 'disappearances' should be reflected in the training of all officials involved in the arrest and custody of prisoners and in the instructions issued to them. They should be instructed that they have the right and duty to refuse to obey any order to participate in a 'disappearance'. An order from a superior officer or a public authority must never be invoked as a justification for taking part in a 'disappearance'.

10 Investigation Governments should ensure that all complaints and reports of 'disappearances' are investigated promptly, impartially and effectively by a body which is independent of those allegedly responsible and has the necessary powers and resources to carry out the investigation. The methods and findings of the investigation should be made public. Officials suspected of responsibility for 'disappearances' should be suspended from active duty during the investigation. Relatives of the victim should have access to information relevant to the investigation and should be entitled to present evidence. Complainants, witnesses, lawyers and others involved in the investigations should be protected from intimidation and reprisals. The investigation should not be curtailed until the fate of the victim is officially clarified.

11 Prosecution Governments should ensure that those responsible for 'disappearances' are brought to justice. This principle should apply wherever such people happen to be, wherever the crime was committed, whatever the nationality of the perpetrators or victims and no matter how much time has elapsed since the commission of the crime. Trials should be in the civilian courts. The perpetrators should not benefit from any legal measures exempting them from criminal prosecution or conviction.

12 Compensation and rehabilitation Victims of 'disappearance' and their dependants should be entitled to compensation. Victims who are released should be provided with appropriate medical care or rehabilitation.

13 Ratification of human rights treaties and implementation of international standards All governments should ratify international treaties containing safeguards and remedies against 'disappearances', including the ICCPR and its first Optional Protocol which provides for individual complaints (see ch 6 at p 135). Governments should ensure full implementation of these and other international instruments, including the UN Declaration on the Protection of All Persons from Enforced Disappearance, and comply with the recommendations of inter-governmental organizations concerning these abuses.

14 International responsibility Governments should use all available channels to intercede with the governments of countries where 'disappearances' have been reported. They should ensure that transfers of equipment, know-how and training for military, security or police use do not facilitate 'disappearances'. No one should be forcibly returned to a country where he or she risks being made to 'disappear' (see Art 13 and commentary at p 42).

Vienna Declaration

> *The World Conference on Human Rights reaffirms that it is the duty of all states, under any circumstances, to make investigations wherever there is reason to believe an enforced disappearance has taken place on a territory under their jurisdiction and, if allegations are confirmed, to prosecute its perpetrators.*
>
> *(Art 62)*

Article 10

(1) All persons deprived of their liberty shall be treated with humanity and with respect for the inherent dignity of the human person.

(2) (a) Accused persons shall, save in exceptional circumstances, be segregated from convicted persons and shall be subject to separate treatment appropriate to their status as unconvicted persons;

(b) Accused juvenile persons shall be separated from adults and brought as speedily as possible for adjudication.

(3) The penitentiary system shall comprise treatment of prisoners the essential aim of which shall be their reformation and social rehabilitation. Juvenile offenders shall be segregated from adults and be accorded treatment appropriate to their age and legal status.

- **Prisoners also have rights.**

Prisoner's rights under Article 10 are
- to be treated with humanity and respect;
- to be kept separate: the unconvicted from convicted prisoners;
- to be kept separate: juvenile from adult prisoners; and
- to reformation and rehabilitation rather than merely punishment.

Commentary

The article applies to any person deprived of his/her liberty by the laws of the state who is held in prison, hospital, psychiatric hospitals, detention camps, correctional institutions or elsewhere.

It is not enough that prisoners are not treated cruelly, inhumanely or in a degrading manner – they *shall be* treated with humanity and respect. Persons deprived of their liberty enjoy all the rights set out in the ICCPR subject to the restrictions that are unavoidable in a closed environment.

Article 10(1) This provision makes it the responsibility of prison, hospital and other authorities to take positive steps to respect the human person. Maltreatment of prisoners such as poor conditions, lengthy periods in solitary confinement, and denial of access to outside visitors violate this article.

Treating all persons deprived of their liberty with humanity and with respect for their dignity is a fundamental and universally applicable rule. Consequently, the application of this rule . . . cannot be dependent on the material resources available in the state party.

(HRC: *General Comment No 21*)

The state cannot point to the conditions outside the walls of the place of detention to excuse or explain the poor conditions inside. People at liberty are free to improve in however small a measure their own conditions – people held in detention are not: they are entirely dependent on the authorities. The state should take measures to monitor the application of these provisions and the rules regarding the treatment of persons deprived of their liberty. Prisoners should have a procedure to complain if these rules are ignored and the right to obtain adequate compensation in the event of a violation.

Article 10(2) Persons awaiting trial should not be forced to mix with convicted prisoners serving a sentence (because they are presumed innocent until proved guilty). Juveniles are a vulnerable group who should be kept apart from adults to prevent intimidation, abuse and the formation of bad habits.

Article 10(3) Prisoners must not be simply locked up all day. The authorities are obliged to establish programmes designed to reform and rehabilitate offenders so that by the time they are released they are able to contribute to society. Juveniles should receive *treatment appropriate to their age*, namely the education and technical training they might have received had they not been imprisoned.

Other relevant information
- Standard Minimum Rules for the Treatment of Prisoners (see ch 3 at p 78; and Appendix 7).
- UN Standard Minimum Rules for the Administration of Juvenile Justice (The Beijing Rules) (see ch 3 at p 78).

Article 11
No one shall be imprisoned merely on the ground of inability to fulfil a contractual obligation.

- **No-one shall be imprisoned for debt.**

This right is NON-DEROGABLE and cannot be suspended under any circumstances.

Commentary
Failure to pay off a debt is not a ground for imprisonment unless the person has been dishonest, grossly negligent or in some way acted criminally.

Article 12

(1) Everyone lawfully within the territory of a state shall, within that territory, have the right to liberty of movement and freedom to choose his residence.

(2) Everyone shall be free to leave any country, including his own.

(3) The above-mentioned rights shall not be subject to any restrictions except those which are provided by law, are necessary to protect national security, public order (ordre public), public health or morals or the rights and freedoms of others, and are consistent with the other rights in the present covenant.

(4) No-one shall be arbitrarily deprived of the right to enter his own country.

Everyone has the right to
- *move around their own country as they wish;*
- *live where they wish; and*
- *enter or leave their country as they wish.*

Commentary

Any restrictions on this right must:
- be provided for by law; and
- be necessary to protect national security, public order, public health or morals, or the rights and freedoms of others; and
- not conflict with the other rights recognized in the ICCPR.

For example: a person's right to set up home in the middle of a national park or tribal reserve is restricted by the greater need to protect the natural resources of the park and preserve the identity of the tribe. On the other hand, official policies that discriminate against certain ethnic or social groups to stop them from moving into a particular area would breach this provision.

Freedom to leave a country   Confiscating a passport prior to departure, or refusal to issue a passport for example, may breach the article. A court has held that if travel increases the risk of illegal acts being committed so does the mere fact of being alive. A right cannot be taken away because someone may commit an illegal act. The illegal act can be punished, the right is inalienable.

What about someone who is kept under close surveillance by the police or security forces?   Someone under close surveillance may be deprived of their freedom of movement for while they can move physically, they cannot move *freely* since all their activities are watched and noted.

Article 13

An alien lawfully in the territory of a state party to the present covenant may be expelled therefrom only in pursuance of a decision reached in accordance with law and shall, except where compelling reasons of national security otherwise require, be allowed to submit the reasons against his expulsion and to have his case

*reviewed by, and be represented for the purpose before, the competent authority or
a person or persons especially designated by the competent authority.*

- **Foreign nationals cannot be expelled arbitrarily.**

Commentary

Expulsion is the order given to a foreign national (alien) to leave the country without
any possibility of returning later. Unless there are very good reasons of national
security, an alien is entitled to argue his/her case against the expulsion order and
have the case reviewed by a competent tribunal. Expulsion should not be confused
with extradition. Extradition is the transfer of one person from one country (or
jurisdiction) to another, for the purpose of standing trial or being sentenced.

What about refugees, what rights do they have?   The ICCPR is silent on this subject.
The UDHR, however, does include a right to seek asylum.

Article 14 UDHR states:

*(1) Everyone has the right to seek and to enjoy in other countries asylum from
persecution.*

*(2) This right may not be invoked in the case of prosecutions genuinely arising
from non-political crimes or from acts contrary to the purposes and principles
of the United Nations.*

- **Everyone has the right to ask for asylum, but not the right to receive it.**

Commentary

A refugee is defined in the *Convention relating to the Status of Refugees* (CR) as a
person who,

> *owing to well-founded fear of being persecuted for reasons of race,
> religion, nationality, membership of a particular social group or political
> opinion, is outside the country of his nationality and is unable or, owing
> to such fear, is unwilling to return to it.*   (CR *Art 1A(2))*

A *well-founded fear* of persecution means a reasonable likelihood of persecution for
reasons of

- race,
- religion,
- nationality,
- social grouping; or
- political opinion

and because of the fear the person is

- outside the country of his/her nationality, and
- unable or unwilling to return.

Although there is no duty on the immigration authorities to admit someone who asks for refugee status, once lawfully in the country the protection offered by Art 13 ICCPR comes into force. The foreign national cannot be simply expelled without a hearing.

Exceptions: The CR does not protect a person where there are serious reasons to believe that:

- S/he has committed
  - a crime against peace;
  - a war crime; or
  - a crime against humanity.
- S/he has committed a serious non-political crime outside the country of his/her residence prior to his/her admission in that country (NB: a 'non-political crime' is an ordinary crime, such as: drugs trafficking, murder, rape etc. Membership of a banned organization, such as a trade union, would constitute a 'political crime').
- S/he has been guilty of acts contrary to the purposes and principles of the United Nations. (CR: Art 1(F))

United Nations High Commissioner for Refugees (UNHCR) The office of UNHCR was established to provide international protection for refugees and to supervise the implementation of the CR and its Protocol.

The protection covers people forced to leave their country because of

- external aggression,
- occupation, or
- other serious disturbance.

The protection covers people seeking asylum, and includes displaced persons who have fled for reasons of

> *conflicts, or radical political, social or economic changes in their own country.*

Protection is given in the following ways:

- supervising the application of the refugee conventions;
- assisting NGOs or governments with the repatriation of people who wish to return to their country, or settle elsewhere;
- assisting the refugees in their resettlement. For example, with transfer of property;
- keeping close contacts with governments and NGOs;
- facilitating the activities of NGOs concerned with the welfare of refugees;

The right to asylum means that the refugee can remain in the place of asylum or at least that s/he will not be sent back to the country where the persecution in question is feared. This prohibition on expulsion or return is known more commonly in its French translation as *non-refoulement.*

Non-refoulement

> *A state must not return any person (whether or not he has entered that country lawfully) to the frontiers of territories where his life or freedom would be threatened on account of his race, religion, nationality, membership of a particular social group or political opinion.*
>
> (CR: *Art 33(1)*)

The principle of non-refoulement is part of international customary law.

There is no obligation on a government to grant asylum; but where states refuse asylum, they are obliged to seek an appropriate solution through

- voluntary repatriation;
- local integration; or
- resettlement in another country.

Stateless persons are people who are not considered as nationals of any state by any other state. They are protected under the *Convention relating to the Status of Stateless Persons* (CS), which has provisions similar to those in the Convention on Refugees.

Organization of African Unity (OAU) The OAU *Convention Governing the Specific Aspects of Refugee Problems* in Africa, provides a broader definition of refugee to include people who flee massive upheavals in their own countries. It is specifically recognized in the OAU Convention that granting asylum to refugees is a peaceful and humanitarian act and shall not be regarded as an unfriendly act by any member state. It is also explicitly stated in the OAU Convention that no refugee shall be turned away at a border.

Vienna Declaration The Vienna Declaration reaffirms Art 14 UDHR and goes on to recognize that *gross violations of human rights including in armed conflicts are among the multiple and complex factors leading to displacement of people.*   (Art 23)

Article 14

14(1) All persons shall be equal before the courts and tribunals. In the determination of any criminal charge against him, or of his rights and obligations in a suit at law, everyone shall be entitled to a fair and public hearing by a competent, independent and impartial tribunal established by law. The press and the public may be excluded from all or part of a trial for reasons of morals, public order (ordre public) or national security in a democratic society, or when the interest of the private lives of the parties so requires, or to the extent strictly necessary in the opinion of the court in special circumstances where publicity would prejudice the interests of justice; but any judgment rendered in a criminal case or in a suit at law

shall be made public except where the interest of juvenile persons otherwise requires
or the proceedings concern matrimonial disputes or the guardianship of children.

- ■ *Everyone is entitled to a fair hearing.*
- ■ *No-one is above the rule of law.*

Commentary

Article 14 lists the minimum guarantees necessary for a fair trial.

It applies to all courts and tribunals whether they are ordinary or specialized. Often military or special courts are created to try civilians and adopt procedures which do not comply with normal standards of justice. The HRC has stated that the circumstances for trying civilians in such courts should be *very exceptional* and nevertheless *genuinely afford the full guarantees* set out in this article (*General Comment No 13*).

Equal before the courts   The law is the same for everyone and should be applied in the same way to all.

. . . a fair and public hearing   The 'equality of arms' between the accused and prosecutor is an essential element of a fair trial. The accused is at an immediate disadvantage when s/he appears in court charged with a crime. In order to ensure a fair trial, every accused person should be guaranteed the following safeguards:
- ■ the right to be presumed innocent until proven guilty;
- ■ time and facilities to prepare a defence;
- ■ free legal representation before and at trial;
- ■ to be present at trial and have the services of an interpreter if necessary;
- ■ to question witnesses and call them on his/her own behalf; and
- ■ the right to appeal.

These guarantees are a *minimum* requirement.

A *public* hearing is one where
- ■ the time and place is made available to members of the public in advance; and
- ■ access is not limited: ordinary members of the public, as well as international observers and members of the press should be allowed free entry so as to verify that justice is done and seen to be done. There must be very good reason for a hearing not to take place in public. The strong public interest in a hearing being held in public may have to be balanced by other considerations owing to
  - – national security and state defence secrets; or
  - – juvenile proceedings involving sexual offences.

NB: A hearing is not 'public' when it is conducted in writing and where the judgment of the court is not published (see ch 4, Trial Observations at p 86).

. . . competent, independent, impartial tribunal . . .   It is a basic principle of any democracy that power should be shared out and not centralized in any one branch of the state. The judges (judiciary) who execute the laws should be separate and independent of Parliament (legislature) who pass those laws. They should also be able to enter judgment against the government (executive) if it acts outside those laws.

The General Assembly of the United Nations endorsed a list of *Basic Principles on the Independence of the Judiciary* drawn up to guide judges and governments on the subject (see ch 3 at p 80 and Appendix 10).

On *competence*, they shall be persons of integrity and ability with appropriate qualifications in law. Selection shall avoid discrimination and improper motives (eg: nepotism, favouritism, etc.).

On *independence*, the independence of the judiciary should be guaranteed by the state and enshrined in the Constitution.

> *A state shall not be able to interfere in a court's proceedings and a court shall not act as an agent for the executive against an individual citizen.*
> *(Draft Declaration on the Right to a Fair Trial and a Remedy)*

On *impartiality*, the judge shall base his/her opinion only on the basis of facts and in accordance with the law. S/he will ensure that proceedings are conducted fairly and the rights of the parties are respected. For example, no judge should try a case in which s/he has an interest.

> *The judiciary shall decide matters before them ... without any restrictions, improper influences, inducements, pressures, threats or interferences, direct or indirect, from any quarter or for any reason.* (Art 2)

Article 7 of the Basic Principles urges each member state of the United Nations to provide adequate resources to enable the judiciary to properly perform its functions. In other words, judges should be adequately paid and protected – particularly in more remote areas.

Is the right to a fair trial a non-derogable right? No. Under Art 4, a government that declares a State of Emergency can suspend the provisions of Art 14.

Isn't it in times of civil war, or armed insurgency, that this right becomes important? Yes. The HRC was concerned enough to issue a General Comment, saying:

> *If states parties decide in circumstances of a public emergency ... to derogate from normal procedures required under Article 14, they should ensure that such derogations do not exceed those strictly required by the exigencies of the actual situation, and respect the other conditions in paragraph 1.*

> *14(2) Everyone charged with a criminal offence shall have the right to be presumed innocent until proved guilty according to law.*

- *Everyone is innocent until proved guilty.*

Commentary

At all times, it is the responsibility of the prosecution to prove the case against an accused person. Any reasonable doubt about the guilt of the accused must be decided in favour of the accused. Suspicion of guilt is not enough – not even strong suspicion – the case must be proved beyond any reasonable doubt before a person can be convicted.

The presumption of innocence further implies a right to be treated as if the person *is* innocent. The public authorities and the press should therefore refrain from making comments that prejudge the issue.

14(3)   In the determination of any criminal charge against him, everyone shall be entitled to the following minimum guarantees, in full equality:
(a)   to be informed promptly and in detail in a language which he understands of the nature and cause of the charge against him;
(b)   to have adequate time and facilities for the preparation of his defence and to communicate with counsel of his own choosing;
(c)   to be tried without undue delay;
(d)   to be tried in his presence and to defend himself in person or through legal assistance of his own choosing; to be informed, if he does not have legal assistance, of this right; and to have legal assistance assigned to him, in any case where the interests of justice so require, and without payment by him in any such case if he does not have sufficient means to pay for it;
(e)   to examine, or have examined, the witness against him and to obtain the attendance and examination of witnesses on his behalf under the same conditions as witnesses against him;
(f)   to have the free assistance of an interpreter if he cannot understand or speak the language used in court;
(g)   not to be compelled to testify against himself or to confess guilt.

Commentary

(a)   An accused person has the right to be told within a reasonable period of time of his/her arrest the charge(s) against him/her. *Promptly* means a matter of days, not weeks (see Art 9 above at p 35).

(b)   Forty-eight hours to prepare a defence in a serious case, would not be an adequate time. Any facilities should include proper access to legal counsel and the opportunity for private consultations with counsel. It also includes access to documents and other evidence which the person accused requires to prepare his/her case. Lawyers should be able to advise and represent their clients privately and *without any restrictions, influences, pressures or undue influence from anyone* (HRC) – see ch 3 at p 81.

(c)   Undue delay amounts to unnecessary delay which will depend on:
  – the complexity of the case;
  – the conduct of the police, prosecution and courts in handling the case;

- the conduct of the accused; and
- whether the accused is in detention awaiting trial;

Detaining a person without trial for four years would amount to undue delay (HRC)

(d) The accused has the right to appear in person before the court. S/he may give up this right if it is done *voluntarily* and *in writing*, and measures must be taken to ensure that counsel provides effective representation in the interests of justice (HRC).

Where the accused person is personally informed of the date, time and place of the trial and fails to appear for trial without any reasonable excuse, s/he may be tried in his/her absence.

However, if the accused subsequently appears and shows that either inadequate notice was given, or some other good and valid reason prevented him/her from appearing, then s/he is entitled to a new hearing.

The accused has the right to represent him/herself in person or to choose his/her own counsel freely from the time the accused is first charged. Where the accused does not have legal assistance, s/he should

- be informed of the right to legal assistance during all stages of any criminal prosecution, including preliminary investigations and appeal proceedings; and
- be provided with free legal assistance in serious cases, if s/he cannot pay for it him/herself and in *all* cases involving the death penalty.

(e) This is an example of the 'equality of arms' principle. The prosecution shall provide the defence with the names of the witnesses it intends calling at the trial and a copy of their statements in good time so that a defence can be prepared. The use of testimony of anonymous witnesses during a trial is a breach of this right. If a witness for the defence is unavailable and is important to the case of the accused, the court must postpone, or adjourn, proceedings to enquire after that witness. Refusal to do so would be a breach of this right and affect the fairness of the hearing as a whole.

(f) If the accused person cannot understand or speak the language used in court s/he is entitled to the assistance of an interpreter free of charge. This right applies to aliens as well as nationals.

It is of basic importance in cases in which ignorance of the language used by a court or difficulty in understanding may constitute a major obstacle to the right of defence (HRC).

(g) This is the legal principle against self-incrimination: no one shall be forced to give evidence against him/herself, or to confess guilt. (Refer to Arts 7 and 10(1): in order to force the accused person to incriminate him/herself, methods are frequently used which violate these two articles. Any confession that has been obtained through force or the threat of force, shall not be admitted as evidence. Judges should have authority to consider any allegations made of violations of the rights of the accused person during any stage of the prosecution, and make appropriate recommendations.) Silence by the accused may not be used as evidence of guilt.

(14)(4)   In the case of juvenile persons, the procedure shall be such as will take account of their age and the desirability of promoting their rehabilitation.

- **Juvenile offenders should not be treated the same as adults.**
- **Special consideration should be given to their youth with emphasis on education not punishment.**

14(5) Everyone convicted of a crime shall have the right to his conviction and sentence being reviewed by a higher tribunal according to law.

- **Everyone has the right to appeal.**

Commentary

The right to review or appeal to a higher court shall provide a thorough and impartial review of the facts of the case within a reasonable period of time. The court shall not order execution of sentence while a case is subject to appeal.

14(6)   When a person has by a final decision been convicted of a criminal offence and when subsequently his conviction has been reversed or he has been pardoned on the ground that a new or newly discovered fact shows conclusively that there has been a miscarriage of justice, the person who has suffered punishment as a result of such conviction shall be compensated according to law, unless it is proved that the non-disclosure of the unknown fact in time is wholly or partly attributable to him.

14(7)   No-one shall be liable to be tried or punished again for an offence for which he has already been finally convicted or acquitted in accordance with the law and penal procedure of each country.

- **No-one can be tried twice for the same offence.**

Commentary

Once a person has been acquitted (or convicted) of a charge, s/he cannot be retried for the same offence – even if evidence later appears that proves conclusively the person's guilt.

Article 15

(1) No-one shall be held guilty of any criminal offence on account of any act or omission which did not constitute a criminal offence, under national or international law, at the time when it was committed. Nor shall a heavier penalty be imposed than the one that was applicable at the time when the criminal offence was committed. If, subsequent to the commission of the offence, provision is made by law for the imposition of a lighter penalty, the offender shall benefit thereby.

(2) Nothing in this article shall prejudice the trial and punishment of any person

for any act or omission which, at the time when it was committed, was criminal according to the general principles of law recognized by the community of nations.

- **No one shall be convicted of an offence that was not a criminal act at the time it was committed.**

This is a NON-DEROGABLE right and cannot be suspended under any circumstances.

Commentary

The purpose of this provision is, firstly, to prevent a new government from creating laws that make acts criminal that were innocent before. For example, where a person is convicted of 'subversive association' under emergency laws, on the grounds of trade union activities that were lawful at the time they were engaged in, or membership of a political party later outlawed. Secondly, it is to prevent new governments imposing heavier penalties for offences for which a person has already been sentenced.

Article 15(2) preserves the right to prosecute crimes recognized by international law even if they are not recognized by national laws, eg: slavery, genocide, and torture.

Article 16

Everyone shall have the right to recognition everywhere as a person before the law.

- *Everyone has the right to be protected by the law.*

This is a NON-DEROGABLE right and cannot be suspended under any circumstances.

Commentary

This article recognizes everyone's legal status. It is the right of every individual to seek the protection of the law through the courts; and it is the duty of the court to recognize and uphold those rights.

What if 'the law' does not recognize the rights you speak of? What if the national law denies an individual this protection? It would appear then that the national law is in breach of international law and the basic standards that have been agreed internationally. The individual then must seek a remedy elsewhere (see ch 6).

Article 17

(1) No-one shall be subjected to arbitrary or unlawful interference with his privacy, family, home or correspondence, nor to unlawful attacks on his honour and reputation.

(2) *Everyone has the right to the protection of the law against such interference or attacks.*

■ **Everyone has the right to be left in peace.**

Commentary

Any interference by the authorities with a person's privacy must be lawful and accounted for. For example, a police search must be accompanied by an official document from a court authorizing the search. Surveillance techniques which include the interception of telephone conversations and correspondence must be authorized. If not, the person has the right to request the courts to order a stop to such interference. Adult consensual sexual activity in private is covered by the notion of 'privacy' in this article. A law prohibiting homosexual activity interferes with a person's privacy under Art 17.

> *The introduction of the concept of arbitrariness is intended to guarantee that even interference provided for by law should be in accordance with the provisions, aims and objectives of the ICCPR and should be, in any event, reasonable in the particular circumstances*
>
> (HRC: *General Comment No 16*)

Article 18

(1) *Everyone shall have the right to freedom of thought, conscience and religion. This right shall include freedom to have or to adopt a religion or belief of his choice, and freedom, either individually or in community with others and in public or private, to manifest his religion or belief in worship, observance, practice and teaching.*

(2) *No one shall be subject to coercion which would impair his freedom to have or to adopt a religion or belief of his choice.*

(3) *Freedom to manifest one's religion or beliefs may be subject only to such limitations as are prescribed by law and are necessary to protect public safety, order, health, or morals or the fundamental rights and freedoms of others.*

(4) *The States Parties to the present Covenant undertake to have respect for the liberty of parents and, when applicable, legal guardians to ensure the religious and moral education of their children in conformity with their own convictions.*

■ **Everyone is free to think or believe what s/he wants.**

This is NON-DEROGABLE and cannot be suspended under any circumstances.

Commentary

The HRC states:

> *Article 18 . . . does not permit any limitations whatsoever on the freedom of thought or conscience or on the freedom to have or adopt a religion or*

belief of one's choice. These freedoms are protected unconditionally . . . no one can be compelled to reveal his thoughts or adherence to a religion or belief (General Comment No 22)

Article 18(1) . . . to have or to adopt a religion . . . This means the freedom to choose a religion or belief, including the right to change one's current religion or belief for another, or none at all. An 'official party line' or an official religion cannot impair the rights of the individual under article 18 or any other rights in the ICCPR. Nor should people who do not accept the official ideology be discriminated against (HRC).

Article 18(2) This paragraph prohibits the use of force (or threat of force or penal sanctions) to compel belief. The HRC has noted that

policies or practices having the same intention or effect, such as, for example . . . restricting access to education, medical care, employment or the rights guaranteed by article 25 and other provisions of the Covenant are . . . inconsistent with article 18(2) (General Comment No 22)

The preamble to the *Declaration on the Elimination of All Forms of Intolerance and of Discrimination Based on Religion or Belief* states that

. . . the disregard and infringement of . . . the right to freedom of thought, conscience and religion or whatever belief, have brought, directly or indirectly, wars and great suffering to mankind . . .
. . . it is essential to promote understanding, tolerance and respect in matters relating to freedom of religion and belief and to ensure that the use of religion or belief for ends inconsistent with the Charter of the United Nations . . . is inadmissible.

The Declaration defines the rights under Art 18 to include the right to:
- assemble to worship in public and keep places for these purposes;
- establish appropriate charitable institutions;
- seek and receive voluntary contributions;
- publish and circulate relevant publications;
- teach a religion or belief in suitable places;
- observe days of rest and celebrate holidays according to one's faith; and
- establish and carry on communications in matters of religion and belief locally and abroad.

Article 18(3) Any limitations that are imposed must
- be set down by law;
- be necessary to protect public safety, order, health or morals* or the rights of others; and

*The concept of morals is not easily definable being a mix of many ingredients. What passes for moral behaviour in one part of the world may be considered immoral in another part. *Consequently,* states the HRC, *limitations on the freedom to manifest a religion or belief for the purpose of protecting morals must be based on principles not deriving exclusively from a single tradition (General Comment No 22).*

- not include any distinction, exclusion, restriction or preference that promote intolerance and discrimination.

All states should take effective measures to put an end to intolerance and discrimination, including the passing of laws.

Article 18(4) Children should enjoy religious education in accordance with the wishes of their parents or guardians and should not be forced to receive religious teaching against the wishes of their parents or guardians. Further, children should be brought up *in a spirit of understanding, tolerance, friendship among peoples . . .* and *. . . respect for freedom of religion or belief of others.*

NB: No manifestation of religion or belief may amount to propaganda for war or advocate national, religious or racial hatred.

Do the rights under article 18 include a right to refuse to perform military service? Increasingly states are including in their laws provisions for 'conscientious objectors' – enabling those persons genuinely holding beliefs that forbid the performance of military service to perform an alternative service. The HRC has said that such a right can be derived from Art 18 *inasmuch as the obligation to use lethal force may seriously conflict with the freedom of conscience and the right to manifest one's religion or belief*

(General Comment No 22)

Article 19

(1) Everyone shall have the right to hold opinions without interference.

(2) Everyone shall have the right to freedom of expression; this right shall include freedom to seek, receive and impart information and ideas of all kinds, regardless of frontiers, either orally, in writing or in print, or in the form of art, or through any other media of his choice.

(3) The exercise of the rights provided for in paragraph 2 of this article carried with it special duties and responsibilities. It may therefore be subject to certain restrictions, but these shall only be such as are provided by law and are necessary:

(a) For respect of the rights or reputations of others;

(b) For the protection of national security or of public order (ordre public), or of public health or morals.

Everyone has the right
- *to their own opinion;*
- *to express themselves; and*
- *to share and discuss information and ideas.*

Commentary

Freedom of expression is one of the cornerstones of democracy for without the freedom to criticize government and freely to express and exchange ideas, there can be no democracy. That said, the 'right to free speech' as it is often called, needs to be balanced by special duties and responsibilities. For example, no-one has the right to shout 'Fire!' in a crowded theatre; nor does my right to say what I like include a right to spread untrue stories about you and ruin your reputation.

A state may be in breach of this article if it passes laws which

- prohibit public speeches unless they have been authorized by the police;
- authorize the detention of people just because of their political views; or
- otherwise restrict the free flow of ideas and information on any other basis than is necessary to protect
  - the rights and reputations of others;
  - national security;
  - public order; or
  - public health or morals.

NB: The right to *hold opinions without interference* (19(1)) is a right to which the ICCPR permits no exception or restriction.

Article 20

(1) Any propaganda for war shall be prohibited by law.

(2) Any advocacy of national, racial or religious hatred that constitutes incitement to discrimination, hostility or violence shall be prohibited by law.

- **Preaching war is prohibited.**

Commentary

After the end of World War II, the chief and overriding purpose of the newly formed United Nations was to maintain peace. As a result, the UN Charter banned all use of force except in self-defence and, theoretically at least, gave itself (ie the UN) a monopoly on the use of force. States could 'go it alone' so long as they did so peacefully. Under the notion of collective security enshrined in the Charter, the monopoly of force by the UN provided security for the weaker states and so made military alliances superfluous.

There have been more wars since the United Nations came into existence; there are more weapons about, more people dying everyday . . . this ban has not been very successful, has it?   The ban is on the *international* use of force; it does not apply to how governments deal with insurrection or liberation movements within its borders. The overwhelming majority of the wars in recent years have been liberation struggles. That said, the ban has not been successful. In part, it is the fault of the member states of the United Nations who deliberately flout the rules or exploit the loopholes in them. In part it is the fault of the UN Charter and its system. A fictitious example illustrates the problem:

The people in a densely wooded area want to co-operate to combat the risk of forest fires. They identify three ways of coping with the matter:

(a) Each village undertakes to put out the fire with its own fire-extinguishers. A fire council is established. Its function is to advise how that duty is to be performed.

(b) The villages agree to co-operate: a fire council is established which decides if a fire has broken out and what must be done to put it out. The fire-extinguishers are owned by each village separately each of whom will use them as directed by the council.

(c) The villages empower the fire council to establish its own fire brigade, under its own authority, complete with its own fire extinguishers and other appliances necessary to put out any fires.

We are presently at the (b) stage. The UN does not have a standing military force available at short notice to police the world putting out conflicts.

So what power does the UN have? The UN Charter sets out the powers the Security Council has concerning *Action with respect to Threats to the Peace, Breaches of the Peace and Acts of Aggression* in Chapter 7 of the Charter. When an incident occurs that threatens international peace, the Security Council can take the following steps:

Step 1: Call on the states parties involved to reach a peaceful settlement.
If this fails:
Step 2: Issue certain measures for the parties to comply with.
If this fails:
Step 3: Call on other member states to use any measures not involving the use of armed force to bring pressure to bear on the parties – for example, economic sanctions, breaking diplomatic and communication links.

If this still does not work and the incident becomes a crisis, such as an invasion –

Step 4: The member state(s) involved can exercise the right of individual or collective self-defence (that is, calling on other member states to help to repel the aggressor).
Alternatively:
Step 5: The Security Council may take such action by air, sea or land forces as may be necessary to maintain or restore international peace.

The UN usually goes in to countries with the consent of the country concerned or at its express invitation.

'Peace' here means international peace; as 'war' means international war. What goes on within the borders of a state is the concern of that state unless the disruption is so severe that it threatens the security and peace of the region.

So states can fall back on the principle of 'national sovereignty' and tell the rest of the world to 'mind their own business'? The U N Charter states firmly: that

> *Nothing . . . shall authorize the United Nations to interfere in matters which are essentially within the domestic jurisdiction of any state.*   *(Art 2(7))*

However, it is increasingly accepted that human rights are not matters which are *essentially* within the domestic jurisdiction. The international community is allowed to call on other states to abide by their obligations under international law. Most recently, this has been supported by the Vienna Declaration stating:

> *The promotion and protection of all human rights is the legitimate concern of the international community (Art 4).*

In Vienna it was recognized that human rights are no longer the exclusive preserve of the state.

Article 20(2) Under the *International Convention on the Elimination of All Forms of Racial Discrimination* (CERD), states parties undertake to take measures to eradicate incitement to discrimination, in particular to criminalize
- the dissemination of ideas based on racial superiority or hatred;
- the incitement of others to racial hatred;
- acts of violence against any race or others of another colour or ethnic origin; and
- the provision of any assistance to racist activities, including financing (Art 4, CERD). For example, using the media to incite hostility and violence between various population groups would breach this article.

The article goes on to outlaw all organizations which incite or promote racial discrimination and makes illegal participation in such organizations.

Article 21
The right of peaceful assembly shall be recognized. No restrictions may be placed on the exercise of this right other than those imposed in conformity with the law and which are necessary in a democratic society in the interests of national security or public safety, public order (ordre public), the protection of public health or morals or the protection of the rights and freedoms of others.

- ***People have the right to meet together peacefully.***

Commentary

The right to freedom of assembly, like the right to freedom of speech, is a fundamental freedom and another cornerstone of a democratic society. Any restrictions, therefore, must be:

- lawful;
- necessary in a democratic society in the interests of
  - security or safety; or
  - order; or
  - public health or moral welfare; or
  - the rights of others.

Laws that impose unnecessary restrictions are found in a 'police state' rather than a democratic society.

When does a restriction become 'necessary'? When a crowd gathers to watch a dangerous spectacle, the police would be justified in dispersing the crowd for their own safety. When a crowd gathers to listen to a political speech, the police would be justified in dispersing the crowd if it was blocking the free movement of the traffic. However, orders that prohibit certain persons from meeting together for fear that they would start plotting, for example, violates this provision. Forbidding more than two persons from gathering at any one time also breaches the article.

Article 22

(1) Everyone shall have the right to freedom of association with others, including the right to form and join trade unions for the protection of his interests.

(2) No restrictions may be placed on the exercise of this right other than those which are prescribed by law and which are necessary in a democratic society in the interests of national security or public safety, public order (ordre public), the protection of public health or morals or the protection of the rights and freedoms of others. This article shall not prevent the imposition of lawful restrictions on members of the armed forces and of the police in their exercise of this right.

(3) Nothing in this article shall authorize States Parties to the International Labour Organization Convention of 1948 concerning Freedom of Association and Protection of the Right to Organize to take legislative measures which would prejudice, or to apply the law in such a manner as to prejudice the guarantees provided for in that Convention.

- ***People are free to join any group, association or organization they wish.***

Commentary

The individual on his/her own is weak; in association with others s/he becomes stronger. Accordingly the group can challenge authority and insist on better conditions of work, or protect the weaker members of the group. Freedom of association allows citizens to come together in organized groups in order to attain various ends, without government interference. The restrictions are the same as those that apply in Art 21.

The principle of freedom of association includes:

- the right of all workers and employers to establish organizations;
- the free functioning of such organizations;
- the right to join federations and confederations and to affiliate with international groupings of occupational organizations;
- the right of organizations not to be suspended or dissolved by administrative authorities;
- protection against anti-union discrimination;
- the right to collective bargaining;
- the right to strike; and
- the right to basic civil liberties which are a necessary precondition to the free exercise of trade union rights.

Other relevant information

1. *The International Covenant on Economic, Social and Cultural Rights* (ICESCR).

Under the ICESCR, this right is non-derogable. It establishes the rights of a Trade Union to:

- establish federations;
- function freely; and
- strike provided that . . . [the right to strike] . . . is exercised in conformity with the laws of the particular country.

Public servants, such as the police and armed forces, are often bound by laws governing strike action.

2. *Convention concerning Freedom of Association and Protection of the Right to Organize* (ILO /87); and

3. *Convention concerning the Application of the Principles of the Right to Organize and to Bargain Collectively* (ILO /98).

These are the two principal Conventions of the International Labour Organization in this area and reflect widely accepted labour law standards (see ch 6 at p 140).

Article 23

(1) The family is the natural and fundamental group unit of society and is entitled to protection by society and the state.

(2) The right of men and women of marriageable age to marry and to found a family shall be recognized.

(3) No marriage shall be entered into without the free and full consent of the intending spouses.

(4) *States parties to the present Covenant shall take appropriate steps to ensure equality of rights and responsibilities of spouses as to marriage, during marriage and at its dissolution. In the case of dissolution, provision shall be made for the necessary protection of any children.*

- ■ *Everyone is free to marry whom they want.*
- ■ *Husband and wife share equal rights and responsibilities.*

Commentary

The family is entitled to protection . . . What is a 'family' may differ from country to country and region to region: no definition is offered. The HRC comments that *when a group of persons is regarded as a family under the legislation and practice of a state, it must be given the protection referred to in article 23 (General Comment No 19).*

The 'protection' a state can afford will vary and depend on different social, economic, cultural and political conditions and traditions. Any protection must not discriminate on the basis of gender.

The right . . . to marry and to found a family . . . The right to have a family and to produce children may include the adoption of children, but does not guarantee a right to adopt.

. . . free and full consent . . . This means a couple must first publicize their intent to marry. Then each freely state, in person and before witnesses, their agreement to marry the other in the presence of a person authorized to marry them.

Marriage by proxy occurs when, for some exceptional reason, one of the parties cannot be physically present and is therefore represented by someone else. It is acceptable if the authorities are satisfied that each party has 'fully and freely' expressed their consent before witnesses and not withdrawn it.

Equality of rights and responsibilities . . .

> *This equality extends to all matters arising from their relationship, such as choice of residence, running of the household, education of the children and administration of assets. Such equality continues to be applicable to arrangements regarding legal separation or dissolution of the marriage*
> *(General Comment No 19)*

The state party is obliged to take appropriate steps (that is, if necessary, enacting laws) to see that its national laws governing marriage and divorce ensure the equal rights and responsibilities of both spouses and make provision for the protection of their children. Acts committed by a wife which give to the husband grounds for divorce but not vice-versa breach this article.

Article 24

(1) Every child shall have, without any discrimination as to race, colour, sex, language and religion, national or social origin, property or birth, the right to such measures of protection as are required by his status as a minor, on the part of his family, society and the State.

(2) Every child shall be registered immediately after birth and shall have a name.

(3) Every child has the right to acquire a nationality.

- **All children have the right to special care and attention.**

Commentary

Article 24(1) requires the state party to take special measures to protect children over and above the requirements of Art 2 (see p 17). In some instances the ICCPR singles out children for special protection (for example, they cannot be executed under Art 6. They must be separated from adults in detention under Art 10. They may be protected from publicity in trial proceedings under Art 14). However, in most cases these 'special measures' are not defined in the ICCPR. They are for each state to determine in view of the needs of the children within its boundaries. They should include the reduction of infant mortality and the eradication of malnutrition among children.

Article 24(2)   The main purpose of the obligation to register children after birth is to reduce the danger of abduction, sale of or traffic in children.

Article 24(3)   This provision prevents a child from receiving less protection from society and the state because s/he is stateless. The right to a nationality provides a child with political status.

Other relevant information

Convention on the Rights of the Child (CRC):   The CRC puts the best interests of the child first. It states that the views of the child should be respected, taking into account the child's evolving capacities. It lists measures to protect children's interests which each state party undertakes to fulfil, including:
- the protection of children from physical or mental harm and neglect, including sexual abuse or exploitation;
- respect for special consideration to be accorded to children in conflict with the law;
- the right of disabled children to special treatment, education and care;
- providing health care to all children, with emphasis on preventive measures, health education and the reduction of infant mortality;
- free and compulsory primary education;
- protection from economic exploitation;
- protection from all forms of sexual abuse and all other forms of exploitation prejudicial to the child's welfare;

- prohibition on the recruitment of children under 15 into the armed forces.

States parties undertake to publicize the principles and provisions of the Convention so that they are widely known.

Vienna Declaration   Article 21 calls for universal ratification of the CRC by 1995 and the effective implementation of its provisions. Attention should be given to the defence and protection of children, in particular
- the girl-child;
- abandoned children;
- street children;
- economically and sexually exploited children – including through child pornography, prostitution or sale of organs;
- children victims of diseases – including AIDS;
- refugee and displaced children;
- children in detention;
- children in armed conflict; and
- children victims of famine and drought.

The rights of the child should be a priority in the UN human rights system.

Article 48 urges all states to address the acute problem of children under especially difficult circumstances. Exploitation and abuse of children should be actively combated including by addressing their root causes. Effective measures are required against
- female infanticide;
- harmful child labour;
- sale of children and organs;
- child prostitution; and
- child pornography, as well as other forms of sexual abuse.

Article 25
Every citizen shall have the right and the opportunity, without any of the distinctions mentioned in article 2 and without unreasonable restrictions:
(a)   To take part in the conduct of public affairs, directly or through freely chosen representatives;
(b) · To vote and to be elected at genuine periodic elections which shall be by universal and equal suffrage and shall be held by secret ballot, guaranteeing the free expression of the will of the electors;
(c)   To have access, on general terms of equality, to public service in his country.

- **Everyone has the right to take part in the political life of his/her country.**

Commentary
If the question is asked: how does 'democracy' work? This article read together with

its twin in the UDHR provides a simple answer in a nutshell. Art 21 UDHR contains the substance:

The will of the people shall be the basis of the authority of government

and Art 25 adds the basic ingredients.

The only restrictions allowed are *reasonable* ones. Reasonable restrictions would involve children and the mentally ill, for example. The right to participate in government would be seriously limited where, for example,

- posts in government are reserved for members of the armed forces;
- elected officials can be removed by the executive;
- the institution of a Presidency-for-Life exists; and
- a political party is refused permission to register itself.

Article 26

All persons are equal before the law and are entitled without any discrimination to the equal protection of the law. In this respect, the law shall prohibit any discrimination and guarantee to all persons equal and effective protection against discrimination on any ground such as race, colour, sex, language, religion, political or other opinion, national or social origin, property, birth or other status.

- **Everyone has the right to the protection of the law from discrimination.**

Commentary

This article prohibits discrimination in law or in fact in any area protected by the authorities. When laws are passed by the state, they must satisfy Art 26 that they are not discriminatory. For example, it prohibits any one class of people from being singled out for 'special attention' to the detriment of that class. This article does not make all differences in treatment discriminatory. A differentiation based on reasonable and objective criteria is not 'discrimination' in the prohibited sense as used in the ICCPR (HRC). It is an additional legal insurance underwriting the promise in Article 2.

Other relevant information

Declaration on Race and Racial Prejudice 1978:

The differences between the achievements of the different peoples are entirely attributable to geographical, historical, political, economic, social and cultural factors. Such differences can in no case serve as a pretext for any rank-ordered classification of nations or peoples. (Art 1)

The differences between people can never be used as an excuse for treating one nation, or a people, as being superior to another. Any theory which involves the claim that racial or ethnic groups are inherently superior or inferior . . . has no scientific foundation and is contrary to the moral and ethical principles of humanity. Racial prejudice, historically linked with inequalities in power, reinforced by economic and social differences between individuals and groups . . . is totally without justification.

(Art 2)

In sum, there is no justification for racial prejudice since there is no foundation for any claim that one racial or ethnic group is superior to another.

Article 27

In those states in which ethnic, religious or linguistic minorities exist, persons belonging to such minorities shall not be denied the right, in community with the other members of their group, to enjoy their own culture, to profess and practise their own religion, or to use their own language.

- **Minority groups have a right to their own identity.**

Commentary

The persons designed to be protected under Art 27 are *those who belong to a group and who share in common a culture, a religion and/or a language.* They need not be citizens of the state party nor permanent residents: migrant workers and even visitors are entitled to the protection of Art 27. The state party is obliged to take positive measures to protect minorities not only against acts committed by the state but also acts committed by others within the state. It may also need to take positive measures to protect the identity of a minority and the rights of its members to enjoy and develop their culture and language and to practise their religion.

> *The protection of these rights is directed towards ensuring the survival and continued development of the cultural, religious and social identity of the minorities concerned, thus enriching the fabric of society as a whole*
>
> *(General Comment No 23)*

'Minorities' has no universally agreed definition. But there are elements a group claiming minority status under Art 27 must contain:
- the minority must be numerically smaller than the rest of the population;
- it must be different from the rest;
- it must occupy a non-dominant position in society; and
- as a group, it must wish to preserve its special characteristics.

Other relevant information

Since minorities are one of the most vulnerable groups in any society, they need particular attention and protection. There are a number of other Conventions that have come into force specifically aimed at minority groups.

1. Convention on the Prevention and Punishment of the Crime of Genocide (GC) The first use of the term 'genocide' in criminal proceedings was in the trials of Nazi war criminals at the Nuremberg War Crimes Tribunal in 1945. It was recognised by the United Nations as a crime under international law under Resolution 96(I) on 11 November 1946 and the Convention was completed in 1948.

Resolution 96(I) defines genocide as *a denial of the right of existence of entire human groups*, as homicide is the denial of the right to live of individual human beings. It instances events when racial, religious, political or other groups have been destroyed, entirely or in part. The punishment of genocide is a matter of international concern and those who commit it, whether individuals, public officials or statesmen are punishable.

It is generally agreed that genocide is a crime under international law.

The preamble to the GC stresses the need for international co-operation in order to deal with *such an odious scourge*. Genocide is defined as:

- *Killing people;*
- *Causing serious bodily harm or mental harm to people;*
- *Deliberately inflicting . . . conditions of life calculated to bring about . . . physical destruction, in whole or in part, of people;*
- *Preventing births;*
- *Forcibly transferring children;*

where *the intention* is to destroy in whole or in part a national, ethnic, racial or religious group. The intention to destroy *a group* is what distinguishes genocide from murder. However atrocious the acts, if they do not have that intention they do not amount to genocide.

In Nuremberg it was said:

> *Crimes against international law are committed by men, not by abstract entities, and only by punishing individuals who commit such crimes can the provisions of international law be enforced.*

Some (very few) rights are considered so fundamental and of such importance that all states can be held to have a legal interest in their protection. The prohibition on genocide is one.

State parties to the GC undertake to prevent and to punish the crime of genocide and any state can call on the UN to take such action as it thinks fit to prevent acts amounting to genocide.

2. Convention against Discrimination in Education This Convention provides, among other things, for the right of minorities to receive education in their own language. For example, a state cannot argue that a child receiving its education in a language that is not its mother tongue is being treated like every other child in the state. In fact, the child's rights are being violated. Equal treatment of minority groups involves the state taking positive measures to safeguard them against discrimination.

3. International Convention on the Elimination of all Forms of Racial Discrimination (CERD)   States parties to the CERD are obliged to make a criminal offence ideas, words or acts that spread racial hatred. They shall outlaw any group or organisation promoting racial discrimination. Further, they undertake to adopt immediate and effective measures to combat prejudices leading to racial hatred and promote tolerance and friendship, particularly in the fields of teaching, education, culture and information.

4. Convention concerning Indigenous and Tribal Peoples in Independent Countries, (ILO/169) (see Appendix 13)   'Tribal peoples' belong to a national community but are distinguished from other members of the community by their customs, laws and language, among other features. Under the Convention, they do not have the rights of 'peoples' to self-determination under international law.

The term 'indigenous peoples' has been defined as: communities, peoples and nations who

- have a historical link with pre-invasion and pre-colonial societies of that territory;
- consider themselves distinct from the post-invasion and post-colonial societies in those territories;
- usually form non-dominant sectors of society; and
- are determined to preserve, develop and transmit to future generations their ancestral territories, and their ethnic identity, in accordance with their own cultural patterns, social institutions and legal systems so that they continue as a people.

ILO 169 provides for

- tribal peoples' land rights;
- the safeguarding of their natural resources;
- the prohibition on forcible relocation of people;
- the need for consultation; and
- penalties for *unauthorized intrusion.*

5. Declaration on the Rights of Persons Belonging to National or Ethnic, Religious and Linguistic Minorities 1992   Stresses the rights of minorities to

- enjoy their own culture;
- profess and practise their own religion;
- use their own language in private and in public freely and without interference or any form of discrimination; and
- participate in decisions on the national and regional level concerning their minority.

States are obliged to:

- ensure that minorities may exercise their rights without discrimination and in full equality before the law;

- enable minorities to develop their culture except where these practices violate national law and international standards;
- take measures to provide opportunities for minorities to learn their mother tongue;
- encourage knowledge of the history, traditions, language and culture of the minorities within a country;
- consider measures to enable minorities to participate in the economic progress and development of the country.

6. International Convention on the Protection of the Rights of All Migrant Workers and Members of their Families 1990 The Convention repeats many of the rights contained in the ICCPR. It includes

- protection from mass expulsion;
- equal treatment with nationals, particularly regarding pay and conditions of work;
- the right to transfer earnings and savings to their own country; and
- respect for the cultural identity of migrant workers.

NB: The Convention is not yet in force as not enough states have ratified it.

Vienna Declaration

States should, in accordance with international law, take concerted positive steps to ensure respect for all human rights and fundamental freedoms of indigenous people, on the basis of equality and non-discrimination, and recognizing the value and diversity of their distinct identities, cultures and social organization.

(Art 20)

In singling out one group for assistance, aren't you discriminating against other groups? A balance is necessary between the interests of society as a whole and a group of persons within that society. Sometimes positive action is required to protect the interests of a group, new laws may be necessary to that end (see: p 18). Articles 28–53 are concerned with the constitution of the Human Rights Committee (HRC) and the reporting procedures for states parties together with other administrative details (see Appendix 4).

Chapter 3

Who monitors human rights

CERTAIN GROUPS in society can be said to have a special role regarding human rights:

medical professionals	students
law enforcement officers	teachers
lawyers and judges	religious organizations
trade unions	women's groups
journalists	business associations
intellectuals, academics, artists	

Because of this they should be:

- REMINDED of their special role and responsibilities;
- ENCOURAGED to apply human rights standards; and
- PARTICIPATE in the human rights NETWORK.

These groups form a key part of any society. If as individuals they cannot prevent human rights violations, they are in a position to communicate and/or expose them. Establishing links with other groups on national, regional and international levels is valuable for communicating information, and creates a network to protect and support the professional or group member. Each may have their own particular concerns and priorities: regular contact avoids duplicating activities and provides a basis for co-operation and mutual assistance. This network can put considerable pressure on any government to observe international human rights standards.

The Human Rights Network:

- Link
- Communication
- Publicity
- Protection.

Link A human rights network links people within a country and with the outside world. It can start with an individual who is concerned about abuses which are occurring in his/her local community. S/he can be the beginning of a network monitoring the situation by establishing links with other like-minded people s/he trusts. These links can form a chain across the country. This chain need not be in the form of an organization (usually it is not); it is simply a network for communicating what is really happening. It need not publish reports or any material. It can quietly and patiently note and observe what is happening and inform others in the network so that the truth cannot be suppressed completely.

Communication A network of individuals or groups automatically establishes a channel of communication. As modern communications technology has improved it is now easy and cheap to transmit information instantaneously to many different points around the world (see ch 6, A P C Network at p 126).

Publicity Exposure embarrasses governments. Television news pictures on millions of screens across the world can mobilize international public opinion to pressurize their governments for action. Even if the state forbids or prevents the national media from reporting effectively, the network can get information out of the country to appropriate international organs (see ch 6).

Exposure is also bad for business: it causes uncertainty and instability in the markets and makes foreign investors nervous.

Protection As part of a network, the monitor is neither alone nor anonymous. International groups can be alerted to pressure the government to release or ensure the safekeeping of individuals within the country. They can also be asked to assist in the urgent evacuation from a country of individuals at serious risk.

Locally, the network provides mutual support and assistance.

All of this puts people in a position to: *know, demand and defend* their human rights.

Setting up the human rights network

Locally

- Foster the development of pressure groups to protect human rights.
- Target professional and religious groups.
- Contact intellectuals and artists.
- Build up links with the national media and foreign correspondents.
- Meet with representatives of international N G Os based in the country.
- Contact foreign delegations or visitors to the country.

Internationally
- Forge links with international human rights organisations and other professional bodies (see: Appendix 14 and ch 6).
- Set up channels of communication with Special Rapporteurs and Working Groups (see ch 6 at p 124).
- Build up regional links and encourage visits.

Some groups have professional codes of conduct or guidelines for their behaviour. They reflect basic human rights standards. They act as a discipline, or a guide where the professional is unsure how to act. Where s/he falls short of the professional standards set out in the code of conduct s/he acts outside the acceptable standards of his/her profession.

While none of the principles enunciated in any of the codes are laws, they do represent standards of conduct which define what is honourable and professional behaviour for the profession.

NB: Even if a professional has not taken such an oath, such oaths exist and represent basic minimum international standards.

Medical professionals

Definition
All doctors, nurses, dentists, their assistants, and others who work in the medical field.

World Medical Association: (WMA)
Formed in 1947, it formulates policies and practices for the medical professions, updating and responding to new developments. All medical professionals are governed and supported by the WMA.

Codes of Conduct

> *The primary task of the medical profession is to preserve health and save life.* (WMA *Regulations in Time of Armed Conflict*)

> *The fundamental responsibility of the nurse is fourfold: to promote health, to prevent illness, to restore health and to alleviate suffering.*
> *(International Council for Nurses Code for Nurses)*

There are a number of professional codes of conduct. Those of particular importance are:
1 Declaration of Geneva;
2 Declaration of Tokyo;
3 Declaration of Hawaii;

4 Statement on the Nurse's role in safeguarding human rights;

5 Resolution of Singapore; and

6 The UN Principles of Medical Ethics relevant to the Role of Health Personnel, particularly Physicians, in the Protection of Prisoners and Detainees against Torture and other Cruel, Inhuman and Degrading Treatment or Punishment.

The Declaration of Geneva   The WMA adopted and amended the earliest known medical code of ethics, the ancient Hippocratic Oath. It was a requirement dating from the fourth century, that all physicians were required to swear this oath.

Declaration of Geneva

At the time of being admitted as a member of the medical profession:

I solemnly pledge myself to consecrate my life to the service of humanity;

I will give to my teachers the respect and gratitude which is their due;

I will practise my profession with conscience and dignity;

The health of my patient will be my first consideration;

I will maintain by all the means in my power, the honour and the noble traditions of the medical profession;

My colleagues will be my brothers;

I will not permit considerations of religion, nationality, race, party politics or social standing to intervene between my duty and my patient;

I will maintain the utmost respect for human life from its beginnings, even under threat, and I will not use my medical knowledge contrary to the laws of humanity;

I make these promises solemnly, freely and upon my honour.

The special role of medical professionals   All medical professionals have a duty to preserve health, save life and alleviate suffering.

- Their professional role gives them a special standing in society;
- they occupy a position of trust;
- they are viewed as *impartial*; and
- they have *access* to places where ordinary people cannot go.

The Declaration of Geneva contains principles corresponding to a number of human rights and fundamental freedoms in the UDHR and ICCPR. In particular

- the right to life and liberty; freedom from discrimination, torture, slavery and inhumane conditions of detention.

For example, under the Declaration of Geneva the medical professional must not discriminate, for whatever reason, when treating a patient: the medical professional has the same duty to save the life of a terrorist as that of a child. S/he must do his/her utmost to alleviate the suffering of any patient, whether they can pay for it or not.

Medical professionals working with police, prisons or security forces are well placed to monitor abuses of human rights and fundamental freedoms. Under the UN *Standard Minimum Rules for the Treatment of Prisoners* (see: Appendix 7), medical professionals should be admitted to places of detention to provide medical care for prisoners.

> *The medical officer shall see and examine every prisoner as soon as possible after his admission and thereafter as necessary, with a view particularly to the discovery of physical or mental illness and the taking of all necessary measures.* *(Rule 24)*

The *Standard Minimum Rules* go on to state that a sick prisoner should be visited by a medical professional daily. The medical professional has a responsibility to report to the prison director if s/he is of the view that the conditions are injurious to the physical or mental health of any prisoner.

It is the medical professional and not the prison administration who has the care of the physical and mental health of prisoners.

Medical professionals and torture   Torture and other cruel, inhuman or degrading treatment or punishment are expressly and absolutely prohibited in international law in every circumstance (see Art 7 ICCPR at p 29). Any participation by 'health personnel' in acts of torture is a gross contravention of medical ethics (Principle 2, UN *Principles of Medical Ethics*).

It is never a defence in law for a person to say that s/he was forced to be involved in acts of this kind. Torture remains in widespread use around the world. The WMA recognized that doctors are involved in torture and issued the Declaration of Tokyo. The Declaration expressly forbids any doctor's involvement – direct or indirect – in the practice of torture or other cruel acts. Nurses have a responsibility to take action to safeguard the rights of persons in detention.

Declaration of Tokyo 1975

Preamble   It is the privilege of the medical doctor to practise medicine in the service of humanity, to preserve and restore bodily and mental health without distinction as to persons, to comfort and ease the suffering of his or her patients. The utmost respect for human life is to be maintained under threat, and no use made of any medical knowledge contrary to the laws of humanity.

For the purpose of this Declaration, torture is defined as the deliberate, systematic or wanton infliction of physical or mental suffering by one or more persons acting alone or on the orders of any authority, to force another person to yield information, to make a confession, or for any other reason.

Declaration
1 The doctor shall not countenance, condone or participate in the practice of torture or other forms of cruel, inhuman or degrading procedures,

whatever the offence of which the victim of such procedures is suspected, accused or guilty, and whatever the victim's beliefs or motives, and in all situations, including armed conflict and civil strife.

2 The doctor shall not provide any premises, instruments, substances or knowledge to facilitate the practice of torture or other forms of cruel, inhuman or degrading treatment or to diminish the ability of the victim to resist such treatment.

3 The doctor shall not be present during any procedure during which torture or other forms of cruel, inhuman or degrading treatment is used or threatened.

4 A doctor must have complete clinical independence in deciding upon the care of a person for whom she or he is medically responsible. The doctor's fundamental role to alleviate the distress of his or her fellow men and no motive whatsoever, be it personal, collective or political, shall prevail against this higher purpose.

5 Where a prisoner refuses nourishment and is considered by the doctor as capable of forming an unimpaired and rational judgement concerning the consequences of such a voluntary refusal of nourishment, he or she shall not be fed artificially. The decision as to the capacity of the prisoner to form such a judgement should be confirmed by at least one other independent doctor. The consequences of the refusal of nourishment shall be explained by the doctor to the prisoner.

6 The World Medical Association will support, and should encourage the international community, the national medical associations and fellow doctors, to support the doctor and his or her family in the face of threats or reprisals resulting from a refusal to condone the use of torture or other forms of cruel, inhuman or degrading treatment.

Nurses The International Council of Nurses issued the *Statement on the Nurse's Role in Safeguarding Human Rights.* The Statement warns nurses:

> *There may be pressures applied to use one's knowledge and skills in ways that are not beneficial to patients or others. Scientific discoveries have brought about more sophisticated forms of torture and resuscitation so that those being tortured can be kept alive for repeated sessions. It is in such circumstances that nurses must be clear about what actions they must take, as in no way, can they participate in such torture, or torture techniques.*

Nurses are advised
- to verify the facts;
- to maintain confidentiality;
- to work within a group;
- to notify the national nurses' association where possible; and

- that personal risk is a factor that has to be considered.

The International Council of Nurses stressed in the *Resolution of Singapore* (1975) that a nurse's first responsibility is towards the patient, notwithstanding considerations of national security and interest; and that nurses with knowledge of torture should report the matter to the appropriate national and/or international bodies.

These codes do not provide a complete set of guidelines to cover every situation which, all too commonly, medical professionals have to face.

Example 1   The police call a medical professional in to sign a document to confirm that no torture has taken place.

There are clear signs that torture has taken place.

Example 2   The police call in a medical professional to revive a prisoner. There are clear signs that the person is being tortured. The doctor suspects that the purpose of reviving him is to continue the torture session.

Example 3   The medical professional notices that the place of detention is 'secret' and other people are being held there incommunicado and in inhuman conditions.

What can the medical professional do?   As a minimum, s/he can:

Note

Write a statement, or detailed note, of what s/he has seen (see ch 4, How to Write a Statement at p 103).

Report

Inform professional colleagues and the network.

Communicate

Write a report to put before those in authority and/or transmit internationally.

Medical Professionals and legal and extra-legal executions

(i) Legal executions   It is a contravention of medical ethics for health personnel, particularly physicians, to be involved in any professional relationship with prisoners or detainees *the purpose of which is not solely to evaluate, protect or improve their physical or mental health.* (UN Principle 3)

Medical professionals who use their skills for any other purpose than *to evaluate, protect or improve* the health of patients in detention contravene medical ethics. The WMA issued a resolution that *it is unethical for physicians to participate in capital punishment.*

The only area of medical involvement ethically permissible is certification of death following capital punishment since family and friends of the executed person have as much need of official evidence of death as the authorities.

(ii) Extra-legal executions Medical professionals have an essential role to play in investigations into deaths that occur in police custody at the hands of a public official in suspicious circumstances, or other possible extra-legal killing, such as the discovery of a secret grave (see Art 9 and Commentary at p 34).

An *autopsy* is an essential step in the investigation process. An autopsy helps to determine the time, cause and manner of death and can help to identify the victim. If the killing was unlawful, the facts discovered by the autopsy can provide important evidence in any commission of enquiry or future criminal proceedings against the persons responsible.

The UN issued *A Model Autopsy Protocol* which sets out international standards to assist governments in establishing proper autopsy procedures (see Appendix 6). Its use, stated in the introduction, will permit early and final resolution of potentially controversial cases and will thwart the speculation and innuendo that are fuelled by unanswered, partially answered or poorly answered questions in the investigation of an apparently suspicious death. The CHR has invited governments to incorporate the Model into their own national rules and practices.

Forensic anthropology is another key area. Friends and relatives spend years searching for those who have 'disappeared'. Unidentified bodies are discovered in secret graves. Forensic anthropology can help to identify the body and explain the fate of the victim. This science applies various anthropological and archaeological techniques to examine the skeletal remains of a corpse to determine the deceased's identity and the manner and cause of death.

When a grave containing the remains of unknown persons is discovered, everything should be left in place and protected from disturbance. Local experts should then be contacted to excavate the area. If they are not available, foreign experts can be contacted through the human rights network. If none of this is possible, the grave should be marked and concealed until a time when it can be investigated.

Commissions of Enquiry should be established when there is no other proper or adequate investigation taking place into human rights violations (see ch 5 at p 116).

In many countries, public enquiries follow all deaths that occur in custody, or suspicious circumstances, as a matter of course. Medical professionals should promote such procedures in their own country and, as impartial and independent individuals, be prepared to sit on any such commissions.

Ways in which medical professionals have been used as tools in a repressive system
- by issuing death certificates which give false causes of death;
- by issuing certificates which state that torture has not taken place in circumstances where it clearly has;

- by making drugs freely available to the 'authorities' for unspecified purposes; and
- by keeping secret the fact that systematic and serious human rights violations take place – eg the widespread use of torture techniques in interrogation and 'disappearing' people to secret places of detention.

Steps medical professionals can take to promote human rights

- Keep informed of the human rights situation.
- Be aware of the international conventions governing human rights.
- Use medical skills properly, in accordance with the relevant professional codes.
- Examine patients thoroughly, with sensitivity and respect.
- Treat according to the medical interests of the patient.
- Treat every patient equally.
- Give every patient the best care possible in the circumstances.
- Keep thorough and accurate medical records, documenting the examination and any conclusions.
- Keep records confidential, use only with the patient's permission or with a proper court order.
- Build up a database with statistics on human rights violations, eg the suspected incidence of torture, rape, civilian mine injuries and the use of chemical weapons.
- Establish links with regional and international professional bodies.
- Build up local links with others concerned with human rights, eg fellow professionals, human rights workers and NGOs.
- Encourage the active and constructive use of commissions of enquiry.

These steps require courage: medical professionals do not want to use their skills against humanity, but if they are threatened by the authorities with physical harm to themselves or their families – what choice do they have?

> *The primary obligation of the physician is his professional duty; in performing his professional duty, the physician's supreme guide is his conscience.*   (WMA: *Regulations in Time of Armed Conflict*)

Under principle 6 of the Declaration of Tokyo, the WMA commits itself to support any doctor and his/her family confronted with such a situation.

Police/Law Enforcement Officials

Definition   The term Law Enforcement Official (LEO) includes all officers of the law, whether appointed or elected, who exercise police powers, especially the powers of arrest and detention.

It includes prison officers, members of the armed forces carrying out police work, or special patrols appointed by the state.

Codes of Conduct

1 UN Code of Conduct for Law Enforcement Officials.
2 UN Basic Principles on the Use of Force and Firearms by LEOs.
3 UN Standard Minimum Rules for the Administration of Juvenile Justice (the Beijing Rules).
4 UN Standard Minimum Rules for the Treatment of Prisoners.
5 UN Body of Principles for the Protection of All Persons under Any Form of Detention or Imprisonment.
6 Geneva Conventions: Common Article 3.

The Vienna Declaration states that governments have a duty to train their LEOs in human rights law (Art 33). The international law of human rights should be part of the training syllabus for LEOs in the same way that soldiers are educated in the rules of war. Emphasis should be placed on the following articles:

Universal Declaration of Human Rights

5 torture and other cruel, inhuman or degrading treatment
6 recognition of everyone before the law
7 equality before the law
9 no arbitrary arrest, detention or exile
10 fair, public hearing, independent impartial tribunal
11 innocent until proven guilty
12 no arbitrary interference with privacy
13 freedom of movement
18 freedom of thought, conscience and religion
19 freedom of opinion and expression
20 peaceful assembly and association

International Covenant on Civil and Political Rights

6 right to life, safeguards for use of death penalty
7 torture and other cruel, inhuman and degrading treatment
9 arbitrary arrest and detention; rules for treatment on arrest
10 treatment of detainees
11 no imprisonment for failing to fulfil a contract
12 freedom of movement in, out and around the country
14 rights when charged with a criminal offence
15 no charging for an act which was not criminal when it was done
16 recognition as a person before the law
17 no arbitrary interference with privacy
18 freedom of thought, conscience and religion
19 freedom of opinion, expression
21 right of peaceful assembly

22 freedom of association
26 equality before the law, protection of the law
(see ch 2 and commentaries on the relevant articles).

Code of conduct for LEOs   The Code stresses that LEOs must uphold the human rights of all individuals and only use force when strictly necessary. It expressly prohibits acts of torture in any circumstances and rejects the defence of superior orders (see Appendix 8).

Basic principles on the use of force and firearms by law enforcement officials   The Basic Principles recognize in their Preamble the great importance of the work performed by LEOs and the vital role they play in society.

The Basic Principles elaborate on when the use of force is justified and outline the conditions that should apply.

Firearms may only be used
- in self-defence;
- in defence of others against the imminent threat of death or serious injury;
- to prevent a crime involving threat to life;
- to arrest a person presenting such a threat and resisting their authority; or
- to prevent the escape of a person presenting such a threat.

In any event, the lethal use of firearms is only allowed when strictly unavoidable in order to protect life.

If the decision to use firearms is taken, LEOs must
- identify themselves; and
- give a clear warning of their intent to use firearms, with enough time for the warning to be observed, unless
  - a warning would place the LEO at undue risk;
  - a warning would place others at serious risk; or
  - a warning would be clearly inappropriate or pointless in the circumstances.

The Basic Principles include guidelines for action on the use of force when it is unavoidable. In such circumstances, LEOs must:
- exercise restraint and act *in proportion to* the seriousness of the offence and legitimate objective to be achieved;
- minimize injury and respect and preserve human life;
- ensure medical assistance is rendered to any injured persons;
- ensure that relatives or close friends of the injured person are notified at the earliest possible moment.

In either case, the *unlawful* use of force or firearms by LEOs should be a criminal offence. Where injury or death is caused by the use of force or firearms by LEOs, the incident must be reported *promptly* to their superiors. Superior officers should be held responsible if they know or should have known that LEOs under their command have used force and firearms unlawfully and they did not take all measures in their power to prevent or report such abuse. These principles are binding at all times including public emergencies (see Appendix 9).

The Beijing Rules The Beijing Rules are concerned with the administration of justice as it affects children and young people (juveniles). Juveniles are a vulnerable group in society and should receive special treatment by LEOs. When a juvenile is arrested, his/her parents or guardian should be immediately informed. The issue of release should be considered without delay either by a court or appropriate authority. LEOs should also exercise their discretion not to charge a juvenile in appropriate cases. Where juveniles are detained in custody, it shall only be a measure of last resort and for the shortest possible period of time. Alternative measures should always be considered. Juveniles should always be kept separate from adult offenders.

Standard Minimum Rules for the Treatment of Prisoners (see Appendix 7) The Standard Minimum Rules provide detailed safeguards to be applied to all prisoners without discrimination of any kind. They issue guidelines on:
- registration of prisoners;
- separation of different categories of prisoners;
- conditions in which prisoners ought to be kept, including:
  - accommodation;
  - personal hygiene;
  - clothing and bedding;
  - food;
  - exercise and sport; and
  - health care;
- discipline and punishment; and
- contact with the outside world.

The Standard Minimum Rules should be made available to all persons in charge of places of detention. Copies of this and other materials can be obtained from the UN Centre for Human Rights in Geneva (see Appendix 14).

The four Geneva Conventions: Common Article 3 The Geneva Conventions deal with the law of war and the rules governing the officers and soldiers in the conduct of war. Article 3 appears in each of the four Conventions. It governs any armed conflict that is not international, for example, civil war.
   Common Article 3 (as it is called) provides that:
- People who are not actively involved in fighting must be treated humanely in all circumstances without any discrimination whatsoever. Included in this category are:
  - combatants who have laid down their weapons and stopped fighting; and
  - combatants who have stopped fighting due to sickness, injuries, detention, or any other reason.

Common Article 3 prohibits:

- murder, mutilation, cruel treatment and torture;
- hostage taking;
- all kinds of humiliating and degrading treatment; and
- arbitrary or summary execution.

Common Article 3 obliges all parties to collect and care for the wounded and the sick. The International Committee of the Red Cross (ICRC), or other impartial humanitarian body, may offer its services to the parties to the conflict.

Are LEOs ever allowed to use force? It depends whether it is reasonable in the circumstances.

For example, where a suspect resists a lawful arrest, the LEO is entitled to use such force as is reasonable to detain the suspect.

What does that mean? The degree of force used must be *proportionate* to the resistance offered and must stop as soon as the suspect no longer resists: a gun can never be used against a fist – it is not proportionate.

So if an LEO is confronted by someone with a gun, the LEO is entitled to shoot that person dead? LEOs should use firearms as a last resort. If the armed suspect ignores all warnings and poses an immediate threat of death or serious injury to others (including the LEO), then the LEO is entitled to shoot that person. LEOs should be issued with a clear set of guidelines and reminded that they too are subject to the law.

Torture and cruel acts are forbidden under any circumstances but they happen all over the world – how are they to be stopped? Torture is a crime. A criminal who wears a uniform is still a criminal. These degrading practices will not stop unless

- individuals refuse to take part and persuade others to do the same;
- LEOs are trained and paid properly;
- the culture of violence within the law enforcement agencies is replaced by a culture of professionalism, where pride is substituted for contempt;
- torturers and those who allow the practice of torture are accountable for their actions in law, enforced through the courts; and
- the courts pass appropriate sentences.

Steps LEOs can take to promote human rights

- Know and follow the relevant codes governing LEOs.
- Know the International Bill of Human Rights.
- Encourage the inclusion of human rights courses into the training of LEOs.
- Defend the rights of others: lead by example.
- Investigate human rights violations and promote the use of inquests, particularly concerning deaths in detention.
- Communicate human rights violations to the human rights network.
- Establish links with national, regional, and professional international bodies.
- Keep accurate records of human rights violations.

Lawyers and Judges

The role of Lawyers and Judges

Lawyers and Judges have a central part to play in maintaining the rule of law which is essential for the protection of human rights and fundamental freedoms. They form part of 'the Establishment' in all societies. There is a firmly established international legal network, connected through Bar Associations and Law Societies to which all lawyers and judges automatically belong.

Codes of Conduct

1 Basic Principles on the Independence of the Judiciary.
2 Basic Principles on the Role of Lawyers.
3 UN Guidelines on the Role of Prosecutors.

Judges

Basic principles on the independence of the judiciary An independent judiciary is one of the cornerstones of a democracy. It is also an essential component in the proper administration of the rule of law.

The Basic Principles set out the principles upon which genuine independence is founded:

- It is the duty of government to respect and observe the independence of the judiciary.
- It is the duty of the judiciary to decide matters impartially.
- Judges must not be subjected to, nor accept
  - restrictions;
  - improper influences;
  - inducements;
  - pressures; or
  - threats or interferences of any kind with the judicial process.
- Judges have exclusive authority to decide all issues that come before them.
- Judges should be properly trained and selected without any discrimination.
- Their appointment as judge should be guaranteed up to a fixed retirement age, or the end of their term of office.
- They may only be removed for incapacity, or behaviour that makes them unfit to discharge their duties.

The preamble to the Basic Principles emphasizes that judges have the ultimate decision over life, freedoms, rights, duties and property of citizens. Accordingly, judges are under a very high duty to have a thorough knowledge of international human rights laws and to give effect to them (see Appendix 10).

The judge who upholds the rule of law often becomes a target of those forces acting outside the law: who protects the judge? The government should protect judges, particularly in remote or rural areas. All judges and lawyers should insist on adequate measures for their protection. The international legal community should also be mobilized to publicize, support, aid or use any other measures to assist their colleagues.

Lawyers

Basic Principles on the Role of Lawyers   The Basic Principles deal, first with the individual's right of access to legal assistance; secondly, with the duties of lawyers; and thirdly, with the protection of lawyers (see: Appendix 11).

Access
- Everyone has the right to have the assistance of a lawyer to protect their rights and defend them in criminal proceedings. The poor shall be assisted by the state.
- Everyone is to be informed of this right on arrest and is to have prompt access to a lawyer no later than 48 hours after detention.
- Everyone shall have a lawyer assigned to him/her, where the interests of justice so require. The lawyer must have the experience and competence to meet the nature of the offence (free of charge if necessary).
- Everyone shall be able to consult in confidence with their lawyer (see ch 2 and commentary under Art 14 at p 47).

Duties of lawyers   The duties of lawyers towards their clients include:
- advising clients of their legal rights and obligations and the workings of the legal system;
- assisting clients in every appropriate way and taking legal action to protect their interests; and
- assisting clients before the courts, tribunals or other administrative authorities.

The lawyer's primary duty is to his/her clients.

Protection of lawyers
- Lawyers should be permitted to carry out their work without any form of intimidation or interference and to consult freely with their clients. They are entitled to protection if their security is at risk.
- Lawyers are not to be identified by the authorities with the interests or causes of their clients.
- Lawyers shall not be prosecuted for statements they make on behalf of their clients in good faith before a court, tribunal, or other administrative authority.
- Lawyers are entitled to early access to all appropriate files and documents in a particular case and all communications with clients must be respected as confidential.
- Disciplinary proceedings against lawyers must be brought before an impartial

disciplinary committee established by the legal profession and subject to independent judicial review proceedings.

The role of prosecutors

Lawyers who prosecute are *essential agents of the administration of justice* and regarded as having distinct duties and responsibilities in carrying out their function. UN *Guidelines on the Role of Prosecutors* deal with the duties of, and protection offered to, lawyers who prosecute (see: Appendix 12).

Duties A prosecutor's duties are:

- to act at all times objectively, fairly, efficiently and to uphold the rights of the individual;
- to prosecute *impartially* without any discrimination whatsoever;
- to pay attention to all the relevant circumstances in a case regardless of whether they are to the advantage or disadvantage of the accused: *the prosecutor must not ignore or suppress any information that favours the accused;*
- to abandon any prosecution where an impartial investigation reveals the charge to be unfounded;
- to refuse to use evidence which the prosecutor knows or reasonably believes has been obtained by torture or other unlawful acts constituting grave violations of the accused's human rights;
- to take all necessary steps to ensure that those responsible for human rights violations are brought to justice; and
- to respect the present guidelines and to prevent and actively oppose any violations of them and to report such violations to the authorities.

Protection

- Prosecutors shall not be intimidated, threatened or interfered with in the course of their duties; and
- they are entitled to the protection of the state where their safety is threatened.

Isn't the main role of the prosecutor to act on behalf of the state to ensure the conviction of the accused? No. The prosecutor is an agent of the administration of justice and, as a lawyer, has a duty at all times to uphold the rule of law. There will be occasions when the highest public official will be prosecuted and for this reason the prosecutor must act, and be seen to act, independently of the state. The prosecutor presents a case to the court on behalf of the people of the country not the government. S/he may present the case forcefully and thoroughly but never unfairly.

Steps lawyers and judges can take to protect human rights

- Lawyers and judges should have a thorough knowledge of international human rights law and should actively promote the safeguards protecting the individual, in particular:

- the codes governing the conduct of LEOs; and
- the treatment of juveniles, persons in detention and persons facing the death penalty.

■ They should actively promote the rule of law at all times, by:
- maintaining the safeguards set out in Art 7–11 UDHR (see ch 2 and commentaries on Art 6, 9, 10, 11);
- insisting on public judicial enquiries into deaths in custody; and
- prosecuting serious human rights violations.

■ They should always act in a manner consistent with the integrity of their profession, by:
- complying with the codes of conduct and guidelines governing their professional duties; and
- maintaining their professional independence.

■ As members of the establishment, they should encourage the government to implement international human rights standards, by:
- reviewing national laws as to their compliance with those standards;
- strictly applying international standards to national laws – particularly in a public emergency;
- holding national conferences and promoting public debate on the rule of law;
- establishing links with the international legal community to support and assist in promoting the rule of law and compliance with international standards, by:
  - holding international conferences;
  - encouraging visits and delegations from outside academics, Bar Associations and Law Societies;
  - keeping in regular contact with colleagues abroad.

Chapter 4

How to monitor, investigate and report in a state in emergency

Introduction

`MONITORING´` means observing a situation, following it closely and reporting at periods on what has been observed and the conclusions that have been reached. What is monitored and how it is monitored will depend on the circumstances of the country or region at the time.

  NB: The monitoring of human rights in a repressive state is highly dangerous. The work puts yourself – and others – at risk.

A country that is suffering increasing state repression and/or a high degree of violence or social unrest has different human rights concerns and challenges to a country in the transitional stage from one-party rule to multiparty democracy.

This chapter is not a blueprint for action, but offers a basic guide to steps that can be taken to monitor human rights violations. Under a repressive state the priority is to document and monitor the violations as they occur and, where possible, communicate the information to people at home and abroad.

Documenting and publicizing human rights violations alerts people both within and without the country of the extent to which power is being abused. A government that controls the information can manipulate the facts for propaganda or other purposes. It can issue denials of reports or rumours that cannot be proved. It enables a government to confuse its critics by turning truth on its head. What you do not know you cannot challenge; what you do know must be communicated.

The condition of ignorance and fear imposed by repressive regimes can be changed by people educating themselves and creating channels of communication to each other and the outside world. No-one can insist on their rights if they do not know what they are and what they mean. Where possible, teams of trainers are needed to go around safe, accessible areas, creating human rights groups, making links between them and developing education programmes. Mass information items can be spread through the media of song, drama, radio, news sheets and other means. This should encourage open debate about the meaning of human rights and the accountability of government.

Monitoring

The information gathered in the course of monitoring builds up a picture of the human rights situation in the country or region. This information – if accurate – challenges, or supports, the legitimate claim of a government to govern. A critical report places the burden on the government to answer or remedy the situation. A refusal by governments to do anything puts their legitimacy in question.

- Information is vital; it must be accurate, objective and clear.
- Because it is vital, it becomes dangerous to possess it. Witnesses are often scared and everyone is vulnerable; therefore it must be kept confidential and safe in order to protect sources, yourself and it.
- Information is useless unless it is communicated; therefore channels of communication must be opened and maintained locally, regionally and internationally.

What to monitor

- Prisons and detention centres (secret and open);
- Trials;
- Hospitals;
- Cemeteries, waste-ground, rivers, lakes etc;
- Vulnerable groups: refugees and internally displaced people (IDPs), women and children, the disabled and mentally ill, and minority groups.

(a) Prisons and detention centres The monitor is not concerned with the guilt or innocence of the prisoner but with:
- the lawfulness of the person's detention:
  - has s/he been detained arbitrarily; or
  - for administrative reasons;
- the conditions of detention:
  - adequate food, water, healthcare;
  - adequate access to a legal representative and/or family members;
- the length of pre-trial detention:
  - how long the person has been detained;
  - what the charges are;
  - the prospect of being tried in a reasonable period of time.

Since the monitor has no legal authority to enter these premises, it is unlikely admittance will be granted. Where practicable, the monitor (accompanied) should visit the governor, or head of the detention centre, in good faith and in a spirit of co-operation. S/he should take along a copy of the *Standard Minimum Rules on the Treatment of Prisoners* (see Appendix 7).

Note whether:
- a register is kept of inmates;
- prisoners are separated: men from women, adults from juveniles and the convicted from the untried;
- food is adequate for health and strength;
- punishment involves: corporal punishment and dark cells or cruel, inhuman or degrading treatment;
- forms of restraint are used: instruments of restraint must never be used as punishments;
- there is contact with the outside world;
- medical visits are made;
- religious services are held and inmates have access to them;
- clothing and bedding are adequate;
- some prisoners exercise control over the others; and
- general health and sanitary conditions are adequate: mosquito nets, blankets, washing and toilet facilities.

The monitor should also ask for a list of the prisoners, and note particularly those:
- under 18 and over 59 years of age;
- accused of politically related offences;
- held for long periods without trial; and
- mentally ill, or with other health problems.

Follow-up is important to ascertain whether people are being tried, released at the end of their sentence or period of detention, and whether the number changes or not. Regular visits should be made. Establish informal contact with the delegate from the International Committee of the Red Cross (ICRC).

Where it is impossible to get access to the places of detention, ex-inmates should be interviewed to get an idea of conditions, numbers of prisoners and the matters noted above.

Secret places of detention/'ghost houses' The monitor should identify the locations of these establishments. The names of those in charge should be noted. A log should be kept of the traffic in and out of these places. A camera would be helpful here. The addresses should be communicated to the ICRC and other international human rights organizations.

(b) Trial observations At any political trial, observer delegations should be invited to attend from trade unions, legal associations and human rights groups abroad.

These are opportunities for the international community to see how the state really works and for international organizations to make known to the court, the national authorities and the general public, the international interest and concern in the trial in question.

It is often the case that, when governments or the courts hear of international observers coming, they move the time or place of the trial without giving notice. This should not discourage the attempt. A trial often focuses the spotlight on governments and raises the veil of secrecy behind which they seek to hide.

A Model Trial Observation   At court:

- The observer should be smartly dressed. S/he should be courteous and impartial at all times. S/he should be in possession of a formal letter of introduction from the organization sending him/her. Copies of this letter should be available.
- Where circumstances allow, a formal letter should be sent to the Minister for Justice. A copy should be given as a matter of courtesy to the presiding judge, prosecutor and defence. The press should be informed that there is an observer presence at the trial. Prudence should be exercised in talking to the press while the trial is in progress.

If confronted by a determined reporter, the observer may wish to state simply:

- by whom s/he is sent;
- the reason why s/he is there (for example, concern to see that the trial proceedings are fair by international standards; or that there have been allegations of mistreatment of prisoners; or the international public interest in the trial; or other such reason).

NB: The observer should not give his/her own opinion about the trial or guilt or innocence of the accused.

Gaining access   All trials must be conducted openly, if they are to be fair. If a trial goes into camera (ie, excludes members of the public) the reasons therefor must be stated in open court. An exclusion order need not affect the trial observer in any event (see ch 2 and Art 14(1) at p 45).

The trial observer should sit in the court if possible where s/he can see and hear clearly – if not, then in the public gallery. Much will depend on the attitude of the officers and staff of the court. Once the presence of an observer is known, s/he will be under scrutiny. The observer therefore should be careful not to be identified with any side, defence or prosecution. The observer is there to note and observe the fairness of the proceedings: s/he should act impartially at all times.

A detailed note should be taken of the evidence heard in court and of all the court proceedings. A report should be written up afterwards.

The observer is usually presumed to have a defence bias. In the interests of balance, an interview should be organized with the prosecutor, or someone from the prosecutor's office. The interview should be carefully prepared in advance and cover the main areas of concern. This is particularly important when the 'audience' granted is not a lengthy one. The interview summary should appear in the report.

The Report   The report on the trial should include the following sub-headings:

Background to the Trial
- Give the outsider a picture of what is happening in the country generally.
- Provide a summary of the political situation giving rise to the arrest of the accused.
- Set out a chronology of the events leading to the trial.
- Briefly summarize the legal system – whether the proceedings are conducted orally or in writing; whether it is adversarial or inquisitorial; trial by jury or by judge.

Particulars of the accused:
- name, age, occupation of the accused person(s) and address;
- date of arrest and circumstances;
- time spent in custody prior to trial and name and address of the place of detention; and
- physical state and demeanour of the accused (for example, whether there are signs of ill-treatment or torture).

The tribunal:
- List the names of the judges/members of the tribunal.
- Give the constitution of the tribunal (for example, one judge and two lay assessors, or three judges, or however it is made up).
- Specify the type of tribunal: military, 'special', civilian. Is it regarded as independent?
- Describe the tribunal's attitude towards the defence: Is there a presumption of innocence? Does the tribunal appear competent, impartial and independent? (see ch 2 and commentary under Art 14 at p 45; and ch 3 at p 80) Does the prosecutor, for example, appear to exercise undue influence over the tribunal?

The prosecution and defence advocates:
- List the names of prosecuting and defending counsel.

Defence counsel:
- Is the accused represented by competent counsel?
- Is counsel able to put the case for the defence without intimidation or interruption?
- Does counsel have any complaint, eg insufficient time to prepare the case, insufficient sight of documents, or about any evidence to be called against the accused, and if so what?

Prosecuting counsel:

- Is prosecuting counsel objective and fair in presenting the case against the accused?
- Has prosecuting counsel ignored or suppressed evidence that may be of use to the accused? (see ch 3 at p 82).

The charge or indictment:

- Set out in full what the accused is charged with, or provide a copy of the charge.
- How does it compare with what s/he was originally charged with?

The relevant laws or decrees:

- Set out the text of the law the accused is alleged to have broken and the date this law came into effect.
- Check that the legislation under which the accused is charged is not retroactive (see ch 2 and Commentary on Art 15 at p 50).
- State whether the charge is brought under any special emergency procedures.

The nature of the prosecution case and a summary of the prosecution evidence:

- What do the prosecution say the accused has done?
- How do they prove the case against each individual accused person?

The nature of the defence and a summary of the defence:

- Set out the defence relied on by the accused.
- State the challenges made of the prosecution case and how far they are successful.
- Note what evidence the defence call or rely on: for example, whether the defence of 'alibi' is raised – ie *I was somewhere else at the time and can prove it.*

The judgment, or decision of the tribunal, and sentence:

- Set out the precise judgement of the tribunal, ie the words used by the judge/ president of the tribunal in passing judgement on the accused.
- Set out the sentence of the court.
- If these are postponed, ascertain the date when judgement will be pronounced and, if it is not possible to observe, then try and arrange for a copy of the judgement to be sent when it becomes available.

The conduct of the trial:

- In your view state whether, or not, the trial was fairly conducted.
- Were the defence/members of the public satisfied with the way it went.
- If the trial was not fairly conducted, then, by referring to the provisions set out in Art 14 (see ch 2 at p 44), state reasons why not.

Comments:
- Note any comments here.
- Introduce incidents extraneous to the court case, whether as background (at (a) above) or that appear to have a bearing on the matter.

Appeal:
- State whether the defence intend to appeal and their assessment of the prospects of success.
- Give the grounds/nature of appeal in outline.

Attach to the report:
- newspaper cuttings (name and date of publication); and
- notes taken of the evidence in the case.

Problem 1: At the court, the observer is refused admittance After explaining the letter of introduction and his/her purpose, the observer should obtain a statement in writing from the highest person in authority present explaining the grounds for refusing access.

Problem 2: In court, the tribunal refuses to allow the observer to take written notes of the proceedings Formally note the tribunal's ruling. Make a mental note of what has taken place and write up the note at convenient moments during the day.

Problem 3: The observer is identified with the cause of the accused The observer should stress that neither the politics of the accused, nor the question of his/her guilt or innocence, is of interest – only the fairness/legitimacy of the proceedings.

Network Co-ordination is necessary with other human rights/legal associations so that the trial can be covered if it is protracted over a long period or delayed. Use the network.

(c) Hospitals Hospitals will disclose considerable amounts of information, for example:
- the type of illness or injury that a person is suffering from;
- the presence of military personnel;
- the availability of medicine; and
- the turnover of patients.

Doctors and nurses should be approached and encouraged to assist the monitoring process (see ch 3 at p 73).

(d) Cemeteries, waste ground, rivers and lakes These should be checked periodically. Any isolated place or area where there are few people about are common places for government agents to dump or bury their victims.

(e) Vulnerable groups   Refugees and displaced persons, women and children, the disabled and mentally ill and minorities (religious, cultural, indigenous groups) are 'vulnerable' groups in international human rights law. They are the first groups to suffer when society experiences difficulties or upheaval. Accordingly, they require special protection. They need to be constantly monitored and – if necessary – a special unit may have to be established. Refugees and displaced people have their own organization (UNHCR) because of the world-wide scale of this situation (see ch 2 and Commentary on Art 13 at p 42).

The monitor should focus particularly on vulnerable groups, such as
- children living on the streets of capital cities;
- orphans;
- the mentally ill or disabled; and
- indigenous people in the rural areas.

If it is not practicable to monitor them and they seem to be particularly at risk, bring their situation to the attention of some body or organization that can assist.

NB: Link up with others at any and every opportunity (see Appendix 14).

While follow-up is important in all human rights activities, it is especially so with vulnerable groups. Their situation can and does alter very swiftly.

There are other categories which require monitoring over and above those just mentioned. The monitor will have to decide on the priorities in his/her country or region. In repressive states, it may appear that every human right is subject to violation.

When such serious and widespread breaches occur the monitor should
- record what occurs;
- concentrate on the most serious abuses; and
- focus on any group that is targeted for particular treatment. Even if the monitor cannot operate in an organization, s/he can witness as an individual human being and, if it is not safe to keep a diary or journal of events, train him/herself to memorize dates, names and places for future testimony.

How to manage a reported human rights violation

(1) Log all reports or incidents in a notebook at the time they happen or they are reported   Take a short note of the facts which will include
- the type of violation and basic details: who, what, where and when.

(2) Establish a procedure
(a)   Calmly review the available facts (however urgent).
- Does the complaint fall into a category so common or widespread that a decision has been taken simply to document the facts for the archive or collective follow-up later.

- Does the complaint received require monitoring; for example, a report of threats to an individual.
- Is a full investigation required immediately; for example, a reported arrest, disappearance or report of a massacre; if so, is some preparation necessary as in the case of torture/rape victims (see: how to take a statement at p 102).

(b)   Conduct further enquiries where:
- on the known facts, there appears to have been a violation; or
- insufficient information is available and the allegation is serious enough to justify further enquiry.

(c)   Establish priorities.
It is often impossible to investigate all complaints. Once it is clear from (1) above what are the principal areas of concern, priorities should be established. Once fixed, they should only be altered in the most exceptional circumstances. Today's priorities will always seem more urgent than yesterday's.

Resources should be so arranged that there is always one team/pair of monitors available to respond to, and cover, emergencies and urgent actions. Those complaints that cannot be investigated or followed up, should be documented for the archives.

(3) Establish a simple system for recording and recalling facts, or data   Such a system will
- provide a statistical basis from which patterns of systematic abuse can be identified;
- be essential for follow-up and reporting; and
- be an accessible store of information for visiting international human rights groups and delegations.

For example:
Files could be arranged by way of a coding system, eg: Subject – Date of incident – Place.
An alleged incident of torture in London on 3 November 1996 would read: Tor:031196:London

Suggested codes:

Wrongful Death	WDt
Injury	Inj
Torture	Tor
Wrongful imprisonment	WIm
Personal Property Seizure	PPS
Land Seizure	LSz
Intimidation	I
Discrimination	Dis

Destruction of Property	DP
Disappearance	D
Forcible Relocation	FR

(4) Follow up all complaints   It may be that they are trivial or unfounded. A simple enquiry may clarify the position one way or another. Follow-up can be time-consuming and dull work but it is vital and must become part of the routine. A close attention to 'follow-up' is a measure of the human rights monitor's commitment and professionalism. In return, it earns credibility and the respect of all parties.

Allegations should never be made without firm evidence in support, for example the incident was witnessed by the monitor; or the place was visited and victims/witnesses spoken to by the monitor. 'Reliable sources said . . . ' may be good enough for journalists, but not for human rights monitors. *Fact must always be separated from rumour.*

If monitors are unable to follow up a complaint, they should say so and give reasons why (lack of resources or the common nature of the complaint, for example). In societies where trust has broken down, a reputation for honest and reliable dealing is an important step in reaffirming human dignity and proper standards of behaviour.

Investigating

Investigations must be thorough and stand up to close examination. The aim is to establish the facts of what took place, prepare a report which contains conclusions and, where appropriate, recommendations.

Investigations will be restricted to cases involving complaints against, or actions by, those in authority or acting under, or for, persons in authority. This includes the government and agents of the government (policemen, security officers, etc) and any opposition to the government where it occupies territory and has set itself up in a position of authority. If the facts and your conclusions support the view that there has been a violation, then – depending on the priorities – evidence will have to be obtained.

Evidence
Evidence is used in a court or formal commission of enquiry to prove an allegation. It takes a number of forms:

Statements   These may be made by
- the witness who tells the story as s/he personally saw or heard it – 'hearsay' is not evidence;
- the doctor who examined the injuries; or
- some other expert, such as the scientist who examined the bullets or chemical sample.

Real evidence   This may consist of
- the physical thing itself;
- the weapon that inflicted the injuries;
- the chemical sample;
- the fingerprint that identifies the person responsible;
- the film of the incident; or
- the sketch of the torture marks on the body.

Important: Blood and other body samples should be preserved for forensic examination, as should bullets and other ballistics fragments.

The importance of evidence is that it forms the basis upon which the case is proved. Therefore, each piece of evidence must be capable of being proved to be what it seems to be so that there is no question of fabrication or falsification. So a witness who makes a statement must sign it as proof that it is his/her statement.

Real evidence must carry a separate statement to say
- when it was taken/found;
- where it was taken/found; and
- who took/found it – and be signed by that person.

This applies to all statements. In this way, when the time comes, the object produced as evidence can be shown to be what it pretends to be, because the court can trace each step it has taken before being produced in court. *Continuity of evidence* is important to maintain (see Exhibits below at p 107).

Corroboration   What one person says s/he saw happen amounts to 'evidence'. Where a vital part of that testimony is supported independently by another person or another piece of evidence, then it *corroborates* the evidence of the first witness.

For example: X complains that s/he was tortured. The marks on the body and examination by a doctor support (corroborate) this complaint.

The investigation   The monitor has no legal authority. S/he relies on the co-operation and good faith of the community. While the monitor has knowingly accepted the risks involved, other people have not.

In an investigation, other people are put at risk, possibly just by being seen talking to an outsider. If people do not wish to talk, they should not be pressured. The monitor can make adequate observations for the purposes of reporting the incident in question without necessarily quoting from, or talking, to other people. For example: *The people I met with were too afraid to talk to me. They said that if they did they would be arrested and taken away.*

Human rights violations occur when – among other things – trust has broken down. The monitor is the link in the chain.

Preliminary Action

(1) The monitor should not go out on an investigation alone, if possible. S/he

should be accompanied by another monitor or trusted companion for reasons of safety, verification and convenience.

(2) The monitor should make sure that someone knows:
- who is going;
- where and by which route;
- the nature of the investigation;
- how long it will take; and
- when they expect to be back.

The person who waits behind should have access to a telephone or other means of raising the alarm.

At the scene:

Situations and circumstances will vary. Generally the monitor should
- exercise caution and discretion;
- listen and observe;
- note his/her own immediate impressions;
- talk to people individually and compare accounts;
- gather as much information (and evidence) as possible, by
  - photographing/filming the scene;
  - recording what people say;
  - collecting or preserving, where possible, real evidence (bullets, clothing, soil, weapons, etc); then
- sitting down quietly and writing up what s/he has observed while it is still fresh in the mind.

A record made at the time, rather than a few hours later, is likely to be more accurate. It may also be used in court proceedings months, even years later, to refresh the memory. Where monitors are working as a team, it may be useful to write up the record jointly, comparing and agreeing accounts in order to achieve the greatest accuracy.

Gathering evidence

Statements:

Identify any witnesses.
- Establish whether they are willing to talk or make a statement either at the time or later (the sooner the better, so that details are still fresh in the witness's mind).
- Make a note of their names and addresses, or where they can be located (see below: How to take a Statement at p 102).

Real evidence:
- Make sure any victim is seen promptly by a medical professional.
- Obtain a copy of the medical report and any sample if possible, for example, blood or semen stains.

PHYSICAL EXAMINATION OF SUSPECTED VICTIM OF VIOLENCE

VICTIM´S NAME/ID REFERENCE

ADDRESS (*WHERE KNOWN*)

AGE (*APPROXIMATE*)

SEX

KNOWN FACTS (*INDICATE STATUS OF THE REPORTER, E G: VICTIM, WITNESS*)

EXAMINATION

A. PUNCTURE WOUNDS (*E G: HOLES MADE BY BULLET OR KNIFE WOUND*)

LOCATION (*E G: BACK OF HEAD/UPPER CHEST*)

SIZE (*MEASURE AREA OF INJURY, E G: 2 CM × 4 CM*)

B. BRUISING

LOCATION

SIZE

C. CUTS

LOCATION

SIZE

TIME

DATE

EXAMINATION CONDUCTED BY

SIGNATURE

Important: List all injuries (bruising, cuts, or puncture wounds) by numbers and mark on the body chart at Table 2 using the appropriate numbers (For example: The victim had three puncture wounds to the upper chest marked 1–3. He had bruising to the arms and wrists marked 4–6 (left arm) and 7–10 (right arm). There were four cuts on his lower back marked 11–14.) Attach any photographs to the report.

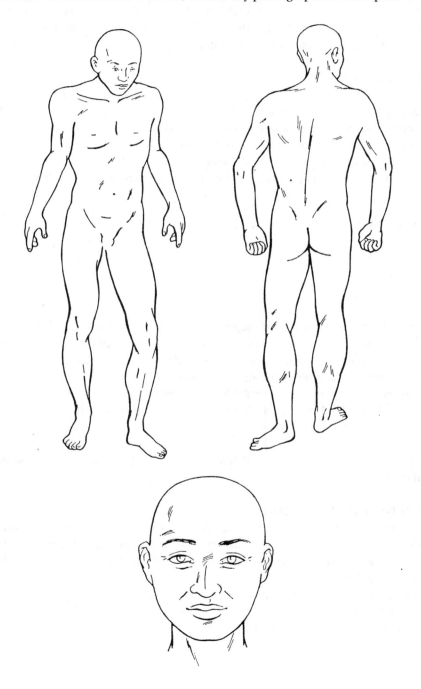

- Note any injuries, or signs of torture, on the body chart at Table A.
- Photograph, film or sketch the scene.
- Collect any bullets, shell fragments, contaminated items, weapons, clothing, and any other articles that may be used in evidence to prove what happened.

NB: Some of the witnesses may be traumatized or terrorized by what they have been through. They should be treated with sensitivity and compassion and given time to decide whether they wish to make a statement.

Action after investigation:
The monitor should
- notify his/her return at once;
- secure the evidence in a safe place – including any statements;
- report initial findings to the appropriate persons for action;
- write up a full report (see below); and
- communicate urgent actions via the human rights network (see ch 6 at p 124).

Reporting

- ACCURACY
- CLARITY
- DISCRETION

A report is a formal account of some event(s), written after some kind of enquiry or investigation has taken place. There are reports to summarize the events of the past week, month, quarter or year. Reports come in all shapes and sizes.
A human rights report aims among other things to
- present a summary of the available evidence; and
- shed light on what actually happened, based on that evidence, and suggest courses of action.

While there is no one single way of writing a report, there are certain elements it should contain.

1. How to write the report
A report must contain an accurate account of the facts. The more serious the allegation, the greater the need for accuracy in describing it. Objectivity helps to achieve accuracy; exaggeration undermines accuracy and causes loss of credibility.
A good report should
- be based on fact not rumour or supposition;
- indicate where the evidence is corroborated;
- provide an impartial account;
- use objective language;
- avoid comment;

- standardize the presentation of the information;
- contain conclusions and the reasons for them; and
- set out recommendations for action.

(i) Be based on fact, not rumour or supposition   The facts emerge from the evidence that has been gathered
- from the statements of the victims and the witnesses;
- from the statements of doctors and any other experts at the scene;
- from photographs; and
- from real evidence and exhibits collected at the scene.

The facts should speak for themselves without comment.

(ii) Indicate where the evidence is corroborated   If it is not possible to find any corroboration, or support, for an allegation, the report should say so. For example:

> *I was unable to confirm the account given by X.*

or

> *Everyone whom I approached in the village was, in my view, too frightened to speak to me. One man who began to speak, stopped as soon as he realized that he was being watched.*

(iii) Provide an impartial account   The report should give a balanced picture of what happened. It should look at all the evidence and include evidence which does not support the allegations being made. For example:

> *One witness said that the attack was carried out by guerrillas and not the army.*

Armed opposition groups   The question of what to do about atrocities committed by armed groups that oppose the state is not an easy one to resolve. States criticize human rights organizations for not presenting a 'balanced' picture if they keep silent. As a matter of international human rights law, it is the state that violates the rights of the individual and not armed opposition groups. It is those rights that the monitor is concerned with.

Atrocities committed by opposition groups can and do happen. It is for the individual monitor, or human rights network, to decide whether to expand the scope of monitoring to include investigating and reporting any such atrocities. The issue is not one of balance or impartiality. Human rights monitors and groups are committed to promoting respect for, and upholding the dignity of, the human person.

All atrocities – whoever commits them – are unacceptable breaches of basic standards of humane behaviour.

(iv) Use objective language   The report should avoid using emotive language.

WRONG: *At this stage he was devastated to see loads of soldiers brutally attacking the terrified defenceless woman. . . .*

BETTER: *At this stage he saw between 10 and 15 uniformed men approach a woman who was alone and unarmed. The men surrounded her. 'They were striking her with the clubs and rifle butts. I counted at least fifty blows' said Y.*

(v) Avoid comment   The report should contain quotations from the statements that have been taken and extracts from the notes made by the author at the time. For example:

> *One woman (who asked not to be named) said that . . .*

and

> *I counted 12 bodies. Two appeared to bear marks of torture (see the photographs in Annexure A at page 5). All had been shot with a single bullet to the head.*

Any comment should be left until the conclusions at the end of the report. (See (vii) below)

(vi) Standardize the presentation of the information   The report should be divided clearly into paragraphs and sections. Each paragraph should be numbered. Each section should carry a heading.

   All quotations or references should state the source they come from, unless a witness has requested that his/her name be withheld – in which case, the quotation can be from 'A witness at the scene'. Where appropriate, the statements should be contained in an Annexure to the report (such as in international proceedings – see ch 6 p 130). Each allegation or series of allegations covered in one section of the report should correspond to an Annexure that contains the evidence from which the report is compiled.

(vii) Contain conclusions and the reasons for them   At the end of the report there should be a separate section headed Conclusions. It may be that the evidence points overwhelmingly in one direction. The report should avoid judgement, however, and use phrases such as:

> *In the circumstances, it appears that. . . .*

or

> *The facts set out above suggest that. . . .*

Sometimes the circumstances are so serious and the evidence is so strong that a clear and unequivocal conclusion is required.

   Comment should also be reserved to this section of the report. For example:

It was my/the monitor's view that . . .
While the situation seemed . . . I/we/the team/the monitor thought/agreed
that. . . .

A 'comment' should be an informed view. Usually comments are made verbally when giving impressions of people, atmosphere, situation and so on. A comment in a report should be carefully considered before it is included. One bad comment can undermine the impartiality and objectivity of an otherwise accurate and clear report.

(viii) Set out recommendations for action   Recommendations suggest the next steps that should be taken. Some reports speak for themselves and do not require recommendations. The monitor is in the best position to assess the situation and identify immediate needs.

A report should not only be accurate in the account of the facts but throw light on the causes of those facts. Propaganda and disinformation confuse and distort facts. The date, time and place; the numbers and identities of the victims may all be accurately stated but each side uses the incident to point the finger of responsibility at the other.

An impartial report with reasoned conclusions clarifies the picture and sensible recommendations point the way ahead.

2. What to do with the report

The report provides an accurate, credible and objective account of a situation. It exposes what is really happening and puts pressure on those responsible for the abuses to stop. Security is important because the perpetrators of the abuses will want to suppress the report and silence the witnesses identified in it. Security of the report protects

- the evidence gathered;
- the witnesses who gave the information; and
- the human rights monitor and his/her network.

Suggestions for keeping the report and evidence secure:

(1)   Keep reports in a secure and safe place until they can be transferred to a Document Centre in a third country.
(2)   Reports and exhibits should not be stored in the same place, unless it is secure.
(3)   Use a code in the reports to identify witnesses, for example initials and/or numbers to protect their identity.
(4)   Establish a network for the swift transfer of the report and evidence to a secure place in or outside the country.

The report should be distributed widely both nationally and internationally. It may be that distribution at a national level is too dangerous.

Organizations to send the report to include:

- press – television, radio, newspapers (a press statement should accompany the report summarizing it and highlighting the most important points);
- human rights groups;

- religious institutions;
- trade unions;
- foreign embassies; and
- foreign NGOs.

The witness statement

1. How to take a statement

LISTEN
NOTE
ENCOURAGE
CLARIFY

The aim of a statement is to set out in writing what a witness to an incident observed. There is much skill involved in taking down a witness' statement. The monitor must

- be sensitive to the witness' feelings;
- take as much time as the witness needs;
- let the witness tell his/her own account without suggesting answers; and
- ensure that the statement is sufficiently detailed.

Confidentiality   The witness must be assured of confidentiality in all situations. The example involving rape underlines this importance. It is usually a matter of common sense. It must be remembered that

- witnesses who make statements are vulnerable because their evidence implicates others; and
- monitors are in a position of trust which they must respect at all times. Cases are not to be related as a 'good story'.

For the same reasons, it is important that the witness understands the implications of giving his/her testimony and the basis upon which s/he shares his/her information.

It must be established whether the witness is

- prepared to give information only as background for the purposes of a report in which the witness is not named; or
- prepared to give the information in the form of a signed statement; and, possibly, to give evidence at a later trial or formal enquiry.

This information should be noted in the report.

LISTEN
Let the witness tell the whole story in his/her own way and time.

NOTE

Make a contemporaneous note of what the witness says.

ENCOURAGE

Do not interrupt this account (except for purposes of taking the note).

CLARIFY

When the witness has finished his/her account, go back over it and clarify points such as dates, times, places, identities, numbers, positions, ages, colours, shapes.

The monitor has the responsibility of ensuring that the report is accurate, objective and factual.

How to listen

- Start with open-ended questions, eg: *Tell me what happened.* . . .
- Use door-opening questions, eg: *Tell me more* . . . and *I hear you.* . . .
- Avoid door-closing statements, eg: *You are wrong* . . . or *that was stupid.* . . .

Ways to listen

- Maintain eye contact.
- Nod the head.
- Put yourself on equal terms. For example, do not stand over someone, or talk from behind a desk.
- Focus on the speaker.
- Avoid judgement or evaluation.
- Make comforting/encouraging sounds.

A good listener   This is a person who

- creates a supportive environment;
- establishes trust; and
- creates a sense of impartiality.

More than usually sensitive cases   Some categories of abuse, such as rape and torture require the interviewer to be especially sensitive.

For example, in the case of rape

- the victim should preferably be interviewed by a woman; or
- at least have a woman present at the interview; and
- the victim should be examined at once by a doctor, preferably female. If this is not possible, a woman should be present at the examination.
- There should be absolute privacy and confidentiality both at the examination and when the statement is made.
- Respect should be shown for the religious and personal concerns of the victim.

2. How to write a statement

A statement is a formal document. It sets out the particulars of the person making it at the beginning, ie

- name,
- address, and
- occupation,

before going on to state what the person wants to say.

It is signed at the end of each page by the person making the statement.

A statement is not evidence by itself. What the person saw or witnessed becomes evidence when that person appears, in person, and testifies in a court of law. The person accused can then question, or cross-examine, the witness as to the accuracy or good faith of the statement.

Step 1 Preliminaries

(a) Heading:	STATEMENT
(b) Name of witness:	Tom Jones
(c) Age:	35
(d) Occupation:	Farmer
(e) Address:	not disclosed
(f) Date of statement:	10 April 1996
(g) Page(s):	1

Step 2 Beginning the statement The witness has already told his/her story. The monitor has made a brief note.

Start at the beginning When and how did the witness become involved? If the context requires going back a number of years to explain relationships and background, do so. Include the date, place, and time:

> *On Friday, 5 April 1996, at about 8 am I was walking along 44th Street in L . . . when I saw . . .*

Begin to tell the story The witness may be emotional. It is important to remain sympathetic and gentle while focusing on the need for clarity and accuracy.

Again, let the witness tell the story in his/her own way and write it down, after all, this is how the person will recount it in a court or at an enquiry. For example:

> *I saw a car speed up to Samuel. Some men jumped out and grabbed him and threw him into the back. The car then sped off.*

Go back over the story This is what the witness saw, but it lacks important details. By asking questions of the witness they can be filled in. For example:

- Can you describe the car?
- Did you see the number plate?
- How did you know it was Samuel?

- Do you remember how many men got out of the car?
- Can you recall what they were wearing?
- Did you see any weapons?
- Would you be able to recognize them again?
- Do you remember which way the car went?

In this way the statement gives the type of detail necessary to prove a case:

> *The car was a black BMW, I cannot remember the number plate, or even if it had one. I know it was Samuel, I'd recognize him anywhere, we have known each other since we were children and he lives in the same village as me. There were two men. They wore civilian clothes, I think. I didn't see any guns. I would not be able to recognize them again. The car drove off in the direction of the army camp.*

Step 3 Ending the statement

(a) When the statement is completed ask the witness to read it over to him/herself, or if the person cannot read, read it out loud.

If the witness disagrees with anything or wants to change something, do so and then ask him/her to initial the corrections.

(b) Check that all pages are numbered and that the witness has signed his/her name at the bottom of each one.

Important: A statement can take a long time to record. Do not rush it. Stop for breaks as necessary. An incomplete statement may mean revisiting the witness and submitting him/her to reliving the ordeal.

Step 4 Making 'further statements'

After a few days, it may be that important matters have been left out of the statement, or need further clarification. Do not alter the statement but ask the witness to make another one. It will carry the same heading: STATEMENT and the same preliminaries as the original.
It will start: *Further to my statement of* . . . (date of first statement):

> *Further to my statement of 10 April 1996, I recall a marked police car drove past me soon after the incident with Samuel. I was too shocked to recall anything else.*

Step 5 Other statements – Producer and Expert

Statements are required for each aspect of the evidence that is used to prove a case.

(a) Producer statements:

A film, tape recording, sketch cannot speak for themselves when it comes to when, where, how they were made. They too require a statement if they are to be used as evidence. So that, if necessary, the person who created them: the photographer, person recording, or artist, can be called before the court and asked questions.

These statements usually are formalities. They are short and to the point. They are called 'Producer statements' because the person makes the statement in order to 'produce' the evidence as an exhibit in court.

The person who, for example, took the photographs

- identifies himself;
- where and when he took the film; and
- the date and the place.

He then 'exhibits' the film and produces it as evidence.
For example:

(a)	Heading:	STATEMENT
(b)	Name:	John Steele
(c)	Age:	30
(d)	Occupation:	Photographer
(e)	Address:	30–44th Street, L. . .
(f)	Date of statement:	15 April 1996
(g)	Page(s)	1

'I am a photographer. On 4 April 1996, I was walking along 44th Street in L . . . when I saw a man being dragged into a black BMW. I took six photographs of the incident and produce them as exhibits JS/1–6.'

The exhibit number for simplicity's sake is the initials of the person followed by a number who finds or makes the real evidence and exhibits, or shows, it to the court.

(b) Expert statements:

An expert's statement is sometimes necessary to prove a specialized piece of evidence. For example, a scientist giving evidence about fingerprints, or bullets (ballistics) or chemical contamination; a forensic anthropologist or doctor. The statement will be the same in format as the others. For example:

- (a)–(g) as above; then
- the expert's statement will begin with details of his/her qualifications and relevant experience:

'My qualifications are . . . . I have been a specialist in the field of (forensic anthropology) for ten years.'

Or:

'I have been a medical practitioner for 25 years. My qualifications are. . . .'

'On 6 April 1996 I examined Mr Sam Wise. He came to me complaining of pain to his chest. On examination, I noticed severe bruising to the right side of his chest. X-rays revealed 3 cracked ribs. I noticed weals on the right side of his back. He was kept in overnight for observation. On 7 April

he was discharged and given pain relievers. I expect him to make a full recovery.'

An expert's evidence should also include
- the date of the examination or analysis;
- the place;
- the names of any other people present;
- from whom the sample/item of evidence was received;
- to whom the sample/item of evidence was given after the examination.

In the same way as any other witness, the document is read over and signed by the maker.

Step 6 Exhibits The actual knife that wounded or killed the victim; the photograph of the scene; these, and other items of real evidence, are produced to a court or commission to prove the allegations.

They are called *exhibits.*

It is important to record carefully what happens to this evidence from the moment of discovery.

If the piece of evidence is handed over to an expert, there must be a statement to say so. Similarly, the expert must say to whom s/he returned it. In this way, the continuity of the exhibit is maintained and the risk of fabrication is reduced.

Statements and exhibits in each case, or series of cases, must be kept in a secure place – preferably in a Document Centre in a third country. This body of evidence can then be sent as an Annexure with the Report to one of the international organs described in ch 6.

Chapter 5

How to promote human rights in a state in transition

IN STATES THAT are emerging into democratic rule, sometimes after years of one-party government during which the rights and freedoms of the individual were restricted, certain factors are common: people are used to expressing the official party line; they are unaccustomed to critical thought and fearful of interfering in matters outside their immediate concerns. They may appear uncaring and selfish.

People cannot change as swiftly as governments and political systems. A country may change from one-party rule to multiparty democracy in a space of months. People require more time to adjust. They need time to learn to trust each other again.

In this political climate, the level of violence and serious human rights violations should have reduced dramatically. Politicians talk less about the demands of national security and more about the need for 'national reconstruction and reconciliation'.

While human rights violations should be continually monitored as before, the transitional period allows greater freedom of movement, assembly and association that were not possible in the repressive state system. The monitor moves from being a passive witness/observer to events and becomes an active participant in the transitional process.

MEC
Mediation:
  – **Peace:** **to prevent violence and intimidation**
  – **Peace:** **to promote reconciliation**
  – **Peace:** **to build trust by opening channels of communication**

Education:
- – Understanding: **to reveal the truth about the past**
- – Understanding: **to discuss the reality of the present**
- – Understanding: **to establish checks and balances on the use of power**
- – Understanding: **to promote respect, equality and dignity**

Communication:
- – Tolerance: **through justice**
- – Tolerance: **through open discussion**
- – Tolerance: **through understanding**

MEC

- Mediation
- Education
- Communication

Mediation

Conflicts between individuals and the state, or among individuals themselves, often end violently when normal procedures are suspended or ignored (as they tend to be in the repressive state).

Conflicts or disputes can arise out of a number of different causes, as when:

- a friendship breaks down;
- a conflict of interest emerges, when two parties compete for power; or
- there is a conflict over values and I try and impose my values on you by telling you my religion is better than yours.

Other causes can be found where there is a limited resource available and both of us want/need it, such as food.

In the transitional period, people have had enough of violence and want to find other ways of solving their differences. But since they do not trust each other nor the institutions that have been taken over by the state, such as the courts, they have no other remedy. Mediation is a form of intervention by an outsider directed at helping opposing parties to reach an agreement or settlement agreeable to both sides.

Steps preparatory to mediation   Preparation is as important as the mediation itself. Decide whether to chair the meeting alone or with a co-chairperson. In racial disputes, it helps to have a representative from each of the parties as co-chair(s).

Similarly in religious disputes, co-chairs who share the religions of the opposing parties and understand each side's standpoint can be extremely helpful. It also helps to have someone to take over when the acting chair is tired or losing patience.

Before the meeting

- The co-chairs should meet the parties, explain how they got involved and explain the role of the mediator. This helps to build credibility and rapport and to get the parties' commitment to the mediation process by explaining its procedures and aims. It also helps in deciding whether the timing is right for mediation to be effective at this stage.

- Gather as much information as possible about the parties and origins of the conflict, eg the degree of trust or bitterness between the parties and their perceptions of each other.
- Obtain a mandate, or authority, from each party to intervene.
- Design the first meeting (there may be a series of meetings) by deciding
  - the number of representatives from each party, by agreement;
  - the venue, date and time convenient to the parties; and
  - the lay-out of the meeting.

Usually tables are arranged in a circle or 3-sided square.

Where the feeling is running very high, it may be advisable to arrange the tables in a V-shape with the mediator's table in the middle at the top of the V, so the parties do not have to talk to each other but through the chair.

A model for mediation

The mediator

In a difficult mediation everything depends on the mediator. The parties are tense, expectant, and emotions are running high. It is a potentially explosive situation that the mediator must be careful in handling: striding in like a schoolmaster will not help.

The mediator should have
- a small ego
- a thick skin
- big ears
- a strong bladder

The mediator should
- believe that people are intelligent;
- believe that each person has a valuable contribution to make;
- be able to conceal his/her own feelings and present a calm and attentive appearance at all times;
- respect the diverse interests of the parties; and
- be aware of power differences between, and among, the parties and be prepared to deal with them.

During the mediation process, the mediator should keep in the background as much as possible and not put forward his/her views.

The mediator should also encourage the negotiation, keep the discussion on the right track and not let it wander off the agenda or stray from the subject.

The mediator should

- clarify group feelings: *You seem to be saying . . .*
- be sensitive to and handle group tensions (suggest a break, going into a caucus, or use humour)
- re-state the parties' interests/positions clearly:
  - *Am I right in saying your position is this . . .*
  - *So is this right, that you are prepared to adopt this position whereby . . .*
- move the negotiation along by asking the other party what their answer is:
  - *What do you say to that?* or invite them to caucus if it would help;
- summarize the discussion of the meeting, eg:
  - *We seem to have reached a position where you on the one hand say this, and you on the other hand say that. So where do we go from here?*
- suggest possible solutions, do not propose them
  - *What if . . .* statements;
- keep the meeting on track and structure the flow of the discussion:
  - *Are we not moving slightly off the point here?*
  - *Isn't the point under discussion that . . ?;* and
- when an agreement is close, push hard to secure it.

At all times the mediator should avoid

- criticizing anyone;
- arrogance, insensitivity, being patronizing;
- making a party look bad;
- making decisions for the parties (assist and guide);
- talking too much (let the parties do that);
- trying to be popular (be prepared to accept rejection);
- letting the meeting drag on when it is clear the parties are not interested in coming to an agreement.

The caucus

What it is and how it is used   A caucus is where the parties separate at any point of the mediation and go into a private meeting among themselves. A caucus can be 'called' by anyone, including the mediator. It is an effective device that enables parties to

- take a break and defuse any tension that may have built up. This will limit destructive exchanges;
- put pressure on parties to explore options and strategies in private but without breaking up the meeting;
- enable the mediator(s), if it would be useful, to enter the private discussions of the party(ies), on the basis that:
  - there is an invitation (even if it has to be requested);
  - strict impartiality and confidentiality is maintained;
  - there is agreement with one party on what it will be acceptable to say or to report to the other; and

- the mediator should make certain of the exact wording of any proposal or offer that is suggested;
- At the end, the party calling for the caucus returns to the room and re-opens the meeting with a report back from the caucus on the position they have reached.

Stage 1: Opening
- Welcome the parties.
- Circulate an attendance list.
- Ensure that all the parties have the authority to act on behalf of the people they represent.
- Establish the ground rules:
  - Everyone will treat each other with respect.
  - No interruption will be permitted while someone is talking (equal opportunities to speak).
  - Explain the taking of 'minutes', or notes of the meeting (decide which of the co-chairs will take them down).
  - Explain caucus procedures.
  - Establish time limitations.

NB: The meeting should not be allowed to go on too long. It may be that an agreement or settlement cannot be reached in the first meeting, or that it depends on the outcome of ongoing events outside. Do not rush matters. If the meeting must go over to another occasion, let it. On the other hand, the pressure of time does focus the mind and can cause the parties to come to a settlement.
- Declare the meeting open.

Stage 2: Minutes and agenda
- If minutes were taken at a previous meeting, check that everybody has seen a copy. They should have been distributed before the meeting so that people have had a chance to read and digest the contents.
- Agree the minutes as an accurate record of what took place.
- If they are not agreed and someone objects: the objection should be heard and the minutes altered accordingly – by agreement.
- Agree an agenda for the meeting. This can be done beforehand by the parties, or at the meeting where each party in turn indicates the point(s) they wish to be discussed and agreed on.

Stage 3: Conflict described
- The first item on the agenda will be the complaint of party A. The spokesperson for party A will state the complaint. When s/he has finished, the spokesperson for party B will reply.
- A full account of the dispute will then emerge, including the attitudes, feelings and perceptions of each party. The mediator clarifies the facts through questions, reflections and summaries.

■ The co-chair takes notes of the facts.

Stage 4: Negotiation
■ The parties talk to each other in turn across the table, or through the chair.
■ The mediator only interrupts during this phase to
  – clarify any unclear points;
  – highlight any points of common ground that both sides seem to be unaware of; and
  – remind the parties of the ground rules where necessary.
■ Parties negotiate to an agreement on each point of the agenda.
■ If the parties are stuck on one point of the agenda, move on to another and come back to it later.
■ It may be that agreement on one point covers other points still on the agenda to be discussed.
■ When agreement is reached, it is taken from the minutes being recorded in the presence of the parties and signed by them.
■ If the press are present, the parties may wish to make a joint press statement. This should be done at the time.
■ Where agreement is not reached, and the parties wish to close the negotiations, then they and not the mediator should end the mediation.

Stage 5: Closure
■ The mediator acknowledges the hard work and good will of the parties and thanks them for attending.
■ A date is fixed for a follow-up meeting if necessary.

Stage 6: The agreement   The agreement should be in writing and signed by the parties.

A good agreement should
■ meet the wishes of the parties as far as possible;
■ be durable and capable of being put into practice;
■ be unambiguous and complete without conditions or reservations;
■ have arisen out of the negotiation;
■ indicate how the agreement is to be monitored (by a person, or persons, from each of the parties; or by setting a date for a future meeting to chart the progress); and
■ make provisions for renegotiations in the event of any breach of the agreement.

Mediation does not only take place in the formal setting described above. It is used every day, for example, a relative may mediate in a family dispute.

It can and does take place wherever there is conflict: in the street between rival political groups of marchers, or at a rally, or in any situation where well-timed intervention could achieve a peaceful outcome.

Some methods of reaching a peaceful resolution in such situations are to

- listen to both sides;
- stress areas of common agreement and interest;
- appeal to and flatter their good sense and maturity
  - *you are clearly intelligent . . .*
  - *there must have been some misunderstanding . . .*
  - *surely we can find a solution to this . . .;*

and so reach an agreed course of conduct.

Good mediation is a matter of timing: knowing when to intervene. When parties are intent on fighting rather than talking, mediation is doomed to failure.

Education

The transitional period should allow people greater freedom of movement, assembly, association and expression. At this time, human rights education must be made a priority. The aim is less to get people to recite the 30 articles of the Universal Declaration of Human Rights and more to get people discussing the meaning of human rights in every day life. In revealing what happened in the past, people have a chance to tell their own stories and to discuss justice and its meaning for them.

In progressing to the present, the discussion may move on to the measures that ought to be taken to ensure as far as possible that what happened does not happen again. What system of checks and balances could be installed to supervise the police, prisons and armed services as well as the government.

People should be encouraged to debate issues affecting civil society. Dissenting views should be heard and accommodated rather than dismissed. Individuals learn in this way *to agree to disagree* without resorting to violence.

Education is a continuing process and the best safeguard against human rights violations. Only people who know what their rights are can demand that the government observe those rights.

Education helps to create a human rights culture. When violations are committed, public outrage insists that those responsible in government are brought to account.

Communication

A society whose members do not communicate with each other is unhealthy and fractured. Without communication there can be no tolerance or trust: a grudge can turn into rage which can turn into hatred and then can end up in open conflict.

Political or military groups used to seizing power when there is a disagreement need to learn to respect the views of others and the rule of law.

The establishment of trained human rights officers throughout the country can help to reconcile local disputes, will facilitate civic education and stimulate public debate. In this way, communities begin to look beyond the uncertainties of the present and forward to see how they can improve their situation in the future.

The Human Rights Commission

The UN Commission on Human Rights adopted *Principles relating to the Status of National Institutions* in 1992.

The Principles provide guidelines to those transitional states in setting up a 'national institution', or permanent Human Rights Commission.

The mandate, or instruction, setting up the Commission should be as broad as possible and the Commission's responsibilities should include:

- comparing national legislation with international human rights law to see that the laws of the country conform to fundamental principles of human rights;
- monitoring human rights violations;
- alerting the government to parts of the country where human rights are violated;
- drawing up human rights programmes for universities, schools and professionals; and
- publicizing human rights through the media to increase public awareness.

Consideration might also be given to authorizing the Commission to:

- investigate reported human rights violations and the conduct of the security forces; and
- conduct wide-ranging national enquiries on human rights concerns.

The UN Principles go on to recommend that members of the Commission should:

- be drawn from a broad cross-section of the community;
- be concerned in the protection and promotion of human rights;
- have adequate funding; and
- be independent of the government.

A Commission's authority should include the power to

- consider any question on the subject of human rights;
- hear any person, obtain any information or documents necessary;
- publicize its opinions and recommendations through the press; and
- set up working groups to assist it.

It might also include

- its own investigative machinery;
- unhindered access to all places of detention;
- obliging public officials to co-operate with the Commission;
- powers to compel the attendance of any witness and the production of any document;
- public hearings; and
- effective remedies: the payment of compensation, free medical treatments where appropriate, and protection of witnesses.

Anyone the Commission alleges to have been involved in human rights violations should be brought to justice.

Commissions of Enquiry

A Commission of enquiry is a body of individual experts (usually) established by the government on a temporary basis to enquire into a defined set of circumstances and to issue a report at the end.

Commissions can vary in approach and scope.

The Ad Hoc Commissions used by the Human Rights and other Committees of the United Nations are set up to study particular situations and report on them (see ch 6 at p 132).

A 'Truth' Commission sets out to establish what happened in a given period and report on the findings within a fixed time-frame.

A Commission is usually delegated the necessary authority to perform its task by the legislature. Its powers can be broad in scope, for example:
- to hear any witness;
- to visit any place of detention without prior notice;
- to undertake investigations; and
- to recommend the removal from office and prosecution of named persons;

or be restricted to an enquiry with limited powers.

Formal commissions are useful mechanisms for
- providing a forum for people to come forward and tell their stories;
- providing people with an objective account of what happened; and
- setting the wheels of justice turning by reintroducing the rule of law.

Any Truth Commission or formal enquiry into past human rights abuses should have a clear mandate and adequate resources to fulfil it.

The mandate should be practicable. Regard should be had to what it is enquiring into and over what period. For example, an enquiry into all human rights violations over a 20 year period may be too ambitious a project for any body to fulfil within a reasonable time. It may be more useful to focus on a particular episode or time period by way of example or specimen.

There is no fixed type of enquiry. It will depend on the purpose for which a Commission is constituted. It may be set up, for example, to apportion blame (to *accuse*) or to find out the objective facts of what happened (to *enquire*). There may be regular reports as the Commission proceeds, or a final report at the close. It may not mention names of individuals but only groups and political parties. It may make recommendations (that are not binding) or make orders (that are). A Commission can do what the circumstances require. The costs of mounting a Commission need not be extravagant. They should never be an argument for not establishing one.

But surely there comes a time when people should get on with life and learn to forgive and forget without always digging up the past? There should be a public record that is incontrovertible, whether in the form of a trial, a report, a book, or an enquiry that is supported by evidence. Hiding the truth about what happened
- perpetuates the suffering of the victims and their families;

- causes deep resentment;
- makes national reconciliation more difficult, if not impossible;
- allows those responsible to get away unpunished; and
- allows history to be rewritten at a later date.

Without some form of public acknowledgement of the past, it is empty to talk of 'reconciliation'.

Monitoring in the transitional state

The period of transition is a turning point in any country's history and development.

The application of MEC is ongoing. Other matters require urgent attention. There may be a referendum and/or an election to be held. People may be calling for a new constitution. It is a crucial time for human rights input. It is not much use having 'rights' if they cannot be enforced.

The constitution

A constitution defines and limits the powers of the three organs of state: the executive, legislature, and judiciary. It represents the highest law in the land: all other laws are subject to the constitution. A law that is 'unconstitutional' can be tested in the courts. A constitution imposes a very useful system of checks and balances on the power of government and individuals in positions of power. Every country is unique and so there is no blueprint for what a constitution should contain. The constitutions of other countries can be discussed and considered but each country needs to develop its own constitution as representing the wishes and desires of the people of that country.

Constitutions also contain certain guarantees that no government can ever suspend under any circumstances, such as the independence of the judiciary and protection of human rights.

There should be a separate chapter or section in the constitution on human rights called: the Bill of Rights, or Human Rights. These rights should be entrenched in the constitution, that is, dug in so that no one person or event can ever justify their suspension or removal in any circumstances (not even when a state of emergency is declared unless specifically allowed for). Other rights should be clearly stated and any reservations or *except* . . . and *unless* . . . clauses should be themselves restricted and closely analysed before inserting them into the text of the constitution.

Action plan
- Lobby for a Bill of Human Rights.
- Lobby for the abolition of the death penalty.
- Lobby for an office of Ombudsman / Human Rights Commission to examine past abuses.
- Lobby for the repeal of laws contrary to international standards.

- Lobby for the ratification of the International Covenants and the Optional Protocols and the entrenchment of their provisions in the new Constitution.

How to lobby
- Convene a national conference/symposium on the constitution, or on a Bill of Rights:
  - Request materials on the International Bill of Rights from the UN Centre for Human Rights in Geneva.
  - Invite a broad cross-section of the society, politicians and members of government, the armed forces, police and prison services, church groups, members of the professions, trade unions and traditional authorities, women's groups and minority organisations, particularly for the disabled. Invite people from abroad and the press.
- Target the media: press releases, articles in the press or radio broadcasts.
- Make direct approaches to politicians, influential individuals or groups, for example, the business community and foreign diplomatic corps.

Important: Throughout this period, it is essential to keep human rights high on the political agenda through sustained and co-ordinated campaigns on issues of particular importance to the country or locality. Use the network.

Elections   Elections are subject to a simple test: were they *free and fair*?

In order to satisfy the test, countries usually set up an Electoral Commission to organize the elections and draw up the electoral law setting out the rules for the elections and a code of conduct for the political parties to follow. They also often invite international government observers to watch the election process to see that it is in fact: free and fair.

In the state in transition, there is increasing tension as those in power face the prospect of losing it. As a result, there can be intimidation of voters at the early stage of voter registration. Serious human rights violations may occur, eg political killings, people disappearing, serious threats to life and property.

The human rights situation during the entire electoral process needs to be monitored. It is a good time to co-ordinate activities with all the human rights organizations in the country and form an umbrella group. It will also strengthen a human rights network throughout the country.

Action plan for monitoring the human rights situation during elections
- Meet with all human rights groups and organizations and discuss the monitoring programme.
- Obtain the support and endorsement of the Electoral Commission, and all the political parties, in writing.
- Organize:
  - timing of the programme stages;
  - recruitment;

- training;
- deployment;
- reporting procedures/channels of communication;
- support; and
- a budget.

(a) Recruitment   Monitors should be mature men and women. Disability alone should not be grounds for disqualification.

Monitors should each be required to sign a Code of Conduct that stresses above all the requirement to act impartially.

Monitors should be strictly advised that no political activity is permissible, as it would be inconsistent with their duties as monitors.

Monitors who breach this rule should be dismissed immediately. Any sign of partiality to a political party or group puts the credibility of the programme at risk and compromises the security of individual monitors.

Monitors should also be informed that their role is to observe and not to intervene.

(b) Training   Training should include some theory and a great deal of practice.
- Theory:
  All monitors should be taught what Human Rights mean in practice and what a human rights violation is. Particular emphasis should be placed on the right to freedom of opinion, expression, thought and belief, assembly, association and movement. They should be made familiar with the electoral law and the code of conduct for political parties.
- Practice:
  - Monitors should be given a daily routine to follow, with a checklist of matters to look out for.
  - They should be provided with notebooks to record incidents in. They should also be required to complete simple daily reports on the human rights situation.
  - They should be taken carefully through the reporting procedures.
  - Examples should be used of situations they would expect to encounter.
  - Use role plays and give them problems to solve.
  - A test at the end of the course would ensure that only the monitors who understood their role would be deployed.

(c) Deployment
- There should be at least two monitors to each voting district or constituency, so that if one is in trouble the other can raise the alarm; or support the other as a witness to an incident; or in a number of ways provide encouragement and guidance.
- They should be equipped with formal identification as monitors. They should be supplied with clothing that clearly identifies who they are.
- A press release should be issued through all the media (radio, television and newspapers) once the monitors have been deployed in their areas.

(d) Reporting procedures

- Daily situation reports should be made available to a central or regional office so that quick and informed assessments of the developing situation can be made.
- The Electoral Commission should be promptly informed of any serious violation, or pattern of intimidation so that it can take the necessary action.
- A spokesman for the programme should be appointed to speak to the press and issue press releases. No one else should speak to the press except the spokesman, as this could undermine the professionalism and credibility of the programme.
- Press releases should be issued at least once a week summarizing the situation throughout the country.
- Clear and efficient channels of communication are essential. They will have to be adapted to the circumstances. If daily reports cannot be communicated, then an alternative arrangement will have to be found.

(e) Support

- The monitors in the field will require regular visits from the central or regional offices, particularly at the beginning. Reassurance is important and there will also be practical problems to be addressed.
- The security of the monitors is of paramount importance. They should always be made aware that central/regional office gives their security priority at all times.

(f) Budget A clear, sensible and detailed budget should be drawn up and submitted to an identified source of funding, such as a government department, the Electoral Commission, an international N G O or donor.

The International Community It is recognized that countries in transition to multiparty democracy require substantial financial support to assist their reconstruction and development. Funding from the international community will depend on the elections being recognized as free and fair. It is important that law and order is not ignored in the process of national reconstruction.

Attention should be focused on

- retraining and overhaul of the police, security and prison services;
- penal reform;
- reviewing the criminal laws; and
- reviewing the appointment and training of judges.

Action plan

- Hold conferences and seminars on these topics to raise public awareness and interest.
- Approach the donor countries, through their embassies and aid programmes.
- Link up with Law Societies and Bar Associations in other parts of the world

who share the same, or have a similar, legal system and invite assistance and support.

The rule of law depends on
- a respected police force with a strong sense of public service;
- an independent, impartial and competent judiciary;
- a humane prison system with conditions that satisfy minimum international standards and a structure that aims at the rehabilitation of the prisoner; and
- adequate resources to service these institutions.

Chapter 6

International reporting and complaints procedures

THERE ARE A number of formal and informal procedures at the international level that can be used to exert pressure on governments to put an end to persistent human rights abuse.

The formal communication procedures are set out in UN resolutions and human rights conventions (see below). They can only be used as a last resort, and while they are time-consuming and often frustrating:

- they do have an impact at the international governmental level;
- they are in place and should be used; (by greater use they must be developed in a more effective way);
- they compel the international community to take notice;

These procedures enlist the support of international experts and expert bodies. On an informal basis reports and statements can be sent to the Special Rapporteurs and Working Groups, communicated through the international computer network to NGOs and press, or sent to the committees established to monitor states' compliance with their treaty obligations (see below). While there is no procedure for enforcing international human rights law, when governments are exposed at the international level

- their international standing is damaged;
- the legitimacy of their right to rule is called into question; and
- they can no longer tell the outside world to 'mind its own business':

> . . . *protection of all human rights is a legitimate concern of the international community* (Article 4, Vienna Declaration)

Vienna Declaration   The Declaration
- calls on all states to accede to Human Rights Conventions (Art 26);
- calls on all states to provide effective remedies (Art 27);
- calls for continued work on the establishment of an International Criminal Court (Art 92);
- calls for the strengthening of present mechanisms (Art 95); and
- calls on the UN to be more active (Art 96).

The available procedures depend on the evidence submitted by human rights organizations. Local human rights groups and individuals play a key role: they provide the primary source of information.

The Commission on Human Rights (CHR)   The CHR, as the principal body in the United Nations dealing with human rights, has developed its own structures, or mechanisms, for dealing with human rights abuse through the Sub-Commission on Prevention of Discrimination and Protection of Minorities.

The Sub-Commission sets international standards for states to follow. It also responds to human rights violations. In 1967, the ECOSOC Council passed Resolution 1235 authorizing the CHR to examine information relevant to gross violations of human rights and fundamental freedoms in *all* countries. These studies were delegated to the Sub-Commission.

As a result, Working Groups of experts were set up, and individual experts who are known as Special Rapporteurs appointed to examine either a country where gross violations exist or a specific type of human rights abuse: for example – torture, arbitrary execution, disappearance. Specific types of abuse such as these are called: *thematic mechanisms.*

Tables A and B list the types of human rights abuse and countries currently under the examination of Special Rapporteurs. Table C lists the themes currently under the scrutiny of Working Groups W/G:

Table A

Extrajudicial Summary or arbitrary executions

Religious Intolerance

Use of Mercenaries as a means of impeding the exercise of the right of peoples to self-determination

Sale of children, child pornography and child prostitution

Racism, racial discrimination & xenophobia

Freedom of Opinion & Expression

Torture, and other cruel, inhuman or degrading treatment

Effects of toxic and dangerous products on enjoyment of human rights

Internally displaced persons

Independence and impartiality of the judiciary, jurors and assessors and the independence of lawyers

Elimination of violence against women

Table B

Myanmar

Iraq

Equatorial Guinea

Afghanistan

Former Yugoslavia

Cuba	**Table C**
Sudan	W/G on enforced or involuntary
Occupied Arab Territories including Palestine	disappearances;
Islamic republic of Iran	W/G on arbitrary detention
Zaïre	
Rwanda	
Burundi	

NB: The Special Rapporteur is distinct from the Special Representative. A Special Representative is appointed directly by the UN Secretary General and reports to him/her on the general political situation.

Urgent action

In cases requiring urgent action, there are a number of channels available:
(1) Special Rapporteurs and Working Groups;
(2) 'Good offices' of the UN Secretary-General, the UN High Commissioner for Human Rights and other public figures;
(3) Amnesty International;
(4) APC Human Rights Network; and
(5) International media.

(1) Special Rapporteurs and Working Groups

Individual experts are appointed by the CHR to examine information and allegations received on a particular subject or country. They transmit cases to the government concerned for comment and can request those governments to investigate matters brought to their attention. When reliable information is received about urgent cases of disappearances, summary or arbitrary executions or torture, for example, the relevant Rapporteur or Working Group can send an urgent action appeal to the government of the country concerned.

An annual report is published by each of these bodies and sent to the CHR. These reports include descriptions of any allegations of violations which have been transmitted to the governments concerned and any response they have received.

Special Representatives and Working Groups rely on experienced NGOs for much of their information. The more tried and trusted a source, the more likely it is the information it is transmitting will be believed and acted upon.

Communicating with the Special Rapporteur

(1) The covering letter should state:
  – the name of the victim;
  – the identity number of the victim, where possible;
  – the date of the incident;
  – the place of the incident;
  – the suspected identity of the perpetrator(s);
  – the official status of the perpetrator(s), or other official connection;

- information detailing the local remedies tried, or, if this is not practicable, a brief explanation as to why (see below).

(2) The letter should be supported by statements from witnesses and/or the victim and any other reliably attested information. Attach these in an annex. Where no evidence is available, but the information received is reliable and speed is essential, then a letter to the Special Rapporteur may be sufficient. S/he will have other sources of information and this communication may provide the piece of independent corroboration required to provoke prompt action.

In cases of enforced or involuntary disappearance state
- the date and place when the missing person was last seen; and
- the steps taken to trace that person.

The covering letter should indicate clearly whether or not the identity of the writer can be disclosed.

If the information relates to both the country and the type of violation, ask that the information be brought to the attention of both Rapporteurs.

Always keep the Special Rapporteur/Working Group informed of subsequent developments.

NB:
- These bodies are able to act on cases in any country.
- The procedures are public and draw a great deal of international attention to the concerns raised.

(See Appendix 14.)

(2) Good offices – the UN Secretary-General and others

The Secretary-General (SG) has the authority to raise any human rights matter with any government. This is usually done on humanitarian grounds.

The SG's 'good offices' means using 'direct contacts' and 'best endeavours' or, put simply, pulling strings.

The exercise of this power is a matter for the private discretion of the SG and not of public record.

The SG has taken up individual cases where there is a pressing humanitarian element. For example, threat to life or limb – an elderly or sick prisoner of conscience.

There is no sure procedure for securing the SG's good offices.

Communicating with the Secretary-General   All communications regarding human rights sent to the Secretariat are channelled to the relevant procedures (see Appendix 14).

The request should make it absolutely clear that its purpose is to seek the exercise of the Secretary-General's good offices.

For example, the letter could begin:

> We respectfully and urgently request the Secretary-General of the United Nations to exercise his good offices to intervene with the Government of . . . on behalf of . . . for the following reasons: . . .

The application could also be addressed to the High Commissioner for Human Rights in the same manner, but changing the title.

Good offices are used by any world figure or leader. Often, international statesmen intervene privately on behalf of an individual, group, or cause. A well-worded letter, especially one that is supported by a number of signatures, may have this effect.

(3) Amnesty International

Amnesty International issues Urgent Actions on behalf of people whose life or physical well-being is in danger.

It is a rapid response system to protect people all over the world who
- are being tortured;
- face immediate execution;
- are being tried unfairly;
- have disappeared; or
- have found asylum and are at risk of being returned to the country from which they fled where they would be victimized.

Amnesty International's Urgent Action procedure mobilizes thousands of volunteers around the world to send express letters, faxes, telegrams and telexes to the government of the person concerned calling for immediate state intervention to protect him/her.

Amnesty has its own verification procedure. Each country has a Research team based at the International Secretariat in London (see Appendix 14).

(4) Association for Progressive Communication (APC) and electronic mail

Electronic mail, known as 'E-Mail', is a development in communication technology that combines speed and efficiency at very low cost. Over the past ten years, computers have played a major role in creating an international human rights network. E-mail enables messages to be sent around the world to other human rights groups, journalists, academics and any other people interested in human rights within a matter of minutes.

APC Human Rights Network

The APC is an international organization of computer networks based in Rio de Janeiro, Brazil and San Francisco, USA. Its goal is to provide low-cost global communications services for individuals and organizations working in such areas as human rights, environment, peace and conflict resolution. It serves over 11 000 users in 92 countries.

Users can communicate with one another, sharing information through electronic mail and the use of noticeboards ('conferences').

Since over 90 % of the world's computers are in the industrialized world, they can be at their most effective when used to put pressure on governments in the industrialized world. For example: when an embassy denied a visa to an indigenous leader on the 28th of the month who was due in the host country on the 7th of the

126 · *The Human Rights Handbook*

next month, an appeal was mounted through the network calling on individuals to send messages to the host government and its embassy. On 4th of the month, a consular official was assigned to review the case and the person concerned received his visa immediately.

The APC networks provide alternative and updated information on the global human rights situation often before the media get it out on their wires. These include: background information, government reports, alerts from activists and first-hand commentary from people on the ground. Its availability does not depend on the interest of the media. The use of computers ensures the information gets out to the international community.

E-mail enables users to

- gather information from many sources;
- collaborate on research, writing and planning;
- distribute and respond to 'Action Alerts'; and
- communicate easily on any subject despite being continents apart.

The costs are small. All that is needed is

- a personal computer
- an ordinary telephone line; and
- a 'modem'.

The costs depend on each network but do not vary a great deal. There is a start-up fee of about $20, which includes training in the installation and use of the equipment and a manual. The monthly membership fee is approximately $10.

It is cheaper and quicker than ordinary means of communication. For example, a 20-page report is transmitted to the network in seconds. The user pays for the time the transmission takes.

The receiver then automatically transmits it to the network around the globe. The whole process can be done in minutes (see Appendix 15).

(5) Foreign media

Contact should be established and maintained with foreign journalists if it is possible/practicable. They can be contacted at the Foreign Correspondents Club in the capital city, or at the various press agencies: Reuters, Agence France Presse (AFP), United Press International (UPI) and Associated Press (AP) have offices in most capitals and major cities. Journalists rely on human rights groups for reliable information. This is often the first step in attracting international attention.

Formal communication procedures

International legal procedures can only be invoked when all domestic (local) remedies have been exhausted.

Local remedies are exhausted when final judgment has been entered by the highest court in the state in question unless:

- there is no legal process to protect the rights alleged to have been violated;
- access to remedies through the local courts has been denied or prevented;

- there has been an unreasonable delay locally in hearing the complaint;
- a consistent pattern of gross violations of human rights makes any prospect of 'remedies' meaningless;
- the victim is prevented from obtaining any form of legal assistance due to the fear in the legal community; or
- the remedies are unlikely to bring effective relief to the victim.

In short, local remedies must be *effective and available* (HRC).

(1) The '1503' Procedure

This procedure applies to all countries, whether or not they are members of the United Nations. It deals with the examination of country situations, rather than individual complaints. It was created by a Resolution of the ECOSOC Council number 1503 – which called for a procedure to identify and eradicate *patterns* of *gross* and *reliably attested* human rights violations.

How to apply the 1503 Procedure

Step 1 What is needed

- Covering letter:
  - Refer to Resolution 1503.
  - Summarize the allegations made.
  - State the purpose of the petition.
- The text of the 'Communication' – describing in detail the consistent pattern of gross violations of human rights.
- Annexures containing the statements of victims and witnesses and other evidence to prove the allegations made in the Communication.
- Prepare, if possible, six copies of the communication.
- Send it to: Secretary-General to the United Nations (see Appendix 14).
- Send a further copy to the Special Rapporteur or Group dealing with the country or specific type of violation.

Step 2 How to prepare

A. The covering letter:

- Refer to the Resolution that created the procedure.

This is a formality so the reader understands what procedure is sought and what authority of the UN is relied on.

- Write at the top of the page:
  - *Further to* ECOSOC *Resolution 1503*
- Summarize the allegations.
  - Draw the attention of the United Nations to a number of gross human rights violations that have occurred over a certain period, and are still occurring, which constitute a consistent pattern.
  - Briefly, set out the allegations one by one in order of time.
  - Explain how domestic remedies have been exhausted, or demonstrate why

these remedies would be ineffective or unreasonably prolonged, or any other reason set out above.

NB: In situations of gross and systematic human rights violations, where there is strong evidence of violations still taking place there is no need to go into detail regarding domestic remedies.

- State the purpose of the communication or petition.
  - It is sufficient to state that you are seeking: *action by the United Nations to end the human rights violations cited in this communication.*
  - Indicate whether the identity of the person making the communication is to be kept secret.

The communication must not be anonymous but it should state clearly whether or not the identity of the author can be disclosed. It will not be divulged if the request for non-disclosure is made. However, no system is foolproof and there will be a risk of the identity becoming known.

It would be helpful to write in one of the UN's official languages: Arabic, Chinese, English, French, Russian or Spanish. If this is not possible, the communication can be translated.

B. The text of the communication:

The 'communication' consists of a report on the violations alleged (see ch 4, How to write the report at p 98).

The communication must show a consistent pattern of gross human rights violations. A couple of individual cases, however 'gross' they may be, will not be sufficient. A number of individual cases over a period (as few as six or seven) may represent a 'pattern'. The key is to provide as much *reliably attested* information as possible – this way, it is harder to ignore or deny.

Each allegation should refer to the article of the UDHR that has been violated. Each allegation should be accompanied by clear evidence. Extracts from the statements of the victims and witnesses should be included and the complete statements attached in the annexures (see below).

Tone of the communication The communication must not have manifestly political motivations.

It must concentrate on the facts and use respectful and objective language. Reports from the media can be included in addition to the substance of any allegations; however the communication cannot be based exclusively on media reports.

C. Annexures:

The annexures contain the completed statements and exhibits relied on to prove the allegations set out in the communication.

An annexure is a way of arranging information in a clear and ordered manner.

Thousands of communications are received every year and a well-presented document is easier to read and understand.

Each allegation made in the text of the communication should be supported by an extract from the complete statement contained in an Annexure. For example:
Set out the first allegation:

- Start with the Article(s) of the UDHR alleged to have been breached.
- State the facts.
- Support the facts with extracts from the statements.

At the end of each extract, refer the reader to the Annexure containing the complete statement – for example: Annexure 'A' page 5.

The next allegation is set down in the same way. At the end of each extract again refer the reader to the complete statement – for example: Annexure 'B' page 2.

Each allegation should be supported by evidence contained in a separate Annexure.

Laying out the Annexure   At the beginning of each Annexure, insert a covering page listing the contents of the Annexure. For example:

ANNEXURE 'A'

1	Statement of the victim, Mr XYZ, on 3 March 1996:	page 1
2	Statement of witness, Mrs ABC, on 10 March 1996:	page 15
3	Statement of Doctor, Dr MNO, on 15 March 1996:	page 20
4	Exhibits:	
	A. Photographs of injuries, produced by Miss STU:	page 22
	B. Press cutting of 18 March 1996:	page 23

The Annexure will then contain the statements and any exhibits as set out on the covering page. It is useful for easy reference to give each page a number, for example, at the bottom of each page of Annexure A, write: A/1, A/2, A/3 etc.

If the statements are not in one of the UN official languages, there are translators at the Centre who can undertake the task.

Step 3 What happens next?

- The UN Secretariat acknowledges receipt and the sender will hear nothing more officially.
- The petition/communication starts its long journey:
  - a copy is sent to the government concerned, inviting a response; and
  - a monthly list, summarizing each communication and government response is circulated confidentially to the CHR and the Sub-Commission on Prevention of Discrimination and Protection of Minorities.

Late July

- The Working Group on Communications meet to review the July communications and determine which appear to reveal a consistent pattern of

gross and reliably attested violations of human rights and fundamental freedoms.
- Those selected go on to the full Sub-Commission. Those that are not go no further.

August
- The full Sub-Commission reviews these communications and decides which country communications appear to reveal a consistent pattern of gross and reliably attested violations of human rights requiring consideration by the Commission.
- Those not forwarded are either dropped from the procedure, or held for further consideration at a later stage.

Late January
- The 'situations', as they now become, are forwarded to the Working Group on Situations, which meets annually one week prior to the annual session of the CHR.
- The Working Group examines the country situations and recommends to the CHR the action it should take.

Early February
- The CHR considers the situations and invites a government representative from each country concerned to address a closed meeting of the CHR and answer any questions put by Commission members.

Step 4 The decisions the CHR can reach
- Drop it from the procedure, because it does not satisfy the test.
- Keep it under confidential review until the next session.
- Subject the situation to a different procedure.
- Order a 'thorough study' through the appointment of a Working Group or Special Rapporteur or Representative.
- Order an investigation by an 'Ad Hoc' committee established for the purpose.

The only information made public is an announcement by the CHR Chairperson stating which countries have been under consideration and against which consideration has been discontinued.

When to use the 1503 Procedure   If the objective is
- public exposure of human rights violations;
- speedy action by the UN; or
- the resolution of an individual case;
the 1503 Procedure is *not* suitable.

It *is* appropriate when the objective is to get the UN to examine a country situation where there is a high level of human rights violations. In any event, consult with experienced NGOs. Any communication is likely to receive closer attention, if it comes through a known channel. Use the network (see Appendix 14).

So once the communication or petition has been sent – nothing more will be heard, apart from an official acknowledgement of receipt?   Correct.

Is the 1503 procedure entirely confidential?   Yes.

So how is it possible to make a public statement at the UN *about the situation in a given country?*   The network should be used to get in touch with an experienced NGO to ask them to intervene at the UN. It is important that this NGO is given all the relevant information. Alternatively, any individual (or group) can attend the public sessions of the CHR in Geneva, or the other committees wherever they sit, or the Third Committee dealing with Human Rights at the UN in New York.

REMEDIES UNDER THE CONVENTIONS

Table A

Committee	Receives Reports from state party	Interstate complaint procedure	Individual complaint procedure	Other
HRC	Yes	Yes	Yes (OPI, ICCPR)	No
CT	Yes	Yes	Yes (Art 22)	Investigation – confidential – state co-operation
CERD	Yes	Yes	Yes (Art 14)	No
CEDAW	Yes	No	No	No
CRC	Yes	No	No	Request SG to order studies on specific issues

1. The UN Committees

Each of the major human rights conventions establishes a Committee of Experts to supervise the implementation of that convention by states parties.

The Committee's effectiveness in acting upon any single country depends in part on the degree to which the government is prepared to co-operate. While the Committees under the conventions can only suggest and recommend that states take action, they can follow up to exert continuing pressure.

The convention creating each of the Committees defines its mandate.

The reports of states parties are examined by the Committees at sessions which are open to the public.

For information about any of the Committees below such as the names of members, dates of sessions and the countries scheduled for review, see Appendix 14.

Why do states 'report' to these Committees? Under these Conventions, each state party is bound to submit a report to the Committee in question on the steps it has taken to implement the terms of the Convention. The Committees monitor the progress states are making through these reports and adopt concluding observations on each. These concluding observations are made public at the end of each session and may be used by NGOs to create publicity and lobby for change.

(a) Human Rights Committee   This was established by the ICCPR. The Committee

- monitors the ICCPR and the first Optional Protocol.
- receives and considers reports from states parties at public meetings, adopts concluding comments on each and may also issue General Comments on particular rights;
- receives and considers complaints from individuals in countries that are states parties to the ICCPR and OP in sessions closed to the public; and
- receives complaints by one country against another. It can appoint an 'ad hoc' commission if all else fails, to work on a friendly solution.

Publicity: The HRC includes in its annual report a summary of its activities under the Covenant and the Optional Protocol and issues concluding comments on each state report considered. A follow-up procedure allows for a highly visible section in the annual report identifying those states that have co-operated with the HRC and those that have not. The HRC also welcomes any information submitted by NGOs as to what measures states parties have taken, or failed to take, of the HRC's views.
Secretariat: Geneva
Date of session: Three sessions each year: March/April in New York; July and October/November in Geneva. Dates available from the International Service for Human Rights (see Appendix 14).

(b) Committee against Torture   This was established by the *Convention against Torture and Other Cruel, Inhuman or Degrading Treatment or Punishment* (CT). The Committee

- receives and considers reports from states parties at public meetings;
- receives and enquires into individual complaints if the state party has recognized the Committee's competence;
- receives and enquires into reports of systematic torture in closed session; and may
- undertake an on-site investigation. Initially, the report is confidential but it may subsequently be made public; and
- receives complaints by one country against another, and may appoint an 'ad hoc' commission.

Publicity: Annual Report and communications it has considered.
Secretariat: Geneva
Date of session: Two sessions each year: April and November in Geneva.

(c) Committee on the Elimination of Racial Discrimination   This was established by the *International Convention on the Elimination of All Forms of Racial Discrimination* (CERD). The Committee

- receives and considers reports from states parties at public meetings;
- receives and enquires into complaints from individuals if the state party has recognized the competence of the Committee;
- receives complaints from one country about another and may appoint an 'ad hoc' commission; and
- may take up violations under its newly adopted early warning and urgent action procedure.

Publicity: Annual Report summarizing all communications with states under the individual petition procedure with the Committee's recommendations and suggestions. It also issues concluding observations on each report considered.
Secretariat: Geneva
Date of session: Two sessions each year: March and August in Geneva.

(d) Committee on the Elimination of Discrimination Against Women   This was established by the *International Convention on the Elimination of All Forms of Discrimination against Women* (CEDAW). The Committee

- receives and considers reports from the states parties at public meetings; and
- adopts general recommendations on specific themes.

It cannot receive complaints from other countries, or from individuals.

The Commission was set up to promote women's rights and to draw the attention of the ECOSOC Council to urgent problems requiring immediate attention. Accordingly, it has the power to receive and enquire into communications from individuals and NGOs and identify those that appear to reveal a consistent pattern of reliably attested injustice and discriminatory practice against women. The Commission then reports, with recommendations, to the ECOSOC Council.

Publicity: Annual report
Secretariat: New York
Date of session: One session each year: January/February in New York.

(e) Committee on the Rights of the Child   This was established by the *Convention on the Rights of the Child* (CRC). The Committee

- receives and considers reports from states parties. Acts confidentially or publicly on urgent appeals which it receives;
- may recommend that the UNGA request the SG to undertake studies on specific issues relating to the rights of the child; and
- encourages the active participation of NGOs in its sessions.

Publicity: Report every two years to the UNGA. The Committee adopts a separate report at each session. It also issues concluding observations on each state report considered.

Secretariat: Geneva

Date of session: Three sessions each year: January, April and September in Geneva.

2. The Individual Complaint Procedure

(a) The first Optional Protocol (OP) to the ICCPR   The OP gives the individual the right to petition under the ICCPR.

IF:

- the country has ratified, or acceded to:

  the ICCPR; and

  the first Optional Protocol.

NB: The OP is a separate treaty. It requires separate ratification/accession.

- All available local remedies have been exhausted.
- The petition is signed by the author.
- The petition is not an abuse of, or incompatible with, the OP, for example, a political attack on the state concerned; or use of language that offends the spirit of the ICCPR.
- The communication is from the alleged victim, victim's family or formal representative.
- It only relates to violations of the ICCPR.
- The complaint is not the subject of another procedure of international investigation or settlement.

NB: This does not apply to the 1503 procedure (see Model Communication at Table B, p 137).

How it works in practice:

- Once satisfied that it is a proper communication, the HRC brings it to the attention of the state party.
- Within six months of receiving the communication, the state party must submit to the HRC:
  - written explanations or statements clarifying the situation; and
  - the remedy, if any, that may have been taken by the state.
- HRC considers all the material before it. The meetings are confidential.
- HRC's views are forwarded to the individual and state party concerned. The HRC subsequently monitors the state's compliance with its decision.

NB: Where there is substantial witness testimony and the state party refuses to co-operate, or summarily dismisses the complaint, the HRC will consider the allegations substantiated. This underlines the importance of having a reliably attested case to present.

What does the HRC **then do?** It is required to determine whether a breach of the Covenant has occurred. The views of the Committee are then sent to the complainant and the state. The HRC can also make recommendations to the state and suggest interim measures to avoid irreparable damage to the victim. Although the views of the HRC are not legally binding, compliance by the state is monitored by a Special Rapporteur especially created for follow-up on views. To make the follow-up procedure more effective, the HRC publishes follow-up activities and includes a *highly visible* section in its annual report.

(b) International Convention on the Elimination of All Forms of Racial Discrimination – Article 14

Individual rights of petition These exist if
- a state has ratified the convention; and
- made the declaration under Article 14 recognizing the Committee's standing to hear the matter;
- the person or persons complaining are the victim(s) of the alleged violation and the communication is not anonymous; and
- the person has exhausted local remedies and brings the case within six months of final judgement.

What happens
- The Committee notifies the state concerned of the substance of the complaint in private. It will not divulge anyone's identity without the express consent of the person(s) involved.
- The state has three months in which to reply and answer the allegation.
- Any suggestions or recommendations made by the Committee are forwarded to the parties – for example, the Committee suggests the state party is in the wrong and recommends that it pays compensation to the victim.
- The annual report of the Committee contains a summary of these proceedings.

NB: A number of European countries have established their own Race Relations Tribunals to hear complaints. These can be rapidly processed. A national remedy should always be tried before an international one.

(See Model Communication Table B – substitute the CERD for ICCPR and OP.)

Model communication

Date: ....

Communication to:
   The Human Rights Committee
   c/o Centre for Human Rights
   United Nations Office
   8–14 avenue de la Paix
   1211 Geneva 10, Switzerland,
submitted for consideration under the Optional Protocol to the International Covenant on Civil and Political Rights.

I. Information concerning the author of the communication

Name .... First name(s) ....
Nationality .... Profession ....
Date and place of birth ....
Present address ....
....
Address for exchange of confidential correspondence (if other than present address)
....
....

Submitting the communication as:
   (a) Victim of the violation or violations set forth below .... ☐
   (b) Appointed representative/legal counsel of the alleged
        victim(s) .... ☐
   (c) Other .... ☐

If box (c) is marked, the author should explain:
  (i) In what capacity he is acting on behalf of the victim(s) (eg family relationship or other personal links with the alleged victim(s)):
       ....
 (ii) Why the victim(s) is (are) unable to submit the communication himself (themselves):
       ....

An unrelated third party having no link to the victim(s) cannot submit a communication on his (their) behalf.

Table B

II. Information concerning the alleged victim(s)
(if other than author)

Name . . . .   First name(s) . . . .
Nationality . . . .   Profession . . . .
Date and place of birth . . . .
Present address or whereabouts . . . .
. . . .

III. State concerned/articles violated/domestic remedies

Name of the state party (country) to the International Covenant and the Optional
Protocol against which the communication is directed:
. . . .
Articles of the International Covenant on Civil and Political Rights allegedly violated:
. . . .
Steps taken by or on behalf of the alleged victim(s) to exhaust domestic remedies –
recourse to the courts or other public authorities, when and with what results (if
possible, enclose copies of all relevant judicial or administrative decisions):
. . . .
If domestic remedies have not been exhausted, explain why:
. . . .

IV. Other international procedures

Has the same matter been submitted for examination under another procedure of
international investigation or settlement (eg the Inter-American Commission on
Human Rights, the European Commission on Human Rights)? If so, when and with
what results?
. . . .

V. Facts of the claim

Detailed description of the facts of the alleged violation or violations (including
relevant dates)*
. . . .
                         Author's signature: . . . .

---

* Add as many pages as need for this description.

(c) Convention Against Torture, and Other Cruel, Inhuman or Degrading Treatment or Punishment – Article 22

The Committee can only consider a 'communication' from an individual where the state:

- has ratified the convention; and
- made the declaration under Article 22 recognizing the Committee's standing to hear the matter.

The other requirements are the same as for the OP (above).

The Vienna Declaration urges

> *all states to put an immediate end to the practice of torture and eradicate this evil forever through full implementation of the* UDHR *as well as the relevant conventions and, where necessary, strengthening of existing mechanisms.* *(Art 57)*

Other procedures under the CT:

Enquiries conducted by the Committee – Article 20.

Where the Committee

- receives reliable information which
- contains well-founded indications that torture
- is being systematically practised in a state,

the Committee can

- invite the state to make observations; and
- decide that an urgent, confidential enquiry should be made and visit the state concerned.

These steps are all strictly confidential. The Committee cannot act without the consent and co-operation of the state concerned. However, the Committee may ultimately decide to make the report on their investigation public.

NB: At the time of ratification, the state is entitled to declare that it does not recognize the competence of the Committee to conduct any such role or enquiry under Art 20 (Art 28) (see Model Communication at Table B – substitute the CT for the ICCPR and OP.)

3 The Committee of Experts under ILO Conventions

The supervision of ILO Conventions is carried out by a Committee of Experts consisting of 20 experts on labour law and social problems from all parts of the world.

The Committee's first step is to issue 'Direct Requests' to governments who fall short of their obligations under a convention. The 'Direct Requests' point out the errors and suggest corrections. These are not published, but sent to the governments and Workers' or Employers' Associations concerned. If the government responds, it is an end of the matter.

Serious, or persistent, violations become the subject of 'Observations'. These are published as part of the Committee's annual report to the International Labour Conference.

The Conference Committee on the Application of Conventions and Recommendations then selects from the Committee's report cases that merit particularly close attention.

The government concerned is requested to send a representative to appear before the Committee and explain the situation. The Committee then reports to the International Labour Conference.

Complaint Procedures

(a) Representations under Article 24, ILO Constitution A 'representation' may be sent to the Director-General of the ILO complaining that a member state has

> *failed to secure in any respect the effective observance within its jurisdiction of any Convention to which it is a party.*

The representation can be sent by any industrial association of employers or workers, ie a trade union or employers' association.

NB: The ILO determines what is an 'industrial association'. The complaint will be more swiftly processed where the organisation submitting the matter is well-known.

Steps
- Send the representation to the Director-General (DG) of the ILO in Geneva (see Appendix 14) in any language. The organization sending the complaint should enclose proof of its status, ie identifying itself.
- The covering letter should
  - refer specifically to Art 24 of the ILO Constitution;
  - refer specifically to the title of the ratified Convention that has been breached; and
  - include a summary of the alleged breach indicating in what respects *the government has failed to secure . . . effective observance.*
- The evidence relied on should be contained in Annexures.

What happens next? If the representation is accepted a special committee is appointed to examine it. This committee may seek further information from the sending organization. It will also communicate with the government concerned for its comments.

When all the comments have been received, the committee reports with its recommendations to the governing body of the ILO.

If the governing body accepts the government's answers, the procedure stops and the representation and replies of the government are published. If it does not, then the report is published and the Committee of Experts will take over the supervision of the case.

(b) Complaints concerning freedom of association   The Committee on Freedom of Association (CFA) was created for the protection of Trade Union rights. It is not necessary for states to have ratified ILO 87 or 98 for this procedure to be invoked. The rights contained in these two ILO Conventions are considered so fundamental that a complaint can be brought under this procedure against any member of the ILO by organizations of employers or workers.

Who can complain to the CFA?
- National organizations directly concerned in the matter;
- International organizations with consultative status with the ILO;
- Other international organizations without consultative status if the allegation relates to matters directly affecting their affiliated organizations.

NB: Even if a government has dissolved an organization, it is for the ILO to determine their status.

Steps
- Send a covering letter to the DG with proof of status (as above).
  - Indicate the matter is addressed to the CFA.
  - Outline the allegation and in what respects the government has failed to observe its obligations.
  - Attach supporting evidence in Annexures.

What happens next?   Further information may be asked for from the sending organization. The government is asked to comment. On occasions, representatives of the DG have visited the country to make on site enquiries.

If the CFA is satisfied that there has been a breach, it can make recommendations to the government to correct the situation, for example to refrain from certain action, or to amend certain laws.

The CFA may refer the case to the Committee of Experts for continued supervision.

Informal procedures

Intervention by NGOs

At the CHR and Sub-Commission in Geneva   The CHR and Sub-Commission provide a forum in which experts, governmental and non-governmental representatives can meet. In particular, the Sub-Commission supplies a platform for

NGOs to bring international attention to human rights violations and facilitates the channelling of information through the Sub-Commission to other UN bodies.

Direct intervention at the CHR or Sub-Commission through written statements or speeches is possible only for the representatives of those NGOs in consultative status with ECOSOC. There are three categories into which these NGOs with 'consultative status' fall:

Category I: organizations concerned with most of the activities of ECOSOC.

Category II: organizations concerned with only a few of the activities covered by ECOSOC (eg human rights).

The Roster: specialized organizations that make occasional and specific contributions to the work of ECOSOC.

These NGOs play an influential role in all aspects of the public work of UN bodies, particularly in the CHR and Sub-Commission. They often take the lead in identifying needs and priorities for UN action. They identify gaps in UN instruments, provide information on countries which are not complying with UN standards, and so on.

NGOs with 'consultative status' will permit other human rights groups to attend the annual session of the CHR under their wing. You will need proper UN credentials. Applications for which should be made in good time to the Centre for Human Rights (see Appendix 14).

For details of timetables and places of UN committee meetings and for practical advice on means of publicizing and drawing attention to a country or region at the CHR or Sub-Commission (see Appendix 14).

The Third Committee at UN headquarters, New York   International human rights organizations should be able to advise on which countries to target, which countries are the key players in the drafting of the resolution you are interested in influencing.

Prepare a briefing paper summarizing the situation being lobbied on and recommendations. The delegates cannot refuse to see you. However, arranging meetings is complicated by sessions starting at the UN at 09h00. It is imperative to telephone the respective missions representative to the Third Committee between 08h00–09h00 to secure a date, time and place of meeting at the UN. Usually a delegate will meet you in the main lobby which is a busy place and open to the public, so stay alert.

If possible meet in the cafe downstairs or outside the building. The main lobby is not suitable as it is very noisy. Alternatively, the delegate may suggest meeting at his/her UN mission.

Keep each meeting as brief as possible as this is a very busy period for delegates. If there are several of you speaking, work out the order beforehand and try not to repeat the others' information.

Follow-up is essential: keep delegates informed of subsequent developments. Send another delegation to lobby in Geneva at the CHR.

For advice consult the organizations in Appendix 14.

Regional reporting and complaints procedures

A. European

The *European Convention for the Protection of Human Rights and Fundamental Freedoms* (1950) contains a procedure for both individual petition and complaints brought by one state against another (interstate). 16 000 individual petitions have been registered to date. The interstate complaint procedure is rarely used.

Like all the other international procedures, it is one of last resort. Unlike the other procedures, there are stricter admissibility requirements before the case can proceed.

The European Court of Human Rights sits in Strasbourg, France. Applications first pass through the European Commission of Human Rights which must

- seek a friendly settlement between the parties; or
- make a judgment on the facts.

The European Commission's decisions are not legally binding.

The Court finally decides cases after they have been referred to it either by the state concerned, or the Commission itself.

The Court's decisions are legally binding on member states, who have all recognized its jurisdiction.

The implementation of the Court's judgements is supervised by the Committee of Ministers (CM). This Committee ensures that states comply with an order of the Court and has the ultimate sanction of suspending or expelling a state from the Council of Europe. The CM also acts where a case is not referred to the Court. The case is then sent to the CM who decide if there has been a violation of the convention and if so, order a state to remedy it.

Bringing a case before the Commission

It is advisable to consult with NGOs and legal experts with knowledge and experience of this procedure in view of the strict admissibility requirements (see Appendix 14).

Requirements

1 The state has accepted the right of individual petition.
2 The petition alleges a breach of a right under the Convention.
3 The domestic remedies in the state have been exhausted.
4 The petition is sent on the proper application form (available from the Commission secretariat).
5 The petition is sent within six months of any final ruling in the state concerned.
6 The petitioner is a 'victim' or someone closely related to the victim, such as a relative. A legal representative can be appointed. Legal aid is available.

Urgent cases

A case can take up to three years before a final report is issued.

The Commission can give priority to urgent cases. A covering letter should set out clearly the reasons for requesting the Commission to take urgent action. The

Commission can then request the state to take measures to suspend or stop or adopt other measures pending the outcome of the petition.

The Commission's requests are not binding on states, though they are usually obeyed.

The procedure through the Commission to the Court and Committee of Ministers is set out in the table below.

TABLE A

State/Individual petition		
Commission examines its admissibility.		
	oral hearing	INADMISSIBLE: END
Commission establishes facts and seeks friendly settlement.		FRIENDLY SETTLEMENT: END
		amendment of legislation or
Commission ensures the settlement is consistent with human rights.		agreement to pay compensation
If unsatisfactory or no friendly settlement, Commission reports to CM.		Report contains Commission's conclusions on facts and if there has been a breach. Report is also sent to the state.
	3-month interval	
1. CM decides if there is a breach. Publishes the Report of the Commission.	OR	1. The State of Commission refers the case to the Court for final decision.
2. CM supervises the implementation of the decision.	OR	2. Public hearing. Final judgment. CM supervises implementation of judgment.

B. American

The Organization of American States (OAS) has 35 member States in the Americas. Under the OAS charter, the Inter-American Commission on Human Rights has the main responsibility for the promotion and protection of human rights. The Commission is based in Washington DC, USA.

The Inter-American Court of Human Rights sits in San José, Costa Rica. Only those states which have ratified the *American Convention on Human Rights* and declared that they accept the competence of the Court are subject to its jurisdiction.

Petitioning the Inter-American Court

A petition may be filed with the Commission against any state which violates its human rights obligations. Those states that have not ratified the American Convention are nevertheless subject to those rights protected by the *American Declaration of the Rights and Duties of Man.*

Any person may submit a petition alleging violation of human rights. The petition may be collective and include a number of victims of a specific incident or practice; or general, alleging widespread human rights violations. In either case, the petition should identify the victim(s) although the victim(s) need not submit or approve the petition themselves.

The petition will include:

- A covering letter.

This includes the matters set out under the 1503 Procedure (see above) with an explanation of the steps taken to exhaust local remedies through the courts. Where domestic remedies have been pursued, the petition must be filed within six months of the date when the final judgment was entered.

- A summary of the facts.

A report summarizing the facts should be included (see ch 4 at p 98).

- Annexures:

The evidence relied on should be attached in the form of Annexures (see above).

The Inter-American system does not share the tight admissibility requirements laid down by the European Commission. Providing the petition

- is filed in time; and
- is not being pursued in another international arena (such as the 1503 Procedure);

and other basic requirements are met, then a file is opened at the Secretariat in Washington and the case is given a number.

The petition is then sent to the government concerned (less any features identifying the person making the petition, if so requested). The government has 90 days to reply. It may seek an extension of time, if it so requires.

The relevant parts of a government's reply will then be sent to the petitioner who has 30 days to comment – an extension may be granted on application.

The petitioner can:

- ask that specific statements made by the government be put to proof;
- request an oral hearing so that witnesses may be called;
- request the Commission to undertake on-site investigations into allegations of widespread human rights violations.

Friendly settlement

The Commission can seek a 'friendly settlement' to the matter if both parties consent to the procedure. If it is agreed on, the Commission appoints a special commission or individual to assess the evidence and, if necessary, conduct an on-site investigation. If friendly settlement is reached, the Commission prepares a report which it places before the parties and the Secretary-General of the OAS for publication. The case stops there.

If a friendly settlement cannot be reached, the Commission prepares a report after examining all the evidence in the case (including exercising its discretion to hold oral hearings), stating the facts and its conclusions. The Commission and the state then have three months to consider whether to refer the matter to the Inter-American Court for a final ruling.

If for whatever reason the matter does not proceed to the court, the Commission adopts an opinion and conclusion, with recommendations which it serves on the state in breach. This opinion is only published if the state does not comply with the recommendations within a specified time period.

The Commission's decisions are not legally binding and it cannot order a state to pay compensation, release a detainee or take any other specific action.

What if a government ignores the petition? The Commission will presume that the allegations contained in the petition are proved. Similarly it is not enough for a government to dismiss the petition or issue a blanket denial, the Commission considers such a response inadequate and is likely to find in favour of the petitioner.

Urgent Action Procedure
In serious or urgent cases, the Commission can ask of governments *the promptest reply . . . using the means it considers most expeditious.* It can further request the government to adopt measures to safeguard the rights allegedly at risk or breached until the outcome of the petition.

The Inter-American Court
After proceedings before the Commission have been completed, the case must go before the Court within three months of the Commission's final report being served on the parties. NB: An individual cannot bring a case before the Court.

The Court then sits in public and listens to the evidence both in written and oral form. Although it decides the case in secret, the judgment is published.

If it finds a violation, it will rule accordingly and order the situation to be remedied. It may award compensation (which can include the costs of legal assistance in preparing and presenting the case). The state party is legally bound by the ruling of the Court.

TABLE B

PETITION	1. Covering letter setting out who you are as above including how local remedies have been exhausted or why they do not apply. 2. Summary of facts contained in Report form (as above). 3. Annexures containing evidence relied on.
1. File opened 2. Case number 3. Petition sent to Government	In urgent cases, Commission requests 'the promptest reply'. Government has 90 days to reply.
Government replies Petitioner comments.	1. Commission will presume case proved from Government silence or dismissal. 2. 30 days for petitioner to reply. 3. Commissioner discretion to order oral hearing.
COMMISSION	FRIENDLY SETTLEMENT PROCEDURE if both parties agree = END
Commission reports with conclusions	

3-month period

1. State or Commission submits case to Inter-American Court for judgment	OR	2. Commission adopts opinion and conclusion and recommendations.

C. African

The African Charter on Human and Peoples' Rights (1981) has been ratified by 49 members of the Organization of African Unity (OAU). It sets out a wide range of human rights. Its implementation is supervised by the African Commission on Human and Peoples' Rights. The secretariat to the OAU has offices in Banjul, The Gambia. The Commission held its first session in 1987 at the OAU head offices in Addis Ababa.

The Charter allows for both interstate and individual complaint procedures in principle. Interstate complaints are not readily used – as elsewhere. While the individual complaint procedure is available, the confidentiality clause in Article 59 of the Charter means that little is known about its findings. Even though it has received over 140 communications, no pressure has been exerted against the states complained of due to the absence of publicity.

The African Commission was established relatively recently. Its priority appears to be to build up its institutions and promote human rights generally.

However, the absence of an African Court of Human and Peoples' Rights which can issue final and binding legal judgments coupled with some enforcement body such as the Committee of Ministers undermines the effectiveness of the Commission's activities.

Appendices

CONTENTS

THE VIENNA DECLARATION AND PROGRAMME OF ACTION (1993)

[Adopted 25 June 1993 by the World Conference on Human Rights]

The World Conference on Human Rights

Considering that the promotion and protection of human rights is a matter of priority for the international community, and that the Conference affords a unique opportunity to carry out a comprehensive analysis of the international human rights system and of the machinery for the protection of human rights, in order to enhance and thus promote a fuller observance of those rights, in a just and balanced manner.

Recognizing and affirming that all human rights derive from the dignity and worth inherent in the human person, and that the human person is the central subject of human rights and fundamental freedoms, and consequently should be the principal beneficiary and should participate actively in the realization of these rights and freedoms.

Reaffirming their commitment to the purposes and principles contained in the Charter of the United Nations and the Universal Declaration of Human Rights.

Reaffirming the commitment contained in Article 56 of the Charter of the United Nations to take joint and separate action, placing proper emphasis on developing effective international co-operation for the realization of the purposes set out in Article 55, including universal respect for, and observance of, human rights and fundamental freedoms for all.

Emphasizing the responsibilities of all states, in conformity with the Charter of the United Nations, to develop and encourage respect for human rights and fundamental freedoms for all, without distinction as to race, sex, language or religion.

Recalling the Preamble to the Charter of the United Nations, in particular the determination to reaffirm faith in fundamental human rights, in the dignity and worth of the human person, and in the equal rights of men and women and of nations large and small.

Recalling also the determination expressed in the Preamble of the Charter of the United Nations to save succeeding generations from the scourge of war, to establish conditions under which justice and respect for obligations arising from treaties and other sources of international law can be maintained, to promote social progress and better standards of life in larger freedom, to practise tolerance and good neighbourliness, and to employ international machinery for the promotion of the economic and social advancement of all peoples.

Emphasizing that the Universal Declaration of Human Rights, which constitutes a common standard of achievement for all peoples and all nations, is the source of inspiration and has been the basis for the United Nations in making advances in standard setting as contained in the existing international human rights instruments, in particular the International Covenant on Civil and Political Rights and the International Covenant on Economic, Social and Cultural Rights.

Considering the major changes taking place on the international scene and the aspirations of all the peoples for an international order based on the principles enshrined in the Charter of the United Nations, including promoting and encouraging respect for human rights and fundamental freedoms for all and respect for the principle of equal rights and self-determination of peoples, peace, democracy, justice, equality, rule of law, pluralism, development, better standards of living and solidarity.

Deeply concerned by various forms of discrimination and violence, to which women continue to be exposed all over the world.

Recognizing that the activities of the United Nations in the field of human rights should be rationalized and enhanced in order to strengthen the United Nations machinery in this field and to further the objectives of universal respect for observance of international human rights standards.

Having taken into account the Declarations adopted by the three regional meetings at Tunis, San José and Bangkok and the contributions made by Governments, and bearing in mind the suggestions made by intergovernmental and non-governmental organizations, as well as the studies prepared by independent experts during the preparatory process leading to the World Conference on Human Rights.

Welcoming the International Year of the World's Indigenous People 1993 as a reaffirmation of the commitment of the international community to ensure their enjoyment of all human rights and fundamental freedoms and to respect the value and diversity of their cultures and identities.

Recognizing also that the international community should devise ways and means to remove the current obstacles and meet challenges to the full realization of all human rights and to prevent the continuation of human rights violations resulting thereof throughout the world.

Invoking the spirit of our age and the realities of our time which call upon the peoples of the world and all states members of the United Nations to rededicate themselves to the global task of promoting and protecting all human rights and fundamental freedoms so as to secure full and universal enjoyment of these rights.

Determined to take new steps forward in the commitment of the international community with a view to achieving substantial progress in human rights endeavours by an increased and sustained effort of international co-operation and solidarity,

Solemnly adopts the Vienna Declaration and Programme of Action

I

1. The World Conference on Human Rights reaffirms the solemn commitment of all states to fulfil their obligations to promote universal respect for, and observance and protection of, all human rights and fundamental freedoms for all in accordance with the Charter of the United Nations, other instruments relating to human rights, and international law. The universal nature of these rights and freedoms is beyond question.

In this framework, enhancement of international co-operation in the field of human rights is essential for the full achievement of the purposes of the United Nations.

Human rights and fundamental freedoms are the birthright of all human beings; their protection and promotion is the first responsibility of Governments.

2. All peoples have the right of self-determination. By virtue of that right they freely determine their political status, and freely pursue their economic, social and cultural development.

Taking into account the particular situation of peoples under colonial or other forms of alien domination or foreign occupation, the World Conference on Human Rights recognizes the right of peoples to take any legitimate action, in accordance with the Charter of the United Nations, to realize their inalienable right of self-determination. The World Conference on Human Rights considers the denial of the right of self-determination as a violation of human rights and underlines the importance of the effective realization of this right.

In accordance with the Declaration on Principles of International Law concerning Friendly Relations and Co-operation Among States in accordance with the Charter of the United Nations, this shall not be construed as authorizing or encouraging any action which would dismember or impair, totally or in part, the territorial integrity or political unity of sovereign and independent states conducting themselves in compliance with the principle of equal rights and self-determination of peoples and thus possessed of a Government representing the whole people belonging to the territory without distinction of any kind.

3. Effective international measures to guarantee and monitor the implementation of human rights standards should be taken in respect of people under foreign occupation, and effective legal protection against the violation of their human rights should be provided, in accordance with human rights norms and international law, particularly the Geneva Convention relative to the Protection of Civilian Persons in Time of War, of 14 August 1949, and other applicable norms of humanitarian law.

4. The promotion and protection of all human rights and fundamental freedoms must be considered as a priority objective of the United Nations in accordance with its purposes and principles, in particular the purpose of international co-operation. In the framework of these purposes and principles, the promotion and protection of all human rights is a legitimate concern of the international community. The organs and specialized agencies related to human rights should therefore further enhance the co-ordination of their activities based on the consistent and objective application of international human rights instruments.

5. All human rights are universal, indivisible and interdependent and interrelated. The international community must treat human rights globally in a fair and equal manner, on the same footing, and with the same emphasis. While the significance of national and regional particularities and various historical, cultural and religious backgrounds must be borne in mind, it is the duty of states, regardless of their political, economic and cultural systems, to promote and protect all human rights and fundamental freedoms.

6. The efforts of the United Nations system towards the universal respect for, and observance of, human rights and fundamental freedoms for all, contribute to the stability and well-being necessary for peaceful and friendly relations among nations, and to improved conditions for peace and security as well as social and economic development, in conformity with the Charter of the United Nations.

7. The processes of promoting and protecting human rights should be conducted in conformity with the purposes and principles of the Charter of the United Nations, and international law.

8. Democracy, development and respect for human rights and fundamental freedoms are interdependent and mutually reinforcing. Democracy is based on the freely expressed will of the people to determine their own political, economic, social and cultural systems and their full participation in all aspects of their lives. In the context of the above, the promotion and protection of human rights and fundamental freedoms at the national and international levels should be universal and conducted without conditions attached.

The international community should support the strengthening and promoting of democracy, development and respect for human rights and fundamental freedoms in the entire world.

9. The World Conference on Human Rights reaffirms that least developed countries committed to the process of democratization and economic reforms, many of which are in Africa, should be supported by the international community in order to succeed in their transition to democracy and economic development.

10. The World Conference on Human Rights reaffirms the right to development, as established in the Declaration on the Right to Development, as a universal and inalienable right and an integral part of fundamental human rights.

As stated in the Declaration on the Right to Development, the human person is the central subject of development.

While development facilitates the enjoyment of all human rights, the lack of development may not be invoked to justify the abridgement of internationally recognized human rights.

States should co-operate with each other in ensuring development and eliminating obstacles to development. The international community should promote an effective international co-operation for the realization of the right to development and the elimination of obstacles to development.

Lasting progress towards the implementation of the right to development requires effective development policies at the national level, as well as equitable economic relations and a favourable economic environment at the international level.

11. The right to development should be fulfilled so as to meet equitably the developmental and environmental needs of present and future generations. The World Conference on Human Rights recognizes that illicit dumping of toxic and dangerous substances and waste potentially constitutes a serious threat to the human rights to life and health of everyone.

Consequently, the World Conference on Human Rights calls on all states to adopt and vigorously implement existing conventions relating to the dumping of toxic and dangerous products and waste and to co-operate in the prevention of illicit dumping.

Everyone has the right to enjoy the benefits of scientific progress and its applications. The World Conference on Human Rights notes that certain advances, notably in the biomedical and life sciences as well as in information technology, may have potentially adverse consequences for the integrity, dignity and human rights of the individual, and calls for international co-operation to ensure that human rights and dignity are fully respected in this area of universal concern.

12. The World Conference on Human Rights calls upon the international community to make all efforts to help alleviate the external debt burden of developing countries, in order to supplement the efforts of the Governments of such countries to attain the full realization of the economic, social and cultural rights of their people.

13. There is a need for states and international organizations, in co-operation with non-governmental organizations, to create favourable conditions at the national, regional and international levels to ensure the full and effective enjoyment of human rights. States should eliminate all violations of human rights and their causes, as well as obstacles to the enjoyment of these rights.

14. The existence of widespread extreme poverty inhibits the full and effective

enjoyment of human rights; its immediate alleviation and eventual elimination must remain a high priority for the international community.

15. Respect for human rights and for fundamental freedoms without distinction of any kind is a fundamental rule of international human rights law. The speedy and comprehensive elimination of all forms of racism and racial discrimination, xenophobia and related intolerance is a priority task for the international community. Governments should take effective measures to prevent and combat them. Groups, institutions, intergovernmental and non-governmental organizations and individuals are urged to intensify their efforts in co-operating and co-ordinating their activities against these evils.

16. The World Conference on Human Rights welcomes the progress made in dismantling apartheid and calls upon the international community and the United Nations system to assist in this process.

The World Conference on Human Rights also deplores the continuing acts of violence aimed at undermining the quest for a peaceful dismantling of apartheid.

17. The acts, methods and practices of terrorism in all its forms and manifestations as well as linkage in some countries to drug trafficking are activities aimed at the destruction of human rights, fundamental freedoms and democracy, threatening territorial integrity, security of states and destabilizing legitimately constituted Governments. The international community should take the necessary steps to enhance co-operation to prevent and combat terrorism.

18. The human rights of women and of the girl-child are an inalienable, integral and indivisible part of universal human rights. The full and equal participation of women in political, civil, economic, social and cultural life, at the national, regional and international levels, and the eradication of all forms of discrimination on grounds of sex are priority objectives of the international community.

Gender-based violence and all forms of sexual harassment and exploitation, including those resulting from cultural prejudice and international trafficking, are incompatible with the dignity and worth of the human person, and must be eliminated. This can be achieved by legal measures and through national action and international co-operation in such fields as economic and social development, education, safe maternity and health care, and social support.

The human rights of women should form an integral part of the United Nations human rights activities, including the promotion of all human rights instruments relating to women.

The World Conference on Human Rights urges Governments, institutions, intergovernmental and non-governmental organizations to intensify their efforts for the protection and promotion of human rights of women and the girl-child.

19. Considering the importance of the promotion and protection of the rights of persons belonging to minorities and the contribution of such promotion and protection to the political and social stability of the states in which such persons live.

The World Conference on Human Rights reaffirms the obligation of states to ensure that persons belonging to minorities may exercise fully and effectively all human rights and fundamental freedoms without any discrimination and in full equality before the law in accordance with the Declaration on the Rights of Persons Belonging to National or Ethnic, Religious and Linguistic Minorities.

The persons belonging to minorities have the right to enjoy their own culture, to profess and practise their own religion and to use their own language in private and in public, freely and without interference or any form of discrimination.

20. The World Conference on Human Rights recognizes the inherent dignity and the unique contribution of indigenous people to the development and plurality of society and strongly reaffirms the commitment of the international community to their economic, social and cultural well-being and their enjoyment of the fruits of sustainable development. States should ensure the full and free participation of indigenous people in all aspects of society, in particular in matters of concern to them.

Considering the importance of the promotion and protection of the rights of indigenous people, and the contribution of such promotion and protection to the political and social stability of the states in which such people live, states should, in accordance with international law, take concerted positive steps to ensure respect for all human rights and fundamental freedoms of indigenous people, on the basis of equality and non-discrimination, and recognize the value and diversity of their distinct identities, cultures and social organization.

21. The World Conference on Human Rights, welcoming the early ratification of the Convention on the Rights of the Child by a large number of states and noting the recognition of the human rights of children in the World Declaration on the Survival, Protection and Development of Children and Plan of Action adopted by the World Summit for Children, urges universal ratification of the Convention by 1995 and its effective implementation by states parties through the adoption of all the necessary legislative, administrative and other measures and the allocation to the maximum extent of the available resources. In all actions concerning children, non-discrimination and the best interest of the child should be primary considerations and the views of the child given due weight. National and international mechanisms and programmes should be strengthened for the defence and protection of children, in particular, the girl-child, abandoned children, street children, economically and sexually exploited children, including through child pornography, child prostitution or sale of organs, children victims of diseases including acquired immunodeficiency syndrome, refugee and displaced children, children in detention, children in armed conflict, as well as children victims of famine and drought and other emergencies. International co-operation and solidarity should be promoted to support the implementation of the Convention and the rights of the child should be a priority in the United Nations system-wide action on human rights.

The World Conference on Human Rights also stresses that the child for the full and harmonious development of his or her personality should grow up in a family environment which accordingly merits broader protection.

22. Special attention needs to be paid to ensuring non-discrimination, and the equal enjoyment of all human rights and fundamental freedoms by disabled persons, including their active participation in all aspects of society.

23. The World Conference on Human Rights reaffirms that everyone, without distinction of any kind, is entitled to the right to seek and to enjoy in other countries asylum from persecution, as well as the right to return to one's own country. In this respect it stresses the importance of the Universal Declaration of Human Rights, the 1951 Convention relating to the Status of Refugees, its 1967 Protocol and regional instruments. It expresses its appreciation to states that continue to admit and host large numbers of refugees in their territories, and to the Office of the United Nations High Commissioner

for Refugees for its dedication to its task. It also expresses its appreciation to the United Nations Relief and Works Agency for Palestine Refugees in the Near East.

The World Conference on Human Rights recognizes that gross violations of human rights, including in armed conflicts, are among the multiple and complex factors leading to displacement of people.

The World Conference on Human Rights recognizes that, in view of the complexities of the global refugee crisis and in accordance with the Charter of the United Nations, relevant international instruments and international solidarity and in the spirit of burden-sharing, a comprehensive approach by the international community is needed in co-ordination and co-operation with the countries concerned and relevant organizations, bearing in mind the mandate of the United Nations High Commissioner for Refugees. This should include the development of strategies to address the root causes and effects of movements of refugees and other displaced persons, the strengthening of emergency preparedness and response mechanisms, the provision of effective protection and assistance, bearing in mind the special needs of women and children, as well as the achievement of durable solutions, primarily through the preferred solution of dignified and safe voluntary repatriation, including solutions such as those adopted by the international refugee conferences.

The World Conference on Human Rights underlines the responsibilities of states, particularly as they relate to the countries of origin.

In the light of the comprehensive approach, the World Conference on Human Rights emphasizes the importance of giving special attention including through inter-governmental and humanitarian organizations and finding lasting solutions to questions related to internally displaced persons including their voluntary and safe return and rehabilitation.

In accordance with the Charter of the United Nations and the principles of humanitarian law, the World Conference on Human Rights further emphasizes the importance of and the need for humanitarian assistance to victims of all natural and man-made disasters.

24. Great importance must be given to the promotion and protection of the human rights of persons belonging to groups which have been rendered vulnerable, including migrant workers, the elimination of all forms of discrimination against them, and the strengthening and more effective implementation of existing human rights instruments. States have an obligation to create and maintain adequate measures at the national level, in particular in the fields of education, health and social support, for the promotion and protection of the rights of persons in vulnerable sectors of their populations and to ensure the participation of those among them who are interested in finding a solution to their own problems.

25. The World Conference on Human Rights affirms that extreme poverty and social exclusion constitute a violation of human dignity and that urgent steps are necessary to achieve better knowledge of extreme poverty and its causes, including those related to the problem of development, in order to promote the human rights of the poorest, and to put an end to extreme poverty and social exclusion and to promote the enjoyment of the fruits of social progress. It is essential for states to foster participation by the poorest people in the decision-making process by the community in which they live, the promotion of human rights and efforts to combat extreme poverty.

26. The World Conference on Human Rights welcomes the progress made in the codification of human rights instruments, which is a dynamic and evolving process, and urges the universal ratification of human rights treaties. All states are encouraged to accede to these international instruments; all states are encouraged to avoid, as far as possible, the resort to reservations.

27. Every state should provide an effective framework of remedies to redress human rights grievances or violations. The administration of justice, including law enforcement and prosecutorial agencies and, especially, an independent judiciary and legal profession in full conformity with applicable standards contained in international human rights instruments, are essential to the full and non-discriminatory realization of human rights and indispensable to the processes of democracy and sustainable development. In this context, institutions concerned with the administration of justice should be properly funded, and an increased level of both technical and financial assistance should be provided by the international community. It is incumbent upon the United Nations to make use of special programmes of advisory services on a priority basis for the achievement of a strong and independent administration of justice.

28. The World Conference on Human Rights expresses its dismay at massive violations of human rights especially in the form of genocide, 'ethnic cleansing' and systematic rape of women in war situations, creating mass exodus of refugees and displaced persons. While strongly condemning such abhorrent practices it reiterates the call that perpetrators of such crimes be punished and such practices immediately stopped.

29. The World Conference on Human Rights expresses grave concern about continuing human rights violations in all parts of the world in disregard of standards as contained in international human rights instruments and international humanitarian law and about the lack of sufficient and effective remedies for the victims.
The World Conference on Human Rights is deeply concerned about violations of human rights during armed conflicts, affecting the civilian population, especially women, children, the elderly and the disabled.
The Conference therefore calls upon states and all parties to armed conflicts strictly to observe international humanitarian law, as set forth in the Geneva Conventions of 1949 and other rules and principles of international law, as well as minimum standards for protection of human rights, as laid down in international conventions.
The World Conference on Human Rights reaffirms the right of the victims to be assisted by humanitarian organizations, as set forth in the Geneva Conventions of 1949 and other relevant instruments of international humanitarian law, and calls for the safe and timely access for such assistance.

30. The World Conference on Human Rights also expresses its dismay and condemnation that gross and systematic violations and situations that constitute serious obstacles to the full enjoyment of all human rights continue to occur in different parts of the world. Such violations and obstacles include, as well as torture and cruel, inhuman and degrading treatment or punishment, summary and arbitrary executions, disappearances, arbitrary detentions, all forms of racism, racial discrimination and apartheid, foreign occupation and alien domination, xenophobia, poverty, hunger and other denials of economic, social and cultural rights, religious intolerance, terrorism, discrimination against women and lack of the rule of law.

31. The World Conference on Human Rights calls upon states to refrain from any unilateral measure not in accordance with international law and the Charter of the

United Nations that creates obstacles to trade relations among states and impedes the full realization of the human rights set forth in the Universal Declaration of Human Rights and international human rights instruments, in particular the rights of everyone to a standard of living adequate for their health and well-being, including food and medical care, housing and the necessary social services. The World Conference on Human Rights affirms that food should not be used as a tool for political pressure.

32. The World Conference on Human Rights reaffirms the importance of ensuring the universality, objectivity and non-selectivity of the consideration of human rights issues.

33. The World Conference on Human Rights reaffirms that states are duty-bound, as stipulated in the Universal Declaration of Human Rights and the International Covenant on Economic, Social and Cultural Rights and in other international human rights instruments, to ensure that education is aimed at strengthening the respect of human rights and fundamental freedoms. The World Conference on Human Rights emphasizes the importance of incorporating the subject of human rights education programmes and calls upon states to do so. Education should promote understanding, tolerance, peace and friendly relations between the nations and all racial or religious groups and encourage the development of United Nations activities in pursuance of these objectives.

Therefore, education on human rights and the dissemination of proper information, both theoretical and practical, play an important role in the promotion and respect of human rights with regard to all individuals without distinction of any kind such as race, sex, language or religion, and this should be integrated in the education policies at the national as well as international levels. The World Conference on Human Rights notes that resource constraints and institutional inadequacies may impede the immediate realization of these objectives.

34. Increased efforts should be made to assist countries which so request to create the conditions whereby each individual can enjoy universal human rights and fundamental freedoms. Governments and the United Nations system as well as other multilateral organizations are urged to increase considerably the resources allocated to programmes aiming at the establishment and strengthening of national legislation, national institutions and related infrastructures which uphold the rule of law and democracy, electoral assistance, human rights awareness through training, teaching and education, popular participation and civil society.

The programmes of advisory services and technical co-operation under the Centre for Human Rights should be strengthened as well as made more efficient and transparent and thus become a major contribution to improving respect for human rights. States are called upon to increase their contributions to these programmes, both through promoting a larger allocation from the United Nations regular budget, and through voluntary contributions.

35. The full and effective implementation of United Nations activities to promote and protect human rights must reflect the high importance accorded to human rights by the Charter of the United Nations and the demands of the United Nations human rights activities, as mandated by member states. To this end, United Nations human rights activities should be provided with increased resources.

36. The World Conference on Human Rights reaffirms the important and constructive role played by national institutions for the promotion and protection of human rights, in particular in their advisory capacity to the competent authorities, their role in remedying

human rights violations, in the dissemination of human rights information, and education in human rights.

The World Conference on Human Rights encourages the establishment and strengthening of national institutions, having regard to the 'Principles relating to the status of national institutions' and recognizing that it is the right of each state to choose the framework which is best suited to its particular needs at the national level.

37. Regional arrangements play a fundamental role in promoting and protecting human rights. They should reinforce universal human rights standards, as contained in international human rights instruments, and their protection. The World Conference on Human Rights endorses efforts under way to strengthen these arrangements and to increase their effectiveness, while at the same time stressing the importance of co-operation with the United Nations human rights activities.

The World Conference on Human Rights reiterates the need to consider the possibility of establishing regional and subregional arrangements for the promotion and protection of human rights where they do not already exist.

38. The World Conference on Human Rights recognizes the important role of non-governmental organizations in the promotion of all human rights and in humanitarian activities at national, regional and international levels. The World Conference on Human Rights appreciates their contribution to increasing public awareness of human rights issues, to the conduct of education, training and research in this field, and to the promotion and protection of all human rights and fundamental freedoms. While recognizing that the primary responsibility for standard-setting lies with states, the Conference also appreciates the contribution of non-governmental organizations to this process. In this respect, the World Conference on Human Rights emphasizes the importance of continued dialogue and co-operation between Governments and non-governmental organizations. Non-governmental organizations and their members genuinely involved in the field of human rights should enjoy the rights and freedoms recognized in the Universal Declaration of Human Rights, and the protection of the national law. These rights and freedoms may not be exercised contrary to the purposes and principles of the United Nations. Non-governmental organizations should be free to carry out their human rights activities, without interference, within the framework of national law and the Universal Declaration of Human Rights.

39. Underlining the importance of objective, responsible and impartial information about human rights and humanitarian issues, the World Conference on Human Rights encourages the increased involvement of the media, for whom freedom and protection should be guaranteed within the framework of national law.

II

A Increased co-ordination on human rights within the United Nations system

1. The World Conference on Human Rights recommends increased co-ordination in support of human rights and fundamental freedoms within the United Nations system. To this end, the World Conference on Human Rights urges all United Nations organs, bodies and the specialized agencies whose activities deal with human rights to co-operate in order to strengthen, rationalize and streamline their activities, taking into account the need to avoid unnecessary duplication. The World Conference on Human Rights also

recommends to the Secretary-General that high-level officials of relevant United Nations bodies and specialized agencies at their annual meeting, besides co-ordinating their activities, also assess the impact of their strategies and policies on the enjoyment of all human rights.

2. Furthermore, the World Conference on Human Rights calls on regional organizations and prominent international and regional finance and development institutions to assess also the impact of their policies and programmes on the enjoyment of human rights.

3. The World Conference on Human Rights recognizes that relevant specialized agencies and bodies and institutions of the United Nations system as well as other relevant intergovernmental organizations whose activities deal with human rights play a vital role in the formulation, promotion and implementation of human rights standards, within their respective mandates, and should take into account the outcome of the World Conference on Human Rights within their fields of competence.

4. The World Conference on Human Rights strongly recommends that a concerted effort be made to encourage and facilitate the ratification of and accession or succession to international human rights treaties and protocols adopted within the framework of the United Nations system with the aim of universal acceptance. The Secretary-General, in consultation with treaty bodies, should consider opening a dialogue with states not having acceded to these human rights treaties, in order to identify obstacles and to seek ways of overcoming them.

5. The World Conference on Human Rights encourages states to consider limiting the extent of any reservations they lodge to international human rights instruments, formulate any reservations as precisely and narrowly as possible, ensure that none is incompatible with the object and purpose of the relevant treaty and regularly review any reservations with a view to withdrawing them.

6. The World Conference on Human Rights, recognizing the need to maintain consistency with the high quality of existing international standards and to avoid proliferation of human rights instruments, reaffirms the guidelines relating to the elaboration of new international instruments contained in General Assembly resolution 41/120 of 4 December 1986 and calls on the United Nations human rights bodies, when considering the elaboration of new international standards, to keep those guidelines in mind, to consult with human rights treaty bodies on the necessity for drafting new standards and to request the Secretariat to carry out technical reviews of proposed new instruments.

7. The World Conference on Human Rights recommends that human rights officers be assigned if and when necessary to regional offices of the United Nations Organization with the purpose of disseminating information and offering training and other technical assistance in the field of human rights upon the request of concerned member states. Human rights training for international civil servants who are assigned to work relating to human rights should be organized.

8. The World Conference on Human Rights welcomes the convening of emergency sessions of the Commission on Human Rights as a positive initiative and that other ways of responding to acute violations of human rights be considered by the relevant organs of the United Nations system.

Resources

9. The World Conference on Human Rights, concerned by the growing disparity between the activities of the Centre for Human Rights and the human, financial and other resources available to carry them out, and bearing in mind the resources needed for other important United Nations programmes, requests the Secretary-General and the General Assembly to take immediate steps to increase substantially the resources for the human rights programme from within the existing and future regular budgets of the United Nations, and to take urgent steps to seek increased extrabudgetary resources.

10. Within this framework, an increased proportion of the regular budget should be allocated directly to the Centre for Human Rights to cover its costs and all other costs borne by the Centre for Human Rights, including those related to the United Nations human rights bodies. Voluntary funding of the Centre's technical co-operation activities should reinforce this enhanced budget; the World Conference on Human Rights calls for generous contributions to the existing trust funds.

11. The World Conference on Human Rights requests the Secretary-General and the General Assembly to provide sufficient human, financial and other resources to the Centre for Human Rights to enable it effectively, efficiently and expeditiously to carry out its activities.

12. The World Conference on Human Rights, noting the need to ensure that human and financial resources are available to carry out the human rights activities, as mandated by intergovernmental bodies, urges the Secretary-General, in accordance with Article 101 of the Charter of the United Nations, and member states to adopt a coherent approach aimed at securing that resources commensurate to the increased mandates are allocated to the Secretariat. The World Conference on Human Rights invites the Secretary-General to consider whether adjustments to procedures in the programme budget cycle would be necessary or helpful to ensure the timely and effective implementation of human rights activities as mandated by member states.

Centre for Human Rights

13. The World Conference on Human Rights stresses the importance of strengthening the United Nations Centre for Human Rights.

14. The Centre for Human Rights should play an important role in co-ordinating system-wide attention for human rights. The focal role of the Centre can best be realized if it is enabled to co-operate fully with other United Nations bodies and organs. The co-ordinating role of the Centre for Human Rights also implies that the office of the Centre for Human Rights in New York is strengthened.

15. The Centre for Human Rights should be assured adequate means for the system of thematic and country rapporteurs, experts, working groups and treaty bodies. Follow-up on recommendations should become a priority matter for consideration by the Commission on Human Rights.

16. The Centre for Human Rights should assume a larger role in the promotion of human rights. This role could be given shape through co-operation with member states and by an enhanced programme of advisory services and technical assistance. The existing voluntary funds will have to be expanded substantially for these purposes and should be managed in a more efficient and co-ordinated way. All activities should follow strict and transparent project management rules and regular programme and project

evaluations should be held periodically. To this end, the results of such evaluation exercises and other relevant information should be made available regularly. The Centre should, in particular, organize at least once a year information meetings open to all member states and organizations directly involved in these projects and programmes.

Adaptation and strengthening of the United Nations machinery for human rights, including the question of the establishment of a United Nations High Commissioner for Human Rights.

17. The World Conference on Human Rights recognizes the necessity for a continuing adaptation of the United Nations human rights machinery to the current and future needs in the promotion and protection of human rights, as reflected in the present Declaration and within the framework of a balanced and sustainable development for all people. In particular, the United Nations human rights organs should improve their co-ordination, efficiency and effectiveness.

18. The World Conference on Human Rights recommends to the General Assembly that, when examining the report of the Conference at its forty-eighth session, it begin, as a matter of priority, consideration of the question of the establishment of a High Commissioner for Human Rights for the promotion and protection of all human rights.

B Equality, dignity and tolerance

1 Racism, racial discrimination, xenophobia and other forms of intolerance

19. The World Conference on Human Rights considers the elimination of racism and racial discrimination, in particular in their institutionalized forms such as apartheid or resulting from doctrines of racial superiority or exclusivity or contemporary forms and manifestations of racism, as a primary objective for the international community and a worldwide promotion programme in the field of human rights. United Nations organs and agencies should strengthen their efforts to implement such a programme of action related to the third decade to combat racism and racial discrimination as well as subsequent mandates to the same end. The World Conference on Human Rights strongly appeals to the international community to contribute generously to the Trust Fund for the Programme for the Decade for Action to Combat Racism and Racial Discrimination.

20. The World Conference on Human Rights urges all Governments to take immediate measures and to develop strong policies to prevent and combat all forms and manifestations of racism, xenophobia or related intolerance, where necessary by enactment of appropriate legislation, including penal measures, and by the establishment of national institutions to combat such phenomena.

21. The World Conference on Human Rights welcomes the decision of the Commission on Human Rights to appoint a Special Rapporteur on contemporary forms of racism, racial discrimination, xenophobia and related intolerance. The World Conference on Human Rights also appeals to all states parties to the International Convention on the Elimination of All Forms of Racial Discrimination to consider making the declaration under article 14 of the Convention.

22. The World Conference on Human Rights calls upon all Governments to take all appropriate measures in compliance with their international obligations and with due regard to their respective legal systems to counter intolerance and related violence based on religion or belief, including practices of discrimination against women and including the desecration of religious sites, recognizing that every individual has the right to

freedom of thought, conscience, expression and religion. The Conference also invites all states to put into practice the provisions of the Declaration on the Elimination of All Forms of Intolerance and of Discrimination Based on Religion or Belief.

23. The World Conference on Human Rights stresses that all persons who perpetrate or authorize criminal acts associated with ethnic cleansing are individually responsible and accountable for such human rights violations, and that the international community should exert every effort to bring those legally responsible for such violations to justice.

24. The World Conference on Human Rights calls on all states to take immediate measures, individually and collectively, to combat the practice of ethnic cleansing to bring it quickly to an end. Victims of the abhorrent practice of ethnic cleansing are entitled to appropriate and effective remedies.

2 Persons belonging to national or ethnic, religious and linguistic minorities

25. The World Conference on Human Rights calls on the Commission on Human Rights to examine ways and means to promote and protect effectively the rights of persons belonging to minorities as set out in the Declaration on the Rights of Persons belonging to National or Ethnic, Religious and Linguistic Minorities. In this context, the World Conference on Human Rights calls upon the Centre for Human Rights to provide, at the request of Governments concerned and as part of its programme of advisory services and technical assistance, qualified expertise on minority issues and human rights, as well as on the prevention and resolution of disputes, to assist in existing or potential situations involving minorities.

26. The World Conference on Human Rights urges states and the international community to promote and protect the rights of persons belonging to national or ethnic, religious and linguistic minorities in accordance with the Declaration on the Rights of Persons belonging to National or Ethnic, Religious and Linguistic Minorities.

27. Measures to be taken, where appropriate, should include facilitation of their full participation in all aspects of the political, economic, social, religious and cultural life of society and in the economic progress and development in their country.

Indigenous people

28. The World Conference on Human Rights calls on the Working Group on Indigenous Populations of the Sub-Commission on Prevention of Discrimination and Protection of Minorities to complete the drafting of a declaration on the rights of indigenous people at its eleventh session.

29. The World Conference on Human Rights recommends that the Commission on Human Rights consider the renewal and updating of the mandate of the Working Group on Indigenous Populations upon completion of the drafting of a declaration on the rights of indigenous people.

30. The World Conference on Human Rights also recommends that advisory services and technical assistance programmes within the United Nations system respond positively to requests by states for assistance which would be of direct benefit to indigenous people. The World Conference on Human Rights further recommends that adequate human and financial resources be made available to the Centre for Human Rights within the overall framework of strengthening the Centre's activities as envisaged by this document.

31. The World Conference on Human Rights urges states to ensure the full and free participation of indigenous people in all aspects of society, in particular in matters of concern to them.

32. The World Conference on Human Rights recommends that the General Assembly proclaim an international decade of the world's indigenous people, to begin from January 1994, including action-orientated programmes, to be decided upon in partnership with indigenous people. An appropriate voluntary trust fund should be set up for this purpose. In the framework of such a decade, the establishment of a permanent forum for indigenous people in the United Nations system should be considered.

Migrant workers

33. The World Conference on Human Rights urges all states to guarantee the protection of the human rights of all migrant workers and their families.

34. The World Conference on Human Rights considers that the creation of conditions to foster greater harmony and tolerance between migrant workers and the rest of the society of the state in which they reside is of particular importance.

35. The World Conference on Human Rights invites states to consider the possibility of signing and ratifying, at the earliest possible time, the International Convention on the Rights of All Migrant Workers and Members of Their Families.

3 The equal status and human rights of women

36. The World Conference on Human Rights urges the full and equal enjoyment by women of all human rights and that this be a priority for Governments and for the United Nations. The World Conference on Human Rights also underlines the importance of the integration and full participation of women as both agents and beneficiaries in the development process, and reiterates the objectives established on global action for women towards sustainable and equitable development set forth in the Rio Declaration on Environment and Development and chapter 24 of Agenda 21, adopted by the United Nations Conference on Environment and Development (Rio de Janeiro, Brazil, 3–14 June 1992).

37. The equal status of women and the human rights of women should be integrated into the mainstream of United Nations system-wide activity. These issues should be regularly and systematically addressed throughout relevant United Nations bodies and mechanisms. In particular, steps should be taken to increase co-operation and promote further integration of objectives and goals between the Commission on the Status of Women, the Commission on Human Rights, the Committee for the Elimination of Discrimination against Women, the United Nations Development Fund for Women, the United Nations Development Programme and other United Nations agencies. In this context, co-operation and co-ordination should be strengthened between the Centre for Human Rights and the Division for the Advancement of Women.

38. In particular, the World Conference on Human Rights stresses the importance of working towards the elimination of violence against women in public and private life, the elimination of all forms of sexual harassment, exploitation and trafficking in women, the elimination of gender bias in the administration of justice and the eradication of any conflicts which may arise between the rights of women and the harmful effects of certain traditional or customary practices, cultural prejudices and religious extremism. The World Conference on Human Rights calls upon the General Assembly to adopt the draft

declaration on violence against women and urges states to combat violence against women in accordance with its provisions. Violations of the human rights of women in situations of armed conflict are violations of the fundamental principles of international human rights and humanitarian law. All violations of this kind, including in particular murder, systematic rape, sexual slavery, and forced pregnancy, require a particularly effective response.

39. The World Conference on Human Rights urges the eradication of all forms of discrimination against women, both hidden and overt. The United Nations should encourage the goal of universal ratification by all States of the Convention on the Elimination of All Forms of Discrimination against Women by the year 2000. Ways and means of addressing the particularly large number of reservations to the Convention should be encouraged. Inter alia, the Committee on the Elimination of Discrimination against Women should continue its review of reservations to the Convention. States are urged to withdraw reservations that are contrary to the object and purpose of the Convention or which are otherwise incompatible with international treaty law.

40. Treaty monitoring bodies should disseminate necessary information to enable women to make more effective use of existing implementation procedures in their pursuits of full and equal enjoyment of human rights and non-discrimination. New procedures should also be adopted to strengthen implementation of the commitment to women's equality and the human rights of women. The Commission on the Status of Women and the Committee on the Elimination of Discrimination against Women should quickly examine the possibility of introducing the right of petition through the preparation of an optional protocol to the Convention on the Elimination of All Forms of Discrimination against Women. The World Conference on Human Rights welcomes the decision of the Commission on Human Rights to consider the appointment of a special rapporteur on violence against women at its fiftieth session.

41. The World Conference on Human Rights recognizes the importance of the enjoyment by women of the highest standard of physical and mental health throughout their life span. In the context of the World Conference on Women and the Convention on the Elimination of All Forms of Discrimination against Women, as well as the Proclamation of Tehran of 1968, the World Conference on Human Rights reaffirms, on the basis of equality between women and men, a woman's right to accessible and adequate health care and the widest range of family planning services, as well as equal access to education at all levels.

42. Treaty monitoring bodies should include the status of women and the human rights of women in their deliberations and findings, making use of gender-specific data. States should be encouraged to supply information on the situation of women de jure and de facto in their reports to treaty monitoring bodies. The World Conference on Human Rights notes with satisfaction that the Commission on Human Rights adopted at its forty-ninth session resolution 1993/46 of 8 March 1993 stating that rapporteurs and working groups in the field of human rights should also be encouraged to do so. Steps should also be taken by the Division for the Advancement of Women in co-operation with other United Nations bodies, specifically the Centre for Human Rights, to ensure that the human rights activities of the United Nations regularly address violations of women's human rights, including gender-specific abuses. Training for United Nations human rights and humanitarian relief personnel to assist them to recognize and deal with human

rights abuses particular to women and to carry out their work without gender bias should be encouraged.

43. The World Conference on Human Rights urges Governments and regional and international organizations to facilitate the access of women to decision-making posts and their greater participation in the decision-making process. It encourages further steps within the United Nations Secretariat to appoint and promote women staff members in accordance with the Charter of the United Nations, and encourages other principal and subsidiary organs of the United Nations to guarantee the participation of women under conditions of equality.

44. The World Conference on Human Rights welcomes the World Conference on Women to be held in Beijing in 1995 and urges that human rights of women should play an important role in its deliberations, in accordance with the priority themes of the World Conference on Women of equality, development and peace.

4 The rights of the child

45. The World Conference on Human Rights reiterates the principle of 'First Call for Children' and, in this respect, underlines the importance of major national and international efforts, especially those of the United Nations Children's Fund, for promoting respect for the rights of the child to survival, protection, development and participation.

46. Measures should be taken to achieve universal ratification of the Convention on the Rights of the Child by 1995 and the universal signing of the World Declaration on the Survival, Protection and Development of Children and Plan of Action adopted by the World Summit for Children, as well as their effective implementation. The World Conference on Human Rights urges states to withdraw reservations to the Convention on the Rights of the Child contrary to the object and purpose of the Convention or otherwise contrary to international treaty law.

47. The World Conference on Human Rights urges all nations to undertake measures to the maximum extent of their available resources, with the support of international co-operation, to achieve the goals in the World Summit Plan of Action. The Conference calls on states to integrate the Convention on the Rights of the Child into their national action plans. By means of these national action plans and through international efforts, particular priority should be placed on reducing infant and maternal mortality rates, reducing malnutrition and illiteracy rates and providing access to safe drinking water and to basic education. Whenever so called for, national plans of action should be devised to combat devastating emergencies resulting from natural disasters and armed conflicts and the equally grave problem of children in extreme poverty.

48. The World Conference on Human Rights urges all states, with the support of international co-operation, to address the acute problem of children under especially difficult circumstances. Exploitation and abuse of children should be actively combated, including by addressing their root causes. Effective measures are required against female infanticide, harmful child labour, sale of children and organs, child prostitution, child pornography, as well as other forms of sexual abuse.

49. The World Conference on Human Rights supports all measures by the United Nations and its specialized agencies to ensure the effective protection and promotion of human rights of the girl child. The World Conference on Human Rights urges states to

repeal existing laws and regulations and remove customs and practices which discriminate against and cause harm to the girl child.

50. The World Conference on Human Rights strongly supports the proposal that the Secretary-General initiate a study into means of improving the protection of children in armed conflicts. Humanitarian norms should be implemented and measures taken in order to protect and facilitate assistance to children in war zones. Measures should include protection for children against indiscriminate use of all weapons of war, especially anti-personnel mines. The need for after-care and rehabilitation of children traumatized by war must be addressed urgently. The Conference calls on the Committee on the Rights of the Child to study the question of raising the minimum age of recruitment into armed forces.

51. The World Conference on Human Rights recommends that matters relating to human rights and the situation of children be regularly reviewed and monitored by all relevant organs and mechanisms of the United Nations system and by the supervisory bodies of the specialized agencies in accordance with their mandates.

52. The World Conference on Human Rights recognizes the important role played by non-governmental organizations in the effective implementation of all human rights instruments and, in particular, the Convention on the Rights of the Child.

53. The World Conference on Human Rights recommends that the Committee on the Rights of the Child, with the assistance of the Centre for Human Rights, be enabled expeditiously and effectively to meet its mandate, especially in view of the unprecedented extent of ratification and subsequent submission of country reports.

5 Freedom from torture

54. The World Conference on Human Rights welcomes the ratification by many member states of the Convention against Torture and Other Cruel, Inhuman or Degrading Treatment or Punishment and encourages its speedy ratification by all other member states.

55. The World Conference on Human Rights emphasizes that one of the most atrocious violations against human dignity is the act of torture, the result of which destroys the dignity and impairs the capability of victims to continue their lives and their activities.

56. The World Conference on Human Rights reaffirms that under human rights law and international humanitarian law, freedom from torture is a right which must be protected under all circumstances, including in times of internal or international disturbance or armed conflicts.

57. The World Conference on Human Rights therefore urges all states to put an immediate end to the practice of torture and eradicate this evil forever through full implementation of the Universal Declaration of Human Rights as well as the relevant conventions and, where necessary, strengthening of existing mechanisms. The World Conference on Human Rights calls on all states to co-operate fully with the Special Rapporteur on the question of torture in the fulfilment of his mandate.

58. Special attention should be given to ensure universal respect for, and effective implementation of, the Principles of Medical Ethics relevant to the Role of Health Personnel, particularly Physicians, in the Protection of Prisoners and Detainees against

Torture and other Cruel, Inhuman or Degrading Treatment or Punishment adopted by the General Assembly of the United Nations.

59. The World Conference on Human Rights stresses the importance of further concrete action within the framework of the United Nations with the view to providing assistance to victims of torture and ensuring more effective remedies for their physical, psychological and social rehabilitation. Providing the necessary resources for this purpose should be given high priority, inter alia, by additional contributions to the United Nations Voluntary Fund for the Victims of Torture.

60. States should abrogate legislation leading to impunity for those responsible for grave violations of human rights such as torture and prosecute such violations, thereby providing a firm basis for the rule of law.

61. The World Conference on Human Rights reaffirms that efforts to eradicate torture should, first and foremost, be concentrated on prevention and, therefore, calls for the early adoption of an optional protocol to the Convention against Torture and Other Cruel, Inhuman and Degrading Treatment or Punishment, which is intended to establish a preventive system of regular visits to places of detention.

Enforced disappearances

62. The World Conference on Human Rights, welcoming the adoption by the General Assembly of the Declaration on the Protection of All Persons from Enforced Disappearance, calls upon all states to take effective legislative, administrative, judicial or other measures to prevent, terminate and punish acts of enforced disappearances. The World Conference on Human Rights reaffirms that it is the duty of all states, under any circumstances, to make investigations whenever there is reason to believe that an enforced disappearance has taken place on a territory under their jurisdiction and, if allegations are confirmed, to prosecute its perpetrators.

6 The rights of the disabled person

63. The World Conference on Human Rights reaffirms that all human rights and fundamental freedoms are universal and thus unreservedly include persons with disabilities. Every person is born equal and has the same rights to life and welfare, education and work, living independently and active participation in all aspects of society. Any direct discrimination or other negative discriminatory treatment of a disabled person is therefore a violation of his or her rights. The World Conference on Human Rights calls on Governments, where necessary, to adopt or adjust legislation to assure access to these and other rights for disabled persons.

64. The place of disabled persons is everywhere. Persons with disabilities should be guaranteed equal opportunity through the elimination of all socially determined barriers, be they physical, financial, social or psychological, which exclude or restrict full participation in society.

65. Recalling the World Programme of Action concerning Disabled Persons, adopted by the General Assembly at its thirty-seventh session, the World Conference on Human Rights calls upon the General Assembly and the Economic and Social Council to adopt the draft standard rules on the equalization of opportunities for persons with disabilities, at their meetings in 1993.

C Co-operation, development and strengthening of human rights

66. The World Conference on Human Rights recommends that priority be given to national and international action to promote democracy, development and human rights.

67. Special emphasis should be given to measures to assist in the strengthening and building of institutions relating to human rights, strengthening of a pluralistic civil society and the protection of groups which have been rendered vulnerable. In this context, assistance provided upon the request of Governments for the conduct of free and fair elections, including assistance in the human rights aspects of elections and public information about elections, is of particular importance.

Equally important is the assistance to be given to the strengthening of the rule of law, the promotion of freedom of expression and the administration of justice, and to the real and effective participation of the people in the decision-making processes.

68. The World Conference on Human Rights stresses the need for the implementation of strengthened advisory services and technical assistance activities by the Centre for Human Rights. The Centre should make available to states upon request assistance on specific human rights issues, including the preparation of reports under human rights treaties as well as for the implementation of coherent and comprehensive plans of action for the promotion and protection of human rights. Strengthening the institutions of human rights and democracy, the legal protection of human rights, training of officials and others, broad-based education and public information aimed at promoting respect for human rights should all be available as components of these programmes.

69. The World Conference on Human Rights strongly recommends that a comprehensive programme be established within the United Nations in order to help states in the task of building and strengthening adequate national structures which have a direct impact on the overall observance of human rights and the maintenance of the rule of law. Such a programme, to be co-ordinated by the Centre for Human Rights, should be able to provide, upon the request of the interested Government, technical and financial assistance to national projects in reforming penal and correctional establishments, education and training of lawyers, judges and security forces in human rights, and any other sphere of activity relevant to the good functioning of the rule of law. That programme should make available to states assistance for the implementation of plans of action for the promotion and protection of human rights.

70. The World Conference on Human Rights requests the Secretary-General of the United Nations to submit proposals to the United Nations General Assembly, containing alternatives for the establishment, structure, operational modalities and funding of the proposed programme.

71. The World Conference on Human Rights recommends that each state consider the desirability of drawing up a national action plan identifying steps whereby that state would improve the promotion and protection of human rights.

72. The World Conference on Human Rights reaffirms that the universal and inalienable right to development, as established in the Declaration on the Right to Development, must be implemented and realized. In this context, the World Conference on Human Rights welcomes the appointment by the Commission on Human Rights of a thematic working group on the right to development and urges that the Working Group, in consultation and co-operation with other organs and agencies of the United Nations system, promptly formulate, for early consideration by the United Nations General Assembly, comprehensive and effective measures to eliminate obstacles to the

implementation and realization of the Declaration on the Right to Development and recommending ways and means towards the realization of the right to development by all states.

73. The World Conference on Human Rights recommends that non-governmental and other grass-roots organizations active in development and/or human rights should be enabled to play a major role on the national and international levels in the debate, activities and implementation relating to the right to development and, in co-operation with Governments, in all relevant aspects of development co-operation.

74. The World Conference on Human Rights appeals to Governments, competent agencies and institutions to increase considerably the resources devoted to building well-functioning legal systems able to protect human rights, and to national institutions working in this area. Actors in the field of development co-operation should bear in mind the mutually reinforcing interrelationship between development, democracy and human rights. Co-operation should be based on dialogue and transparency.

The World Conference on Human Rights also calls for the establishment of comprehensive programmes, including resource banks of information and personnel with expertise relating to the strengthening of the rule of law and of democratic institutions.

75. The World Conference on Human Rights encourages the Commission on Human Rights, in co-operation with the Committee on Economic, Social and Cultural Rights, to continue the examination of optional protocols to the International Covenant on Economic, Social and Cultural Rights.

76. The World Conference on Human Rights recommends that more resources be made available for the strengthening or the establishment of regional arrangements for the promotion and protection of human rights under the programmes of advisory services and technical assistance of the Centre for Human Rights. States are encouraged to request assistance for such purposes as regional and subregional workshops, seminars and information exchanges designed to strengthen regional arrangements for the promotion and protection of human rights in accord with universal human rights standards as contained in international human rights instruments.

77. The World Conference on Human Rights supports all measures by the United Nations and its relevant specialized agencies to ensure the effective promotion and protection of trade union rights, as stipulated in the International Covenant on Economic, Social and Cultural Rights and other relevant international instruments. It calls on all states to abide fully by their obligations in this regard contained in international instruments.

D Human rights education

78. The World Conference on Human Rights considers human rights education, training and public information essential for the promotion and achievement of stable and harmonious relations among communities and for fostering mutual understanding, tolerance and peace.

79. States should strive to eradicate illiteracy and should direct education towards the full development of the human personality and to the strengthening of respect for human rights and fundamental freedoms. The World Conference on Human Rights calls on all states and institutions to include human rights, humanitarian law, democracy and rule of

law as subjects in the curricula of all learning institutions in formal and non-formal settings.

80. Human rights education should include peace, democracy, development and social justice, as set forth in international and regional human rights instruments, in order to achieve common understanding and awareness with a view to strengthening universal commitment to human rights.

81. Taking into account the World Plan of Action on Education for Human Rights and Democracy, adopted in March 1993 by the International Congress on Education for Human Rights and Democracy of the United Nations Educational, Scientific and Cultural Organization, and other human rights instruments, the World Conference on Human Rights recommends that states develop specific programmes and strategies for ensuring the widest human rights education and the dissemination of public information, taking particular account of the human rights needs of women.

82. Governments, with the assistance of intergovernmental organizations, national institutions and non-governmental organizations, should promote an increased awareness of human rights and mutual tolerance. The World Conference on Human Rights underlines the importance of strengthening the World Public Information Campaign for Human Rights carried out by the United Nations. They should initiate and support education in human rights and undertake effective dissemination of public information in this field. The advisory services and technical assistance programmes of the United Nations system should be able to respond immediately to requests from states for educational and training activities in the field of human rights as well as for special education concerning standards as contained in international human rights instruments and in humanitarian law and their application to special groups such as military forces, law enforcement personnel, police and the health profession. The proclamation of a United Nations decade for human rights education in order to promote, encourage and focus these educational activities should be considered.

E Implementation and monitoring methods

83. The World Conference on Human Rights urges Governments to incorporate standards as contained in international human rights instruments in domestic legislation and to strengthen national structures, institutions and organs of society which play a role in promoting and safeguarding human rights.

84. The World Conference on Human Rights recommends the strengthening of United Nations activities and programmes to meet requests for assistance by states which want to establish or strengthen their own national institutions for the promotion and protection of human rights.

85. The World Conference on Human Rights also encourages the strengthening of co-operation between national institutions for the promotion and protection of human rights, particularly through exchanges of information and experience, as well as co-operation with regional organizations and the United Nations.

86. The World Conference on Human Rights strongly recommends in this regard that representatives of national institutions for the promotion and protection of human rights convene periodic meetings under the auspices of the Centre for Human Rights to examine ways and means of improving their mechanisms and sharing experiences.

87. The World Conference on Human Rights recommends to the human rights treaty

bodies, to the meetings of chairpersons of the treaty bodies and to the meetings of states parties that they continue to take steps aimed at co-ordinating the multiple reporting requirements and guidelines for preparing state reports under the respective human rights conventions and study the suggestion that the submission of one overall report on treaty obligations undertaken by each state would make these procedures more effective and increase their impact.

88. The World Conference on Human Rights recommends that the states parties to international human rights instruments, the General Assembly and the Economic and Social Council should consider studying the existing human rights treaty bodies and the various thematic mechanisms and procedures with a view to promoting greater efficiency and effectiveness through better co-ordination of the various bodies, mechanisms and procedures, taking into account the need to avoid unnecessary duplication and overlapping of their mandates and tasks.

89. The World Conference on Human Rights recommends continued work on the improvement of the functioning, including the monitoring tasks, of the treaty bodies, taking into account multiple proposals made in this respect, in particular those made by the treaty bodies themselves and by the meetings of the chairpersons of the treaty bodies. The comprehensive national approach taken by the Committee on the Rights of the Child should also be encouraged.

90. The World Conference on Human Rights recommends that states parties to human rights treaties consider accepting all the available optional communication procedures.

91. The World Conference on Human Rights views with concern the issue of impunity of perpetrators of human rights violations, and supports the efforts of the Commission on Human Rights and the Sub-Commission on Prevention of Discrimination and Protection of Minorities to examine all aspects of the issue.

92. The World Conference on Human Rights recommends that the Commission on Human Rights examine the possibility for better implementation of existing human rights instruments at the international and regional levels and encourages the International Law Commission to continue its work on an international criminal court.

93. The World Conference on Human Rights appeals to states which have not yet done so to accede to the Geneva Conventions of 12 August 1949 and the Protocols thereto, and to take all appropriate national measures, including legislative ones, for their full implementation.

94. The World Conference on Human Rights recommends the speedy completion and adoption of the draft declaration on the right and responsibility of individuals, groups and organs of society to promote and protect universally recognized human rights and fundamental freedoms.

95. The World Conference on Human Rights underlines the importance of preserving and strengthening the system of special procedures, rapporteurs, representatives, experts and working groups of the Commission on Human Rights and the Sub-Commission on the Prevention of Discrimination and Protection of Minorities, in order to enable them to carry out their mandates in all countries throughout the world, providing them with the necessary human and financial resources. The procedures and mechanisms should be enabled to harmonize and rationalize their work through periodic meetings. All states are asked to co-operate fully with these procedures and mechanisms.

96. The World Conference on Human Rights recommends that the United Nations

assume a more active role in the promotion and protection of human rights in ensuring full respect for international humanitarian law in all situations of armed conflict, in accordance with the purposes and principles of the Charter of the United Nations.

97. The World Conference on Human Rights, recognizing the important role of human rights components in specific arrangements concerning some peace-keeping operations by the United Nations, recommends that the Secretary-General take into account the reporting, experience and capabilities of the Centre for Human Rights and human rights mechanisms, in conformity with the Charter of the United Nations.

98. To strengthen the enjoyment of economic, social and cultural rights, additional approaches should be examined, such as a system of indicators to measure progress in the realization of the rights set forth in the International Covenant on Economic, Social and Cultural Rights. There must be a concerted effort to ensure recognition of economic, social and cultural rights at the national, regional and international levels.

F Follow-up to the World Conference on Human Rights

99. The World Conference on Human Rights recommends that the General Assembly, the Commission on Human Rights and other organs and agencies of the United Nations system related to human rights consider ways and means for the full implementation, without delay, of the recommendations contained in the present Declaration, including the possibility of proclaiming a United Nations decade for human rights. The World Conference on Human Rights further recommends that the Commission on Human Rights annually review the progress towards this end.

100. The World Conference on Human Rights requests the Secretary-General of the United Nations to invite on the occasion of the fiftieth anniversary of the Universal Declaration of Human Rights all states, all organs and agencies of the United Nations system related to human rights, to report to him on the progress made in the implementation of the present Declaration and to submit a report to the General Assembly at its fifty-third session, through the Commission on Human Rights and the Economic and Social Council. Likewise, regional and, as appropriate, national human rights institutions, as well as non-governmental organizations, may present their views to the Secretary-General on the progress made in the implementation of the present Declaration. Special attention should be paid to assessing the progress towards the goal of universal ratification of international human rights treaties and protocols adopted within the framework of the United Nations system.

UNIVERSAL DECLARATION OF HUMAN RIGHTS

[Adopted and proclaimed by United Nations General Assembly resolution 217A(III) on 10 December 1948.]

PREAMBLE

Whereas recognition of the inherent dignity and of the equal and inalienable rights of all members of the human family is the foundation of freedom, justice and peace in the world.

Whereas disregard and contempt for human rights have resulted in barbarous acts which have outraged the conscience of mankind, and the advent of a world in which human beings shall enjoy freedom of speech and belief and freedom from fear and want has been proclaimed as the highest aspiration of the common people.

Whereas it is essential, if man is not to be compelled to have recourse, as a last resort, to rebellion against tyranny and oppression, that human rights should be protected by the rule of law.

Whereas it is essential to promote the development of friendly relations between nations.

Whereas the peoples of the United Nations have in the Charter reaffirmed their faith in fundamental human rights, in the dignity and worth of the human person and in the equal rights of men and women and have determined to promote social progress and better standards of life in larger freedom.

Whereas member states have pledged themselves to achieve, in co-operation with the United Nations, the promotion of universal respect for and observance of human rights and fundamental freedoms.

Whereas a common understanding of these rights and freedoms is of the greatest importance for the full realization of this pledge.

Now, therefore

The General Assembly

Proclaims this Universal Declaration of Human Rights as a common standard of achievement for all peoples and all nations, to the end that every individual and every organ of society, keeping this Declaration constantly in mind, shall strive by teaching and education to promote respect for these rights and freedoms and by progressive measures, national and international, to secure their universal and effective recognition and observance, both among the peoples of member states themselves and among the peoples of territories under their jurisdiction.

Article 1

All human beings are born free and equal in dignity and rights. They are endowed with reason and conscience and should act towards one another in a spirit of brotherhood.

Article 2

Everyone is entitled to all the rights and freedoms set forth in this Declaration, without distinction of any kind, such as race, colour, sex, language, religion, political or other opinion, national or social origin, property, birth or other status.

Furthermore, no distinction shall be made on the basis of the political, jurisdictional or international status of the country or territory to which a person belongs, whether it be independent, trust, non-selfgoverning or under any other limitation of sovereignty.

Article 3

Everyone has the right to life, liberty and security of person.

Article 4

No one shall be held in slavery or servitude; slavery and the slave trade shall be prohibited in all their forms.

Article 5

No one shall be subjected to torture or to cruel, inhuman or degrading treatment or punishment.

Article 6

Everyone has the right to recognition everywhere as a person before the law.

Article 7

All are equal before the law and are entitled without any discrimination to equal protection of the law. All are entitled to equal protection against any discrimination in violation of this Declaration and against any incitement to such discrimination.

Article 8

Everyone has the right to an effective remedy by the competent national tribunals for acts violating the fundamental rights granted him by the constitution or by law.

Article 9

No one shall be subjected to arbitrary arrest, detention or exile.

Article 10

Everyone is entitled in full equality to a fair and public hearing by an independent and impartial tribunal, in the determination of his rights and obligations and of any criminal charge against him.

Article 11

1. Everyone charged with a penal offence has the right to be presumed innocent until proved guilty according to law in a public trial at which he has had all the guarantees necessary for his defence.

2. No one shall be held guilty of any penal offence on account of any act or omission which did not constitute a penal offence, under national or international law, at the time when it was committed. Nor shall a heavier penalty be imposed than the one that was applicable at the time the penal offence was committed.

Article 12

No one shall be subjected to arbitrary interference with his privacy, family, home or correspondence, nor to attacks upon his honour and reputation. Everyone has the right to the protection of the law against such interference or attacks.

Article 13

1. Everyone has the right to freedom of movement and residence within the borders of each state.

2. Everyone has the right to leave any country, including his own, and to return to his country.

Article 14

1. Everyone has the right to seek and to enjoy in other countries asylum from persecution.

2. This right may not be invoked in the case of prosecutions genuinely arising from non-political crimes or from acts contrary to the purposes and principles of the United Nations.

Article 15

1. Everyone has the right to a nationality.

2. No one shall be arbitrarily deprived of his nationality nor denied the right to change his nationality.

Article 16

1. Men and women of full age, without any limitation due to race, nationality or religion, have the right to marry and to found a family. They are entitled to equal rights as to marriage, during marriage and at its dissolution.

2. Marriage shall be entered into only with the free and full consent of the intending spouses.

3. The family is the natural and fundamental group unit of society and is entitled to protection by society and the state.

Article 17

1. Everyone has the right to own property alone as well as in association with others.

2. No one shall be arbitrarily deprived of his property.

Article 18

Everyone has the right to freedom of thought, conscience and religion; this right includes freedom to change his religion or belief, and freedom, either alone or in community with others and in public or private, to manifest his religion or belief in teaching, practice, worship and observance.

Article 19

Everyone has the right to freedom of opinion and expression; this right includes freedom to hold opinions without interference and to seek, receive and impart information and ideas through any media and regardless of frontiers.

Article 20

1. Everyone has the right to freedom of peaceful assembly and association.

2. No one may be compelled to belong to an association.

Article 21

1. Everyone has the right to take part in the government of his country, directly or through freely chosen representatives.

2. Everyone has the right to equal access to public service in his country.

3. The will of the people shall be the basis of the authority of government; this will shall be expressed in periodic and genuine elections which shall be by universal and equal suffrage and shall be held by secret vote or by equivalent free voting procedures.

Article 22

Everyone, as a member of society, has the right to social security and is entitled to realization, through national effort and international co-operation and in accordance with the organization and resources of each state, of the economic, social and cultural rights indispensable for his dignity and the free development of his personality.

Article 23

1. Everyone has the right to work, to free choice of employment, to just and favourable conditions of work and to protection against unemployment.

2. Everyone, without any discrimination, has the right to equal pay for equal work.

3. Everyone who works has the right to just and favourable remuneration ensuring for himself and his family an existence worthy of human dignity, and supplemented, if necessary, by other means of social protection.

4. Everyone has the right to form and to join trade unions for the protection of his interests.

Article 24

Everyone has the right to rest and leisure, including reasonable limitation of working hours and periodic holidays with pay.

Article 25

1. Everyone has the right to a standard of living adequate for the health and well-being of himself and of his family, including food, clothing, housing and medical care and necessary social services, and the right to security in the event of unemployment, sickness, disability, widowhood, old age or other lack of livelihood in circumstances beyond his control.

2. Motherhood and childhood are entitled to special care and assistance. All children, whether born in or out of wedlock, shall enjoy the same social protection.

Article 26

1. Everyone has the right to education. Education shall be free, at least in the elementary and fundamental stages. Elementary education shall be compulsory.

Technical and professional education shall be made generally available and higher education shall be equally accessible to all on the basis of merit.

2. Education shall be directed to the full development of the human personality and to the strengthening of respect for human rights and fundamental freedoms. It shall promote understanding, tolerance and friendship among all nations, racial or religious groups, and shall further the activities of the United Nations for the maintenance of peace.

3. Parents have a prior right to choose the kind of education that shall be given to their children.

Article 27

1. Everyone has the right freely to participate in the cultural life of the community, to enjoy the arts and to share in scientific advancement and its benefits.

2. Everyone has the right to the protection of the moral and material interests resulting from any scientific, literary or artistic production of which he is the author.

Article 28

Everyone is entitled to a social and international order in which the rights and freedoms set forth in this Declaration can be fully realized.

Article 29

1. Everyone has duties to the community in which alone the free and full development of his personality is possible.

2. In the exercise of his rights and freedoms, everyone shall be subject only to such limitations as are determined by law solely for the purpose of securing due recognition and respect for the rights and freedoms of others and of meeting the just requirements of morality, public order and the general welfare in a democratic society.

3. These rights and freedoms may in no case be exercised contrary to the purposes and principles of the United Nations.

Article 30

Nothing in this Declaration may be interpreted as implying for any state, group or person any right to engage in any activity or to perform any act aimed at the destruction of any of the rights and freedoms set forth herein.

APPENDIX 3

INTERNATIONAL COVENANT ON ECONOMIC, SOCIAL, AND CULTURAL RIGHTS

[Adopted and opened for signature, ratification, and accession by United Nations General Assembly resolution 2200A(XXI) on 16 December 1966.

Entered into force on 3 January 1976 in accordance with article 27.]

PREAMBLE

The states parties to the present Covenant

Considering that, in accordance with the principles proclaimed in the Charter of the United Nations, recognition of the inherent dignity and of the equal and inalienable rights of all members of the human family is the foundation of freedom, justice and peace in the world.

Recognizing that these rights derive from the inherent dignity of the human person.

Recognizing that, in accordance with the Universal Declaration of Human Rights, the ideal of free human beings enjoying freedom from fear and want can only be achieved if conditions are created whereby everyone may enjoy his economic, social and cultural rights, as well as his civil and political rights.

Considering the obligation of states under the Charter of the United Nations to promote universal respect for, and observance of, human rights and freedoms.

Realizing that the individual, having duties to other individuals and to the community to which he belongs, is under a responsibility to strive for the promotion and observance of the rights recognized in the present Covenant.

Agree upon the following articles:

PART I

Article 1

1. All peoples have the right of self-determination. By virtue of that right they freely determine their political status and freely pursue their economic, social and cultural development.

2. All peoples may, for their own ends, freely dispose of their natural wealth and resources without prejudice to any obligations arising out of international economic co-operation, based upon the principle of mutual benefit, and international law. In no case may a people be deprived of its own means of subsistence.

3. The states parties to the present Covenant, including those having responsibility for the administration of Non-Self-Governing and Trust Territories, shall promote the realization of the right of self-determination, and shall respect that right, in conformity with the provisions of the Charter of the United Nations.

PART II

Article 2

1. Each state party to the present Covenant undertakes to take steps, individually and through international assistance and co-operation, especially economic and technical, to the maximum of its available resources, with a view to achieving progressively the full realization of the rights recognized in the present Covenant by all appropriate means, including particularly the adoption of legislative measures.

2. The states parties to the present Covenant undertake to guarantee that the rights enunciated in the present Covenant will be exercised without discrimination of any kind as to race, colour, sex, language, religion, political or other opinion, national or social origin, property, birth or other status.

3. Developing countries, with due regard to human rights and their national economy, may determine to what extent they would guarantee the economic rights recognized in the present Covenant to non-nationals.

Article 3

The states parties to the present Covenant undertake to ensure the equal right of men and women to the enjoyment of all economic, social and cultural rights set forth in the present Covenant.

Article 4

The states parties to the present Covenant recognize that, in the enjoyment of those rights provided by the state in conformity with the present Covenant, the state may subject such rights only to such limitations as are determined by law only in so far as this may be compatible with the nature of these rights and solely for the purpose of promoting the general welfare in a democratic society.

Article 5

1. Nothing in the present Covenant may be interpreted as implying for any state, group or person any right to engage in any activity or to perform any act aimed at the destruction of any of the rights or freedoms recognized herein, or at their limitation to a greater extent than is provided for in the present Covenant.

2. No restriction upon or derogation from any of the fundamental human rights recognized or existing in any country in virtue of law, conventions, regulations or custom shall be admitted on the pretext that the present Covenant does not recognize such rights or that it recognizes them to a lesser extent.

PART III

Article 6

1. The states parties to the present Covenant recognize the right to work, which includes the right of everyone to the opportunity to gain his living by work which he freely chooses or accepts, and will take appropriate steps to safeguard this right.

2. The steps to be taken by a state party to the present Covenant to achieve the full realization of this right shall include technical and vocational guidance and training programmes, policies and techniques to achieve steady economic, social and cultural

development and full and productive employment under conditions safeguarding fundamental political and economic freedoms to the individual.

Article 7

The states parties to the present Covenant recognize the right of everyone to the enjoyment of just and favourable conditions of work which ensure, in particular:

(a) Remuneration which provides all workers, as a minimum, with:

    (i) Fair wages and equal remuneration for work of equal value without distinction of any kind, in particular women being guaranteed conditions of work not inferior to those enjoyed by men, with equal pay for equal work;

    (ii) A decent living for themselves and their families in accordance with the provisions of the present Covenant;

(b) Safe and healthy working conditions;

(c) Equal opportunity for everyone to be promoted in his employment to an appropriate higher level, subject to no considerations other than those of seniority and competence;

(d) Rest, leisure and reasonable limitation of working hours and periodic holidays with pay, as well as remuneration for public holidays.

Article 8

1. The states parties to the present Covenant undertake to ensure:

(a) The right of everyone to form trade unions and join the trade union of his choice, subject only to the rules of the organization concerned, for the promotion and protection of his economic and social interests. No restrictions may be placed on the exercise of this right other than those prescribed by law and which are necessary in a democratic society in the interests of national security or public order or for the protection of the rights and freedoms of others;

(b) The right of trade unions to establish national federations or confederations and the right of the latter to form or join international trade-union organizations;

(c) The right of trade unions to function freely subject to no limitations other than those prescribed by law and which are necessary in a democratic society in the interests of national security or public order or for the protection of the rights and freedoms of others;

(d) The right to strike, provided that it is exercised in conformity with the laws of the particular country.

2. This article shall not prevent the imposition of lawful restrictions on the exercise of these rights by members of the armed forces or of the police or of the administration of the state.

3. Nothing in this article shall authorize states parties to the International Labour Organisation Convention of 1948 concerning Freedom of Association and Protection of the Right to Organize to take legislative measures which would prejudice, or apply the law in such a manner as would prejudice, the guarantees provided for in that Convention.

Article 9

The states parties to the present Covenant recognize the right of everyone to social security, including social insurance.

Article 10

The states parties to the present Covenant recognize that:

1. The widest possible protection and assistance should be accorded to the family, which is the natural and fundamental group unit of society, particularly for its establishment and while it is responsible for the care and education of dependent children. Marriage must be entered into with the free consent of the intending spouses.

2. Special protection should be accorded to mothers during a reasonable period before and after childbirth. During such period working mothers should be accorded paid leave or leave with adequate social security benefits.

3. Special measures of protection and assistance should be taken on behalf of all children and young persons without any discrimination for reasons of parentage or other conditions. Children and young persons should be protected from economic and social exploitation. Their employment in work harmful to their morals or health or dangerous to life or likely to hamper their normal development should be punishable by law. States should also set age limits below which the paid employment of child labour should be prohibited and punishable by law.

Article 11

1. The states parties to the present Covenant recognize the right of everyone to an adequate standard of living for himself and his family, including adequate food, clothing and housing, and to the continuous improvement of living conditions. The states parties will take appropriate steps to ensure the realization of this right, recognizing to this effect the essential importance of international co-operation based on free consent.

2. The states parties to the present Covenant, recognizing the fundamental right of everyone to be free from hunger, shall take, individually and through international co-operation, the measures, including specific programmes, which are needed:
(a) To improve methods of production, conservation and distribution of food by making full use of technical and scientific knowledge, by disseminating knowledge of the principles of nutrition and by developing or reforming agrarian systems in such a way as to achieve the most efficient development and utilization of natural resources;
(b) Taking into account the problems of both food-importing and food-exporting countries, to ensure an equitable distribution of world food supplies in relation to need.

Article 12

1. The states parties to the present Covenant recognize the right of everyone to the enjoyment of the highest attainable standard of physical and mental health.

2. The steps to be taken by the states parties to the present Covenant to achieve the full realization of this right shall include those necessary for:
(a) The provision for the reduction of the stillbirth-rate and of infant mortality and for the healthy development of the child;
(b) The improvement of all aspects of environmental and industrial hygiene;
(c) The prevention, treatment and control of epidemic, endemic, occupational and other diseases;
(d) The creation of conditions which would assure to all medical service and medical attention in the event of sickness.

Article 13

1. The states parties to the present Covenant recognize the right of everyone to education. They agree that education shall be directed to the full development of the human personality and the sense of its dignity, and shall strengthen the respect for human rights and fundamental freedoms. They further agree that education shall enable all persons to participate effectively in a free society, promote understanding, tolerance and friendship among all nations and all racial, ethnic or religious groups, and further the activities of the United Nations for the maintenance of peace.

2. The states parties to the present Covenant recognize that, with a view to achieving the full realization of this right:
(a) Primary education shall be compulsory and available free to all;
(b) Secondary education in its different forms, including technical and vocational secondary education, shall be made generally available and accessible to all by every appropriate means, and in particular by the progressive introduction of free education;
(c) Higher education shall be made equally accessible to all, on the basis of capacity, by every appropriate means, and in particular by the progressive introduction of free education;
(d) Fundamental education shall be encouraged or intensified as far as possible for those persons who have not received or completed the whole period of their primary education;
(e) The development of a system of schools at all levels shall be actively pursued, an adequate fellowship system shall be established, and the material conditions of teaching staff shall be continuously improved.

3. The states parties to the present Covenant undertake to have respect for the liberty of parents and, when applicable, legal guardians to choose for their children schools, other than those established by the public authorities, which conform to such minimum educational standards as may be laid down or approved by the state and to ensure the religious and moral education of their children in conformity with their own convictions.

4. No part of this article shall be construed so as to interfere with the liberty of individuals and bodies to establish and direct educational institutions, subject always to the observance of the principles set forth in paragraph 1 of this article and to the requirement that the education given in such institutions shall conform to such minimum standards as may be laid down by the state.

Article 14

Each state party to the present Covenant which, at the time of becoming a Party, has not been able to secure in its metropolitan territory or other territories under its jurisdiction compulsory primary education, free of charge, undertakes within two years, to work out and adopt a detailed plan of action for the progressive implementation, within a reasonable number of years, to be fixed in the plan, of the principle of compulsory education free of charge for all.

Article 15

1. The states parties to the present Covenant recognize the right of everyone:
(a) To take part in cultural life;
(b) To enjoy the benefits of scientific progress and its applications;

(c) To benefit from the protection of the moral and material interests resulting from any scientific, literary or artistic production of which he is the author.

2. The steps to be taken by the states parties to the present Covenant to achieve the full realization of this right shall include those necessary for the conservation, the development and the diffusion of science and culture.

3. The states parties to the present Covenant undertake to respect the freedom indispensable for scientific research and creative activity.

4. The states parties to the present Covenant recognize the benefits to be derived from the encouragement and development of international contacts and co-operation in the scientific and cultural fields.

PART IV

Article 16

1. The states parties to the present Covenant undertake to submit in conformity with this part of the Covenant reports on the measures which they have adopted and the progress made in achieving the observance of the rights recognized herein.

2. *(a)* All reports shall be submitted to the Secretary-General of the United Nations, who shall transmit copies to the Economic and Social Council for consideration in accordance with the provisions of the present Covenant;
(b) The Secretary-General of the United Nations shall also transmit to the specialized agencies copies of the reports, or any relevant parts therefrom, from states parties to the present Covenant which are also members of these specialized agencies in so far as these reports, or parts therefrom, relate to any matters which fall within the responsibilities of the said agencies in accordance with their constitutional instruments.

Article 17

1. The states parties to the present Covenant shall furnish their reports in stages, in accordance with a programme to be established by the Economic and Social Council within one year of the entry into force of the present Covenant after consultation with the states parties and the specialized agencies concerned.

2. Reports may indicate factors and difficulties affecting the degree of fulfilment of obligations under the present Covenant.

3. Where relevant information has previously been furnished to the United Nations or to any specialized agency by any state party to the present Covenant, it will not be necessary to reproduce that information, but a precise reference to the information so furnished will suffice.

Article 18

Pursuant to its responsibilities under the Charter of the United Nations in the field of human rights and fundamental freedoms, the Economic and Social Council may make arrangements with the specialized agencies in respect of their reporting to it on the progress made in achieving the observance of the provisions of the present Covenant falling within the scope of their activities. These reports may include particulars of decisions and recommendations on such implementation adopted by their competent organs.

Article 19

The Economic and Social Council may transmit to the Commission on Human Rights for study and general recommendation or, as appropriate, for information the reports concerning human rights submitted by states in accordance with Articles 16 and 17, and those concerning human rights submitted by the specialized agencies in accordance with Article 18.

Article 20

The states parties to the present Covenant and the specialized agencies concerned may submit comments to the Economic and Social Council on any general recommendation under Article 19 or reference to such general recommendation in any report of the Commission on Human Rights or any documentation referred to therein.

Article 21

The Economic and Social Council may submit from time to time to the General Assembly reports with recommendations of a general nature and a summary of the information received from the states parties to the present Covenant and the specialized agencies on the measures taken and the progress made in achieving general observance of the rights recognized in the present Covenant.

Article 22

The Economic and Social Council may bring to the attention of other organs of the United Nations, their subsidiary organs and specialized agencies concerned with furnishing technical assistance any matters arising out of the reports referred to in this part of the present Covenant which may assist such bodies in deciding, each within its field of competence, on the advisability of international measures likely to contribute to the effective progressive implementation of the present Covenant.

Article 23

The states parties to the present Covenant agree that international action for the achievement of the rights recognized in the present Covenant includes such methods as the conclusion of conventions, the adoption of recommendations, the furnishing of technical assistance and the holding of regional meetings and technical meetings for the purpose of consultation and study organized in conjunction with the Governments concerned.

Article 24

Nothing in the present Covenant shall be interpreted as impairing the provisions of the Charter of the United Nations and of the constitutions of the specialized agencies which define the respective responsibilities of the various organs of the United Nations and of the specialized agencies in regard to the matters dealt with in the present Covenant.

Article 25

Nothing in the present Covenant shall be interpreted as impairing the inherent right of all peoples to enjoy and utilize fully and freely their natural wealth and resources.

PART V

Article 26

1. The present Covenant is open for signature by any state member of the United Nations or member of any of its specialized agencies, by any state party to the Statute of the international Court of Justice, and by any other state which has been invited by the General Assembly of the United Nations to become a party to the present Covenant.

2. The present Covenant is subject to ratification. Instruments of ratification shall be deposited with the Secretary-General of the United Nations.

3. The present Covenant shall be open to accession by any state referred to in paragraph 1 of this article.

4. Accession shall be effected by the deposit of an instrument of accession with the Secretary-General of the United Nations.

5. The Secretary-General of the United Nations shall inform all states which have signed the present Covenant or acceded to it of the deposit of each instrument of ratification or accession.

Article 27

1. The present Covenant shall enter into force three months after the date of the deposit with the Secretary-General of the United Nations of the thirty-fifth instrument of ratification or instrument of accession.

2. For each state ratifying the present Covenant or acceding to it after the deposit of the thirty-fifth instrument of ratification or instrument of accession, the present Covenant shall enter into force three months after the date of the deposit of its own instrument of ratification or instrument of accession.

Article 28

The provisions of the present Covenant shall extend to all parts of federal states without any limitations or exceptions.

Article 29

1. Any state party to the present Covenant may propose an amendment and file it with the Secretary-General of the United Nations. The Secretary-General shall thereupon communicate any proposed amendments to the states parties to the present Covenant with a request that they notify him whether they favour a conference of states parties for the purpose of considering and voting upon the proposals. In the event that at least one third of the states parties favours such a conference, the Secretary-General shall convene the conference under the auspices of the United Nations. Any amendment adopted by a majority of the states parties present and voting at the conference shall be submitted to the General Assembly of the United Nations for approval.

2. Amendments shall come into force when they have been approved by the General Assembly of the United Nations and accepted by a two-thirds majority of the states parties to the present Covenant in accordance with their respective constitutional processes.

3. When amendments come into force they shall be binding on those states parties

which have accepted them, other states parties still being bound by the provisions of the present Covenant and any earlier amendment which they have accepted.

Article 30

Irrespective of the notifications made under Article 26, paragraph 5, the Secretary-General of the United Nations shall inform all states referred to in paragraph 1 of the same article of the following particulars:

(a) Signatures, ratifications and accessions under Article 26;

(b) The date of the entry into force of the present Covenant under Article 27 and the date of the entry into force of any amendments under Article 29.

Article 31

1. The present Covenant, of which the Chinese, English, French, Russian and Spanish texts are equally authentic, shall be deposited in the archives of the United Nations.

2. The Secretary-General of the United Nations shall transmit certified copies of the present Covenant to all states referred to in Article 26.

INTERNATIONAL COVENANT ON CIVIL AND POLITICAL RIGHTS

[Adopted and opened for signature, ratification, and accession by United Nations General Assembly resolution 2200A(XXI) on 16 December 1966.

Entered into force on 23 March 1976 in accordance with Article 49.]

PREAMBLE

The states parties to the present Covenant

Considering that, in accordance with the principles proclaimed in the Charter of the United Nations, recognition of the inherent dignity and of the equal and inalienable rights of all members of the human family is the foundation of freedom, justice and peace in the world.

Recognizing that these rights derive from the inherent dignity of the human person.

Recognizing that, in accordance with the Universal Declaration of Human Rights, the ideal of free human beings enjoying civil and political freedom and freedom from fear and want can only be achieved if conditions are created whereby everyone may enjoy his civil and political rights, as well as his economic, social and cultural rights.

Considering the obligation of states under the Charter of the United Nations to promote universal respect for, and observance of, human rights and freedoms.

Realizing that the individual, having duties to other individuals and to the community to which he belongs, is under a responsibility to strive for the promotion and observance of the rights recognized in the present Covenant,

Agree upon the following articles:

PART I

Article 1

1. All peoples have the right of self-determination. By virtue of that right they freely determine their political status and freely pursue their economic, social and cultural development.

2. All peoples may, for their own ends, freely dispose of their natural wealth and resources without prejudice to any obligations arising out of international economic co-operation, based upon the principle of mutual benefit, and international law. In no case may a people be deprived of its own means of subsistence.

3. The states parties to the present Covenant, including those having responsibility for the administration of Non-Self-Governing and Trust Territories, shall promote the realization of the right of self-determination, and shall respect that right, in conformity with the provisions of the Charter of the United Nations.

PART II

Article 2

1. Each state party to the present Covenant undertakes to respect and to ensure to all individuals within its territory and subject to its jurisdiction the rights recognized in the present Covenant, without distinction of any kind, such as race, colour, sex, language, religion, political or other opinion, national or social origin, property, birth or other status.

2. Where not already provided for by existing legislative or other measures, each state party to the present Covenant undertakes to take the necessary steps, in accordance with its constitutional processes and with the provisions of the present Covenant, to adopt such legislative or other measures as may be necessary to give effect to the rights recognized in the present Covenant.

3. Each state party to the present Covenant undertakes:

(a) To ensure that any person whose rights or freedoms as herein recognized are violated shall have an effective remedy, notwithstanding that the violation has been committed by persons acting in an official capacity;

(b) To ensure that any person claiming such a remedy shall have his right thereto determined by competent judicial, administrative or legislative authorities, or by any other competent authority provided for by the legal system of the state, and to develop the possibilities of judicial remedy;

(c) To ensure that the competent authorities shall enforce such remedies when granted.

Article 3

The states parties to the present Covenant undertake to ensure the equal right of men and women to the enjoyment of all civil and political rights set forth in the present Covenant.

Article 4

1. In time of public emergency which threatens the life of the nation and the existence of which is officially proclaimed, the states parties to the present Covenant may take measures derogating from their obligations under the present Covenant to the extent strictly required by the exigencies of the situation, provided that such measures are not inconsistent with their other obligations under international law and do not involve discrimination solely on the ground of race, colour, sex, language, religion or social origin.

2. No derogation from Articles 6, 7, 8 (paragraphs 1 and 2), 11, 15, 16 and 18 may be made under this provision.

3. Any state party to the present Covenant availing itself of the right of derogation shall immediately inform the other states parties to the present Covenant, through the intermediary of the Secretary-General of the United Nations, of the provisions from which it has derogated and of the reasons by which it was actuated. A further communication shall be made, through the same intermediary, on the date on which it terminates such derogation.

Article 5

1. Nothing in the present Covenant may be interpreted as implying for any state, group or person any right to engage in any activity or perform any act aimed at the destruction

of any of the rights and freedoms recognized herein or at their limitation to a greater extent than is provided for in the present Covenant.

2. There shall be no restriction upon or derogation from any of the fundamental human rights recognized or existing in any state party to the present Covenant pursuant to law, conventions, regulations or custom on the pretext that the present Covenant does not recognize such rights or that it recognizes them to a lesser extent.

PART III

Article 6

1. Every human being has the inherent right to life. This right shall be protected by law. No one shall be arbitrarily deprived of his life.

2. In countries which have not abolished the death penalty, sentence of death may be imposed only for the most serious crimes in accordance with the law in force at the time of the commission of the crime and not contrary to the provisions of the present Covenant and to the Convention on the Prevention and Punishment of the Crime of Genocide. This penalty can only be carried out pursuant to a final judgment rendered by a competent court.

3. When deprivation of life constitutes the crime of genocide, it is understood that nothing in this article shall authorize any state party to the present Covenant to derogate in any way from any obligation assumed under the provisions of the Convention on the Prevention and Punishment of the Crime of Genocide.

4. Anyone sentenced to death shall have the right to seek pardon or commutation of the sentence. Amnesty, pardon or commutation of the sentence of death may be granted in all cases.

5. Sentence of death shall not be imposed for crimes committed by persons below eighteen years of age and shall not be carried out on pregnant women.

6. Nothing in this article shall be invoked to delay or to prevent the abolition of capital punishment by any state party to the present Covenant.

Article 7

No one shall be subjected to torture or to cruel, inhuman or degrading treatment or punishment. In particular, no one shall be subjected without his free consent to medical or scientific experimentation.

Article 8

1. No one shall be held in slavery; slavery and the slave-trade in all their forms shall be prohibited.

2. No one shall be held in servitude.

3. *(a)* No one shall be required to perform forced or compulsory labour;

(b) Paragraph 3 *(a)* shall not be held to preclude, in countries where imprisonment with hard labour may be imposed as a punishment for a crime, the performance of hard labour in pursuance of a sentence to such punishment by a competent court;

(c) For the purpose of this paragraph the term 'forced or compulsory labour' shall not include:

(i)   Any work or service, not referred to in subparagraph *(b)*, normally required of a person who is under detention in consequence of a lawful order of a court, or of a person during conditional release from such detention;

(ii) Any service of a military character and, in countries where conscientious objection is recognized, any national service required by law of conscientious objectors;

(iii) Any service exacted in cases of emergency or calamity threatening the life or well-being of the community;

(iv) Any work or service which forms part of normal civil obligations.

Article 9

1. Everyone has the right to liberty and security of person. No one shall be subjected to arbitrary arrest or detention. No one shall be deprived of his liberty except on such grounds and in accordance with such procedure as are established by law.

2. Anyone who is arrested shall be informed, at the time of arrest, of the reasons for his arrest and shall be promptly informed of any charges against him.

3. Anyone arrested or detained on a criminal charge shall be brought promptly before a judge or other officer authorized by law to exercise judicial power and shall be entitled to trial within a reasonable time or to release. It shall not be the general rule that persons awaiting trial shall be detained in custody, but release may be subject to guarantees to appear for trial, at any other stage of the judicial proceedings, and, should occasion arise, for execution of the judgment.

4. Anyone who is deprived of his liberty by arrest or detention shall be entitled to take proceedings before a court, in order that that court may decide without delay on the lawfulness of his detention and order his release if the detention is not lawful.

5. Anyone who has been victim of unlawful arrest or detention shall have an enforceable right to compensation.

Article 10

1. All persons deprived of their liberty shall be treated with humanity and with respect for the inherent dignity of the human person.

2. *(a)* Accused persons shall, save in exceptional circumstances, be segregated from convicted persons and shall be subject to separate treatment appropriate to their status as unconvicted persons;

(b) Accused juvenile persons shall be separated from adults and brought as speedily as possible for adjudication.

3. The penitentiary system shall comprise treatment of prisoners the essential aim of which shall be their reformation and social rehabilitation. Juvenile offenders shall be segregated from adults and be accorded treatment appropriate to their age and legal status.

Article 11

No one shall be imprisoned merely on the ground of inability to fulfil a contractual obligation.

Article 12

1. Everyone lawfully within the territory of a state shall, within that territory, have the right to liberty of movement and freedom to choose his residence.

2. Everyone shall be free to leave any country, including his own.

3. The above-mentioned rights shall not be subject to any restrictions except those which are provided by law, are necessary to protect national security, public order (ordre public), public health or morals or the rights and freedoms of others, and are consistent with the other rights recognized in the present Covenant.

4. No one shall be arbitrarily deprived of the right to enter his own country.

Article 13

An alien lawfully in the territory of a state party to the present Covenant may be expelled therefrom only in pursuance of a decision reached in accordance with law and shall, except where compelling reasons of national security otherwise require, be allowed to submit the reasons against his expulsion and to have his case reviewed by, and be represented for the purpose before, the competent authority or a person or persons especially designated by the competent authority.

Article 14

1. All persons shall be equal before the courts and tribunals. In the determination of any criminal charge against him, or of his rights and obligations in a suit at law, everyone shall be entitled to a fair and public hearing by a competent, independent and impartial tribunal established by law. The Press and the public may be excluded from all or part of a trial for reasons of morals, public order (ordre public) or national security in a democratic society, or when the interest of the private lives of the parties so requires, or to the extent strictly necessary in the opinion of the court in special circumstances where publicity would prejudice the interests of justice; but any judgment rendered in a criminal case or in a suit at law shall be made public except where the interest of juvenile persons otherwise requires or the proceedings concern matrimonial disputes or the guardianship of children.

2. Everyone charged with a criminal offence shall have the right to be presumed innocent until proved guilty according to law.

3. In the determination of any criminal charge against him, everyone shall be entitled to the following minimum guarantees, in full equality:
(a) To be informed promptly and in detail in a language which he understands of the nature and cause of the charge against him;
(b) To have adequate time and facilities for the preparation of his defence and to communicate with counsel of his own choosing;
(c) To be tried without undue delay;
(d) To be tried in his presence, and to defend himself in person or through legal assistance of his own choosing; to be informed, if he does not have legal assistance, of this right; and to have legal assistance assigned to him, in any case where the interests of justice so require, and without payment by him in any such case if he does not have sufficient means to pay for it;
(e) To examine, or have examined, the witnesses against him and to obtain the attendance and examination of witnesses on his behalf under the same conditions as witnesses against him;

(f) To have the free assistance of an interpreter if he cannot understand or speak the language used in court;

(g) Not to be compelled to testify against himself or to confess guilt.

4. In the case of juvenile persons, the procedure shall be such as will take account of their age and the desirability of promoting their rehabilitation.

5. Everyone convicted of a crime shall have the right to his conviction and sentence being reviewed by a higher tribunal according to law.

6. When a person has by a final decision been convicted of a criminal offence and when subsequently his conviction has been reversed or he has been pardoned on the ground that a new or newly discovered fact shows conclusively that there has been a miscarriage of justice, the person who has suffered punishment as a result of such conviction shall be compensated according to law, unless it is proved that the non-disclosure of the unknown fact in time is wholly or partly attributable to him.

7. No one shall be liable to be tried or punished again for an offence for which he has already been finally convicted or acquitted in accordance with the law and penal procedure of each country.

Article 15

1. No one shall be held guilty of any criminal offence on account of any act or omission which did not constitute a criminal offence, under national or international law, at the time when it was committed. Nor shall a heavier penalty be imposed than the one that was applicable at the time when the criminal offence was committed. If, subsequent to the commission of the offence, provision is made by law for the imposition of the lighter penalty, the offender shall benefit thereby.

2. Nothing in this article shall prejudice the trial and punishment of any person for any act or omission which, at the time when it was committed, was criminal according to the general principles of law recognized by the community of nations.

Article 16

Everyone shall have the right to recognition everywhere as a person before the law.

Article 17

1. No one shall be subjected to arbitrary or unlawful interference with his privacy, family, home or correspondence, nor to unlawful attacks on his honour and reputation.

2. Everyone has the right to the protection of the law against such interference or attacks.

Article 18

1. Everyone shall have the right to freedom of thought, conscience and religion. This right shall include freedom to have or to adopt a religion or belief of his choice, and freedom, either individually or in community with others and in public or private, to manifest his religion or belief in worship, observance, practice and teaching.

2. No one shall be subject to coercion which would impair his freedom to have or to adopt a religion or belief of his choice.

3. Freedom to manifest one's religion or beliefs may be subject only to such limitations

as are prescribed by law and are necessary to protect public safety, order, health, or morals or the fundamental rights and freedoms of others.

4. The states parties to the present Covenant undertake to have respect for the liberty of parents and, when applicable, legal guardians to ensure the religious and moral education of their children in conformity with their own convictions.

Article 19

1. Everyone shall have the right to hold opinions without interference.

2. Everyone shall have the right to freedom of expression; this right shall include freedom to seek, receive and impart information and ideas of all kinds, regardless of frontiers, either orally, in writing or in print, in the form of art, or through any other media of his choice.

3. The exercise of the rights provided for in paragraph 2 of this article carries with it special duties and responsibilities. It may therefore be subject to certain restrictions, but these shall only be such as are provided by law and are necessary:
(a) For respect of the rights or reputations of others;
(b) For the protection of national security or of public order (ordre public), or of public health or morals.

Article 20

1. Any propaganda for war shall be prohibited by law.

2. Any advocacy of national, racial or religious hatred that constitutes incitement to discrimination, hostility or violence shall be prohibited by law.

Article 21

The right of peaceful assembly shall be recognized. No restrictions may be placed on the exercise of this right other than those imposed in conformity with the law and which are necessary in a democratic society in the interests of national security or public safety, public order (ordre public), the protection of public health or morals or the protection of the rights and freedoms of others.

Article 22

1. Everyone shall have the right to freedom of association with others, including the right to form and join trade unions for the protection of his interests.

2. No restrictions may be placed on the exercise of this right other than those which are prescribed by law and which are necessary in a democratic society in the interests of national security or public safety, public order (ordre public), the protection of public health or morals or the protection of the rights and freedoms of others. This article shall not prevent the imposition of lawful restrictions on members of the armed forces and of the police in their exercise of this right.

3. Nothing in this article shall authorize states parties to the International Labour Organization Convention of 1948 concerning Freedom of Association and Protection of the Right to Organize to take legislative measures which would prejudice, or to apply the law in such a manner as to prejudice the guarantees provided for in that Convention.

Article 23

1. The family is the natural and fundamental group unit of society and is entitled to protection by society and the state.

2. The right of men and women of marriageable age to marry and to found a family shall be recognized.

3. No marriage shall be entered into without the free and full consent of the intending spouses.

4. States parties to the present Covenant shall take appropriate steps to ensure equality of rights and responsibilities of spouses as to marriage, during marriage and at its dissolution. In the case of dissolution, provision shall be made for the necessary protection of any children.

Article 24

1. Every child shall have, without any discrimination as to race, colour, sex, language, religion, national or social origin, property or birth, the right to such measures of protection as are required by his status as a minor, on the part of his family, society and the state.

2. Every child shall be registered immediately after birth and shall have a name.

3. Every child has the right to acquire a nationality.

Article 25

Every citizen shall have the right and the opportunity, without any of the distinctions mentioned in Article 2 and without unreasonable restrictions:
(a) To take part in the conduct of public affairs, directly or through freely chosen representatives;
(b) To vote and to be elected at genuine periodic elections which shall be by universal and equal suffrage and shall be held by secret ballot, guaranteeing the free expression of the will of the electors;
(c) To have access, on general terms of equality, to public service in his country.

Article 26

All persons are equal before the law and are entitled without any discrimination to the equal protection of the law. In this respect, the law shall prohibit any discrimination and guarantee to all persons equal and effective protection against discrimination on any ground such as race, colour, sex, language, religion, political or other opinion, national or social origin, property, birth or other status.

Article 27

In those states in which ethnic, religious or linguistic minorities exist, persons belonging to such minorities shall not be denied the right, in community with the other members of their group, to enjoy their own culture, to profess and practise their own religion, or to use their own language.

PART IV

Article 28

1. There shall be established a Human Rights Committee (hereafter referred to in the present Covenant as the Committee). It shall consist of eighteen members and shall carry out the functions hereinafter provided.

2. The Committee shall be composed of nationals of the states parties to the present Covenant who shall be persons of high moral character and recognized competence in the field of human rights, consideration being given to the usefulness of the participation of some persons having legal experience.

3. The members of the Committee shall be elected and shall serve in their personal capacity.

Article 29

1. The members of the Committee shall be elected by secret ballot from a list of persons possessing the qualifications prescribed in Article 28 and nominated for the purpose by the states parties to the present Covenant.

2. Each state party to the present Covenant may nominate not more than two persons. These persons shall be nationals of the nominating state.

3. A person shall be eligible for renomination.

Article 30

1. The initial election shall be held no later than six months after the date of the entry into force of the present Covenant.

2. At least four months before the date of each election to the Committee, other than an election to fill a vacancy declared in accordance with Article 34, the Secretary-General of the United Nations shall address a written invitation to the states parties to the present Covenant to submit their nominations for membership of the Committee within three months.

3. The Secretary-General of the United Nations shall prepare a list in alphabetical order of all the persons thus nominated, with an indication of the states parties which have nominated them, and shall submit it to the states parties to the present Covenant no later than one month before the date of each election.

4. Elections of the members of the Committee shall be held at a meeting of the states parties to the present Covenant convened by the Secretary-General of the United Nations at the Headquarters of the United Nations. At that meeting, for which two thirds of the states parties to the present Covenant shall constitute a quorum, the persons elected to the Committee shall be those nominees who obtain the largest number of votes and an absolute majority of the votes of the representatives of states parties present and voting.

Article 31

1. The Committee may not include more than one national of the same state.

2. In the election of the Committee, consideration shall be given to equitable geographical distribution of membership and to the representation of the different forms of civilization and of the principal legal systems.

Article 32

1. The members of the Committee shall be elected for a term of four years. They shall be eligible for re-election if renominated. However, the terms of nine of the members elected at the first election shall expire at the end of two years; immediately after the first election, the names of these nine members shall be chosen by lot by the Chairman of the meeting referred to in Article 30, paragraph 4.

2. Elections at the expiry of office shall be held in accordance with the preceding articles of this part of the present Covenant.

Article 33

1. If, in the unanimous opinion of the other members, a member of the Committee has ceased to carry out his functions for any cause other than absence of a temporary character, the Chairman of the Committee shall notify the Secretary-General of the United Nations, who shall then declare the seat of that member to be vacant.

2. In the event of the death or the resignation of a member of the Committee, the Chairman shall immediately notify the Secretary-General of the United Nations, who shall declare the seat vacant from the date of death or the date on which the resignation takes effect.

Article 34

1. When a vacancy is declared in accordance with Article 33 and if the term of office of the member to be replaced does not expire within six months of the declaration of the vacancy, the Secretary-General of the United Nations shall notify each of the states parties to the present Covenant, which may within two months submit nominations in accordance with Article 29 for the purpose of filling the vacancy.

2. The Secretary-General of the United Nations shall prepare a list in alphabetical order of the persons thus nominated and shall submit it to the states parties to the present Covenant. The election to fill the vacancy shall then take place in accordance with the relevant provisions of this part of the present Covenant.

3. A member of the Committee elected to fill a vacancy declared in accordance with Article 33 shall hold office for the remainder of the term of the member who vacated the seat on the Committee under the provisions of that article.

Article 35

The members of the Committee shall, with the approval of the General Assembly of the United Nations, receive emoluments from United Nations resources on such terms and conditions as the General Assembly may decide, having regard to the importance of the Committee's responsibilities.

Article 36

The Secretary-General of the United Nations shall provide the necessary staff and facilities for the effective performance of the functions of the Committee under the present Covenant.

Article 37

1. The Secretary-General of the United Nations shall convene the initial meeting of the Committee at the Headquarters of the United Nations.

2. After its initial meeting, the Committee shall meet at such times as shall be provided in its rules of procedure.

3. The Committee shall normally meet at the Headquarters of the United Nations or at the United Nations Office at Geneva.

Article 38

Every member of the Committee shall, before taking up his duties, make a solemn declaration in open committee that he will perform his functions impartially and conscientiously.

Article 39

1. The Committee shall elect its officers for a term of two years. They may be re-elected.

2. The Committee shall establish its own rules of procedure, but these rules shall provide, inter alia, that:
(a) Twelve members shall constitute a quorum;
(b) Decisions of the Committee shall be made by a majority vote of the members present.

Article 40

1. The states parties to the present Covenant undertake to submit reports on the measures they have adopted which give effect to the rights recognized herein and on the progress made in the enjoyment of those rights:
(a) Within one year of the entry into force of the present Covenant for the states parties concerned;
(b) Thereafter whenever the Committee so requests.

2. All reports shall be submitted to the Secretary-General of the United Nations, who shall transmit them to the Committee for consideration. Reports shall indicate the factors and difficulties, if any, affecting the implementation of the present Covenant.

3. The Secretary-General of the United Nations may, after consultation with the Committee, transmit to the specialized agencies concerned copies of such parts of the reports as may fall within their field of competence.

4. The Committee shall study the reports submitted by the states parties to the present Covenant. It shall transmit its reports, and such general comments as it may consider appropriate, to the states parties. The Committee may also transmit to the Economic and Social Council these comments along with the copies of the reports it has received from states parties to the present Covenant.

5. The states parties to the present Covenant may submit to the Committee observations on any comments that may be made in accordance with paragraph 4 of this article.

Article 41

1. A state party to the present Covenant may at any time declare under this article that

it recognizes the competence of the Committee to receive and consider communications to the effect that a state party claims that another state party is not fulfilling its obligations under the present Covenant. Communications under this article may be received and considered only if submitted by a state party which has made a declaration recognizing in regard to itself the competence of the Committee. No communication shall be received by the Committee if it concerns a state party which has not made such a declaration. Communications received under this article shall be dealt with in accordance with the following procedure:

(a) If a state party to the present Covenant considers that another state party is not giving effect to the provisions of the present Covenant, it may, by written communication, bring the matter to the attention of that state party. Within three months after the receipt of the communication the receiving state shall afford the state which sent the communication an explanation, or any other statement in writing clarifying the matter which should include, to the extent possible and pertinent, reference to domestic procedures and remedies taken, pending, or available in the matter;

(b) If the matter is not adjusted to the satisfaction of both states parties concerned within six months after the receipt by the receiving state of the initial communication, either state shall have the right to refer the matter to the Committee, by notice given to the Committee and to the other state;

(c) The Committee shall deal with a matter referred to it only after it has ascertained that all available domestic remedies have been invoked and exhausted in the matter, in conformity with the generally recognized principles of international law. This shall not be the rule where the application of the remedies is unreasonably prolonged;

(d) The Committee shall hold closed meetings when examining communications under this article;

(e) Subject to the provisions of subparagraph (c), the Committee shall make available its good offices to the states parties concerned with a view to a friendly solution of the matter on the basis of respect for human rights and fundamental freedoms as recognized in the present Covenant;

(f) In any matter referred to it, the Committee may call upon the states parties concerned, referred to in subparagraph (b), to supply any relevant information;

(g) The states parties concerned, referred to in subparagraph (b), shall have the right to be represented when the matter is being considered in the Committee and to make submissions orally and/or in writing;

(h) The Committee shall, within twelve months after the date of receipt of notice under subparagraph (b), submit a report:

    (i) If a solution within the terms of subparagraph (e) is reached, the Committee shall confine its report to a brief statement of the facts and of the solution reached;

    (ii) If a solution within the terms of subparagraph (e) is not reached, the Committee shall confine its report to a brief statement of the facts; the written submissions and record of the oral submissions made by the states parties concerned shall be attached to the report. In every matter, the report shall be communicated to the states parties concerned.

2. The provisions of this article shall come into force when ten states parties to the present Covenant have made declarations under paragraph 1 of this article. Such declarations shall be deposited by the states parties with the Secretary-General of the

United Nations, who shall transmit copies thereof to the other states parties. A declaration may be withdrawn at any time by notification to the Secretary-General. Such a withdrawal shall not prejudice the consideration of any matter which is the subject of a communication already transmitted under this article; no further communication by any state party shall be received after the notification of withdrawal of the declaration has been received by the Secretary-General, unless the state party concerned has made a new declaration.

Article 42

1. *(a)* If a matter referred to the Committee in accordance with Article 41 is not resolved to the satisfaction of the states parties concerned, the Committee may, with the prior consent of the states parties concerned, appoint an ad hoc Conciliation Commission (hereinafter referred to as the Commission). The good offices of the Commission shall be made available to the states parties concerned with a view to an amicable solution of the matter on the basis of respect for the present Covenant;

(b) The Commission shall consist of five persons acceptable to the states parties concerned. If the states parties concerned fail to reach agreement within three months on all or part of the composition of the Commission, the members of the Commission concerning whom no agreement has been reached shall be elected by secret ballot by a two-thirds majority vote of the Committee from among its members.

2. The members of the Commission shall serve in their personal capacity. They shall not be nationals of the states parties concerned, or of a state not party to the present Covenant, or of a state party which has not made a declaration under Article 41.

3. The Commission shall elect its own Chairman and adopt its own rules of procedure.

4. The meetings of the Commission shall normally be held at the Headquarters of the United Nations or at the United Nations Office at Geneva. However, they may be held at such other convenient places as the Commission may determine in consultation with the Secretary-General of the United Nations and the states parties concerned.

5. The secretariat provided in accordance with Article 36 shall also service the commissions appointed under this article.

6. The information received and collated by the Committee shall be made available to the Commission and the Commission may call upon the states parties concerned to supply any other relevant information.

7. When the Commission has fully considered the matter, but in any event not later than twelve months after having been seized of the matter, it shall submit to the Chairman of the Committee a report for communication to the states parties concerned:

(a) If the Commission is unable to complete its consideration of the matter within twelve months, it shall confine its report to a brief statement of the status of its consideration of the matter;

(b) If an amicable solution to the matter on the basis of respect for human rights as recognized in the present Covenant is reached, the Commission shall confine its report to a brief statement of the facts and of the solution reached;

(c) If a solution within the terms of subparagraph *(b)* is not reached, the Commission's report shall embody its findings on all questions of fact relevant to the issues between the states parties concerned, and its views on the possibilities of an amicable solution of the matter. This report shall also contain the written

submissions and a record of the oral submissions made by the states parties concerned;

(d) If the Commission's report is submitted under subparagraph (c), the states parties concerned shall, within three months of the receipt of the report, notify the Chairman of the Committee whether or not they accept the contents of the report of the Commission.

8. The provisions of this article are without prejudice to the responsibilities of the Committee under Article 41.

9. The states parties concerned shall share equally all the expenses of the members of the Commission in accordance with estimates to be provided by the Secretary-General of the United Nations.

10. The Secretary-General of the United Nations shall be empowered to pay the expenses of the members of the Commission, if necessary, before reimbursement by the states parties concerned, in accordance with paragraph 9 of this article.

Article 43

The members of the Committee, and of the ad hoc conciliation commissions which may be appointed under Article 42, shall be entitled to the facilities, privileges and immunities of experts on mission for the United Nations as laid down in the relevant sections of the Convention on the Privileges and Immunities of the United Nations.

Article 44

The provisions for the implementation of the present Covenant shall apply without prejudice to the procedures prescribed in the field of human rights by or under the constituent instruments and the conventions of the United Nations and of the specialized agencies and shall not prevent the states parties to the present Covenant from having recourse to other procedures for settling a dispute in accordance with general or special international agreements in force between them.

Article 45

The Committee shall submit to the General Assembly of the United Nations, through the Economic and Social Council, an annual report on its activities.

PART V

Article 46

Nothing in the present Covenant shall be interpreted as impairing the provisions of the Charter of the United Nations and of the constitutions of the specialized agencies which define the respective responsibilities of the various organs of the United Nations and of the specialized agencies in regard to the matters dealt with in the present Covenant.

Article 47

Nothing in the present Covenant shall be interpreted as impairing the inherent right of all peoples to enjoy and utilize fully and freely their natural wealth and resources.

PART VI

Article 48

1. The present Covenant is open for signature by any state member of the United Nations or member of any of its specialized agencies, by any state party to the Statute of the International Court of Justice, and by any other state which has been invited by the General Assembly of the United Nations to become a Party to the present Covenant.

2. The present Covenant is subject to ratification. Instruments of ratification shall be deposited with the Secretary-General of the United Nations.

3. The present Covenant shall be open to accession by any state referred to in paragraph 1 of this article.

4. Accession shall be effected by the deposit of an instrument of accession with the Secretary-General of the United Nations.

5. The Secretary-General of the United Nations shall inform all states which have signed this Covenant or acceded to it of the deposit of each instrument of ratification or accession.

Article 49

1. The present Covenant shall enter into force three months after the date of the deposit with the Secretary-General of the United Nations of the thirty-fifth instrument of ratification or instrument of accession.

2. For each state ratifying the present Covenant or acceding to it after the deposit of the thirty-fifth instrument of ratification or instrument of accession, the present Covenant shall enter into force three months after the date of the deposit of its own instrument of ratification or instrument of accession.

Article 50

The provisions of the present Covenant shall extend to all parts of federal states without any limitations or exceptions.

Article 51

1. Any state party to the present Covenant may propose an amendment and file it with the Secretary-General of the United Nations. The Secretary-General of the United Nations shall thereupon communicate any proposed amendments to the states parties to the present Covenant with a request that they notify him whether they favour a conference of states parties for the purpose of considering and voting upon the proposals. In the event that at least one third of the states parties favours such a conference, the Secretary-General shall convene the conference under the auspices of the United Nations. Any amendment adopted by a majority of the states parties present and voting at the conference shall be submitted to the General Assembly of the United Nations for approval.

2. Amendments shall come into force when they have been approved by the General Assembly of the United Nations and accepted by a two-thirds majority of the states parties to the present Covenant in accordance with their respective constitutional processes.

3. When amendments come into force, they shall be binding on those states parties

which have accepted them, other states parties still being bound by the provisions of the present Covenant and any earlier amendment which they have accepted.

Article 52

Irrespective of the notifications made under Article 48, paragraph 5, the Secretary-General of the United Nations shall inform all states referred to in paragraph 1 of the same article of the following particulars:

(a) Signatures, ratifications and accessions under Article 48;

(b) The date of the entry into force of the present Covenant under Article 49 and the date of the entry into force of any amendments under Article 51.

Article 53

1. The present Covenant, of which the Chinese, English, French, Russian and Spanish texts are equally authentic, shall be deposited in the archives of the United Nations.

2. The Secretary-General of the United Nations shall transmit certified copies of the present Covenant to all states referred to in Article 48.

OPTIONAL PROTOCOL TO THE INTERNATIONAL COVENANT ON CIVIL AND POLITICAL RIGHTS

[Adopted and opened for signature, ratification, and accession by United Nations General Assembly resolution 2200A(XXI) on 16 December 1966.

Entered into force on 23 March 1976 in accordance with Article 9.]

The states parties to the present Protocol

Considering that in order further to achieve the purposes of the Covenant on Civil and Political Rights (hereinafter referred to as the Covenant) and the implementation of its provisions it would be appropriate to enable the Human Rights Committee set up in Part IV of the Covenant (hereinafter referred to as the Committee) to receive and consider, as provided in the present Protocol, communications from individuals claiming to be victims of violations of any of the rights set forth in the Covenant.

Have agreed as follows:

Article 1

A state party to the Covenant that becomes a Party to the present Protocol recognizes the competence of the Committee to receive and consider communications from individuals subject to its jurisdiction who claim to be victims of a violation by that state party of any of the rights set forth in the Covenant. No communication shall be received by the Committee if it concerns a state party to the Covenant which is not a Party to the present Protocol.

Article 2

Subject to the provisions of Article 1, individuals who claim that any of their rights enumerated in the Covenant have been violated and who have exhausted all available domestic remedies may submit a written communication to the Committee for consideration.

Article 3

The Committee shall consider inadmissible any communication under the present Protocol which is anonymous, or which it considers to be an abuse of the right of submission of such communications or to be incompatible with the provisions of the Covenant.

Article 4

1. Subject to the provisions of Article 3, the Committee shall bring any communications submitted to it under the present Protocol to the attention of the state party to the present Protocol alleged to be violating any provision of the Covenant.

2. Within six months, the receiving state shall submit to the Committee written

explanations or statements clarifying the matter and the remedy, if any, that may have been taken by that state.

Article 5

1. The Committee shall consider communications received under the present Protocol in the light of all written information made available to it by the individual and by the state party concerned.

2. The Committee shall not consider any communication from an individual unless it has ascertained that:

(a) The same matter is not being examined under another procedure of international investigation or settlement;

(b) The individual has exhausted all available domestic remedies. This shall not be the rule where the application of the remedies is unreasonably prolonged.

3. The Committee shall hold closed meetings when examining communications under the present Protocol.

4. The Committee shall forward its views to the state party concerned and to the individual.

Article 6

The Committee shall include in its annual report under Article 45 of the Covenant a summary of its activities under the present Protocol.

Article 7

Pending the achievement of the objectives of Resolution 1514(XV) adopted by the General Assembly of the United Nations on 14 December 1960 concerning the Declaration on the Granting of Independence to Colonial Countries and Peoples, the provisions of the present Protocol shall in no way limit the right of petition granted to these peoples by the Charter of the United Nations and other international conventions and instruments under the United Nations and its specialized agencies.

Article 8

1. The present Protocol is open for signature by any state which has signed the Covenant.

2. The present Protocol is subject to ratification by any state which has ratified or acceded to the Covenant. Instruments of ratification shall be deposited with the Secretary-General of the United Nations.

3. The present Protocol shall be open to accession by any state which has ratified or acceded to the Covenant.

4. Accession shall be effected by the deposit of an instrument of accession with the Secretary-General of the United Nations.

5. The Secretary-General of the United Nations shall inform all states which have signed the present Protocol or acceded to it of the deposit of each instrument of ratification or accession.

Article 9

1. Subject to the entry into force of the Covenant, the present Protocol shall enter into

force three months after the date of the deposit with the Secretary-General of the United Nations of the tenth instrument of ratification or instrument of accession.

2. For each state ratifying the present Protocol or acceding to it after the deposit of the tenth instrument of ratification or instrument of accession, the present Protocol shall enter into force three months after the date of the deposit of its own instrument of ratification or instrument of accession.

Article 10

The provisions of the present Protocol shall extend to all parts of federal states without any limitations or exceptions.

Article 11

1. Any state party to the present Protocol may propose an amendment and file it with the Secretary-General of the United Nations. The Secretary-General shall thereupon communicate any proposed amendments to the states parties to the present Protocol with a request that they notify him whether they favour a conference of states parties for the purpose of considering and voting upon the proposal. In the event that at least one third of the states parties favours such a conference, the Secretary-General shall convene the conference under the auspices of the United Nations. Any amendment adopted by a majority of the states parties present and voting at the conference shall be submitted to the General Assembly of the United Nations for approval.

2. Amendments shall come into force when they have been approved by the General Assembly of the United Nations and accepted by a two-thirds majority of the states parties to the present Protocol in accordance with their respective constitutional processes.

3. When amendments come into force, they shall be binding on those states parties which have accepted them, other states parties still being bound by the provisions of the present Protocol and any earlier amendment which they have accepted.

Article 12

1. Any state party may denounce the present Protocol at any time by written notification addressed to the Secretary-General of the United Nations. Denunciation shall take effect three months after the date of receipt of the notification by the Secretary-General.

2. Denunciation shall be without prejudice to the continued application of the provisions of the present Protocol to any communication submitted under Article 2 before the effective date of denunciation.

Article 13

Irrespective of the notifications made under Article 8, paragraph 5, of the present Protocol, the Secretary-General of the United Nations shall inform all states referred to in Article 48, paragraph 1, of the Covenant of the following particulars:
(a) Signatures, ratifications and accessions under Article 8;
(b) The date of the entry into force of the present Protocol under Article 9 and the date of the entry into force of any amendments under Article 11;
(c) Denunciations under Article 12.

Article 14

1. The present Protocol, of which the Chinese, English, French, Russian and Spanish texts are equally authentic, shall be deposited in the archives of the United Nations.

2. The Secretary-General of the United Nations shall transmit certified copies of the present Protocol to all states referred to in article 48 of the Covenant.

APPENDIX 6

UNITED NATIONS MODEL
AUTOPSY PROTOCOL

A Introduction

Difficult or sensitive cases should ideally be the responsibility of an objective, well-equipped and well-trained prosector (the person performing the autopsy and preparing the written report) who is separate from a potentially involved political organization or entity. Unfortunately, this ideal is often unattainable. This proposed model autopsy protocol includes a comprehensive checklist of the steps in a basic forensic postmortem examination that should be followed to the extent possible given the resources available. Use of this autopsy protocol will permit early and final resolution of potentially controversial cases and will thwart the speculation and innuendo that are fuelled by unanswered, partially answered to poorly answered questions in the investigation of an apparently suspicious death.

This model autopsy protocol is intended to have several applications and may be of value to the following categories of individuals:

(a) Experienced forensic pathologists may follow this model autopsy protocol to ensure a systematic examination and to facilitate meaningful positive or negative criticism by later observers. While trained pathologists may justifiably abridge certain aspects of this postmortem examination or written descriptions of their findings in routine cases, abridged examinations or reports are never appropriate in potentially controversial cases. Rather, a systematic and comprehensive examination and report are required to prevent the omission or loss of important details;

(b) General pathologists or other physicians who have not been trained in forensic pathology but are familiar with basic postmortem examination techniques may supplement their customary autopsy procedures with this model autopsy protocol. It may also alert them to situations in which they should seek consultation, as written material cannot replace the knowledge gained through experience;

(c) Independent consultants whose expertise has been requested in observing, performing or reviewing an autopsy may cite this model autopsy protocol and its proposed minimum criteria as a basis for their actions or opinions;

(d) Governmental authorities, international political organizations, law enforcement agencies, families or friends of decedents, or representatives of potential defendants charged with responsibility for a death may use this model autopsy protocol to establish appropriate procedures for the postmortem examination prior to its performance;

(e) Historians, journalists, attorneys, judges, other physicians and representatives of the public may also use this model autopsy protocol as a benchmark for evaluating an autopsy and its findings;

(f) Governments or individuals who are attempting either to establish or upgrade their medicolegal system for investigating deaths may use this model autopsy protocol as a guideline, representing the procedures and goals to be incorporated into an ideal medicolegal system.

While performing any medicolegal death investigation, the prosector should collect information that will establish the identity of the deceased, the time and place of death, the cause of death, and the manner or mode or death (homicide, suicide, accident or natural). It is of the utmost importance that an autopsy performed following a controversial death be thorough in scope. The documentation and recording of the autopsy findings should be equally thorough so as to permit meaningful use of the autopsy results (see Annexure II below). It is important to have as few omissions or discrepancies as possible, as proponents of different interpretations of a case may take advantage of any perceived shortcomings in the investigation. An autopsy performed in a controversial death should meet certain minimum criteria if the autopsy report is to be proffered as meaningful or conclusive by the prosector, the autopsy's sponsoring agency or governmental unit, or anyone else attempting to make use of such an autopsy's findings or conclusions.

This model autopsy protocol is designed to be used in diverse situations. Resources such as autopsy rooms, X-ray equipment or adequately trained personnel are not available everywhere. Forensic pathologists must operate under widely divergent political systems. In addition, social and religious customs vary widely throughout the world; and autopsy is an expected and routine procedure in some areas, while it is abhorred in others. A prosector, therefore, may not always be able to follow all of the steps in this protocol when performing autopsies. Variation from this protocol may be inevitable or even preferable in some cases. It is suggested, however, that any major deviations, with the supporting reasons, should be noted.

It is important that the body should be made available to the prosector for a minimum of 21 hours in order to assure an adequate and unhurried examination. Unrealistic limits or conditions are occasionally placed upon the prosector with respect to the length of time permitted for the examination or the circumstances under which an examination is allowed. When conditions are imposed, the prosector should be able to refuse to perform a compromised examination and should prepare a report explaining this position. Such a refusal should not be interpreted as indicating that an examination was unnecessary or inappropriate. If the prosector decided to proceed with the examination notwithstanding difficult conditions or circumstances, he or she should include in the autopsy report and explanation of the limitations or impediments.

Certain steps in this model autopsy protocol have been emphasized by the use of boldface type. These represent the most essential elements of the protocol.

B Proposed Model Autopsy Protocol

1 Scene investigation

The prosector(s) and medical investigators should have the right of access to the scene where the body was found. The medical personnel should be notified immediately to assure that no alteration of the body has occurred. If access to the scene was denied, if the body was altered or if information was withheld, this should be stated in the prosector's report.

A system for co-ordination between the medical and non-medical investigators (eg law enforcement agencies) should be established. This should address such issues as how the prosector will be notified and who will be in charge of the scene. Obtaining certain types of evidence is often the role of the non-medical investigators, but the medical investigators who have access to the body at the scene of death should perform the following steps:

(a) Photograph the body as it is found and after it has been moved;

(b) Record the body position and condition, including body warmth or coolness, lividity and rigidity;

(c) Protect the deceased's hands, eg with paper bags;

(d) Note the ambient temperature. In cases where the time of death is an issue, rectal temperature should be recorded and any insects present should be collected for forensic entomological study. Which procedure is applicable will depend on the length of the apparent postmortem interval.

(e) Examine the scene for blood, as this may be useful in identifying suspects;

(f) Record the identities of all persons at the scene;

(g) Obtain information from scene witnesses, including those who last saw the decedent alive, and when, where and under what circumstances. Interview any emergency medical personnel who may have had contact with the body;

(h) Obtain identification of the body and other pertinent information from friends or relatives. Obtain the deceased's medical history from his or her physician(s) and hospital charts, including any previous surgery, alcohol or drug use, suicide attempts and habits;

(i) Place the body in a body pouch or its equivalent. Save this pouch after the body has been removed from it;

(j) Store the body in a secure refrigerated location so that tampering with the body and its evidence cannot occur;

(k) Make sure that projectiles, guns, knives and other weapons are available for examination by the responsible medical personnel;

(l) If the decedent was hospitalized prior to death, obtain admission or blood specimens and any X-rays, and review and summarize hospital records;

(m) Before beginning the autopsy, become familiar with the types of torture or violence that are prevalent in that country or locale (see Annexure III).

2 Autopsy

The following protocol should be followed during the autopsy:

(a) Record the date, starting and finishing times, and place of the autopsy (a complex autopsy may take as long as an entire working day).

(b) Record the name(s) of the prosector(s), the participating assistant(s), and all other persons present during the autopsy, including the medical and/or scientific degrees and professional, political or administrative affiliation(s) of each. Each person's role in the autopsy should be indicated, and one person should be designated as the principal prosector who will have the authority to direct the performance of the autopsy. Observers and other team members are subject to direction by, and should not interfere with, the principal prosector. The time(s) during the autopsy when each person is present should be included. The use of a 'sign-in' sheet is recommended;

(c) Adequate photographs are crucial for thorough documentation of autopsy findings;

    (i) Photographs should be in colour (transparency or negative/print), in focus, adequately illuminated, and taken by a professional or good quality camera. Each photograph should contain a ruled reference scale, an identifying case name or number, and a sample of standard grey. A description of the camera (including the lens 'f-number' and focal length), film and the lighting system must be included in the autopsy report. If more than one camera is utilized, the identifying information should be recorded for each. Photographs should also include information indicating which camera took each picture, if more than one camera is used. The identity of the person taking the photographs should be recorded;

(ii)   Serial photographs reflecting the course of the external examination must be included. Photograph the body prior to and following undressing, washing, cleaning and shaving;

(iii)   Supplement close-up photographs with distant and/or immediate range photographs to permit orientation and identification of the close-up photographs;

(iv)   Photographs should be comprehensive in scope and must confirm the presence of all demonstrable signs of injury or disease commented upon in the autopsy report;

(v)   Identifying facial features should be portrayed (after washing or cleaning the body), with photographs of a full frontal aspect of the face, and right and left profiles of the face with hair in normal position and with hair retracted, if necessary, to reveal the ears;

(d)   Radiograph the body before it is removed from its pouch or wrappings. X-rays should be repeated both before and after undressing the body. Fluoroscopy may also be performed. Photograph all X-ray films;

(i)   Obtain dental X-rays, even if identification has been established in other ways;

(ii)   Document any skeletal system injury by X-ray. Skeletal X-rays may also record anatomic defects or surgical procedures. Check especially for fractures of the fingers, toes and other bones in the hands or feet. Skeletal X-rays may also aid in the identification of the deceased, but detecting identifying characteristics, estimating age and height, and determining sex and race. Frontal sinus films should also be taken, as these can be particularly useful for identification purposes;

(iii)   Take X-rays in gunshot cases to aid in locating the projectile(s). Recover, photograph and save any projectile or major projectile fragment that is seen on an X-ray. Other radio-opaque objects (pacemakers, artificial joints or valves, knife fragments etc) documented with X-rays should also be removed, photographed and saved;

(iv)   Skeletal X-rays are essential in children to assist in determining age and developmental status;

(e)   Before clothing is removed, examine the body and the clothing. Photograph the clothed body. Record any jewellery present;

(f)   The clothing should be carefully removed over a clean sheet or body pouch. Let the clothing dry if it is bloody or wet. Describe the clothing that is removed and label it in a permanent fashion. Either place the clothes in the custody of a responsible person or keep them, as they may be useful as evidence or for identification;

(g)   The external examination, focusing on a search for external evidence of injury is, in most cases, the most important portion of the autopsy;

(i)   Photograph all surfaces – 100 per cent of the body area. Take good quality, well-focused, colour photographs with adequate illumination;

(ii)   Describe and document the means used to make the identification. Examine the body and record the deceased's apparent age, length, weight, sex, head hair style and length, nutritional status, muscular development and colour of skin, eyes and hair (head, facial and body);

(iii) In children, measure also the head circumference, crown-rump length and crown-heel length;

(iv) Record the degree, location and fixation of rigor and livor mortis;

(v) Note body warmth or coolness and state of preservation; note any decomposition changes, such as skin slippage. Evaluate the general condition of the body and note adipocere formation, maggots, eggs or anything else that suggests the time or place of death;

(vi) With all injuries, record the size, shape, patter, location (related to obvious anatomic landmarks), colour, course, direction, depth and structure involved. Attempt to distinguish injuries resulting from therapeutic measures from those unrelated to medical treatment. In the description of projectile wounds, note the presence or absence of soot, gunpowder or singeing. If gunshot residue is present, document it photographically and save it for analysis. Attempt to determine whether the gunshot wound is an entry or exit wound. If an entry wound is present and no exit wound is seen, the projectile must be found and saved or accounted for. Excise wound tract tissue samples for microscopic examination. Tape together the edges of knife wounds to assess the blade size and characteristics;

(vii) Photograph all injuries, taking two colour pictures of each, labelled with the autopsy identification number on a scale that is oriented parallel or perpendicular to the injury. Shave hair where necessary to clarify an injury, and take photographs both before and after shaving. Save all hair removed from the site of the injury. Take photographs before and after washing the site of an injury. Wash the body only after any blood or materials that may have come from an assailant has been collected and saved;

(viii) Examine the skin. Note and photograph any scars, areas of keloid formation, tattoos, prominent moles, areas of increased or decreased pigmentation, and anything distinctive or unique such as birthmarks. Note any bruises and incise them for delineation of their extent. Excise them for microscopic examination. The head and genital area should be checked with special care. Note any injection sites or puncture wounds and excise them to use for toxicological evaluation. Note any abrasions and excise them; microscopic sections may be useful for attempting to date the time of injury. Note any bite marks; these should be photographed to record the dental pattern, swabbed for saliva testing (before the body is washed) and excised for microscopic examination. Bite marks should also be analysed by a forensic odontologist, if possible. Note any burn marks and attempt to determine the cause (burning rubber, a cigarette, electricity, a blowtorch, acid, hot oil etc.). Excise any suspicious areas for microscopic examination, as it may be possible to distinguish microscop-ically between burns caused by electricity and those caused by heat;

(ix) Identify and label any foreign object that is recovered, including its relation to specific injuries. Do not scratch the sides or tip of any projectiles. Photograph each projectile and large projectile fragment with an identifying label, and then place each in a sealed, padded and labelled container in order to maintain the chain of custody;

(x) Collect a blood specimen of at least 50 cc from a subclavian or femoral vessel;

(xi) Examine the head and external scalp, bearing in mind that injuries may be hidden by the hair. Shave hair where necessary. Check for fleas and lice, as these may indicate unsanitary conditions prior to death. Note any alopecia as this may be caused by malnutrition, heavy metals (eg thallium), drugs or traction. Pull, do not cut, 20 representative head hairs and save them, as hair may also be useful for detecting some drugs and poisons;

(xii) Examine the teeth and note their condition. Record any that are absent, loose or damaged, and record all dental work (restorations, fillings etc), using a dental identification system to identify each tooth. Check the gums for periodontal disease. Photograph dentures, if any, and save them if the decedent's identity is unknown. Remove the mandible and maxilla if necessary for identification. Check the inside of the mouth and note any evidence of trauma, injection sites, needle marks or biting of the lips, cheeks or tongue. Note any articles or substances in the mouth. In cases of suspected sexual assault, save oral fluid or get a swab for spermatozoa and acid phosphatase evaluation. (Swabs taken at the tooth-gum junction and samples from between the teeth provide the best specimens for identifying spermatozoa.) Also take swabs from the oral cavity for seminal fluid typing. Dry the swabs quickly with cool, blown air if possible, and preserve them in clean plain paper envelopes. If rigor mortis prevents an adequate examination, the masseter muscles may be cut to permit better exposure;

(xiii) Examine the face and note if it is cyanotic or if petechiae are present:

(a) Examine the eyes and view the conjunctiva of both the globes and the eyelids. Note any petechiae in the upper or lower eyelids. Note any scleral icterus. Save contact lenses, if they are present. Collect at least 1 ml of vitreous humor from each eye;

(b) Examine the nose and ears and note any evidence of trauma, haemorrhage or other abnormalities. Examine the tympanic membranes;

(xiv) Examine the neck externally on all aspects and note any contusions, abrasions or petechiae. Describe and document injury patterns to differentiate manual, ligature and hanging strangulation. Examine the neck at the conclusion of the autopsy, when the blood has drained out of the area and the tissues are dry;

(xv) Examine all surfaces of the extremities: arms, forearms, wrists, hands, legs and feet, and note any 'defence' wounds. Dissect and describe any injuries. Note any bruises about the wrists or ankles that may suggest restraints such as handcuffs or suspension. Examine the medial and lateral surfaces of the fingers, the anterior forearms and the backs of the knees for bruises;

(xvi) Note any broken or missing fingernails. Note any gunpowder residue on the hands, document photographically and save it for analysis. Take fingerprints in all cases. If the decedent's identity is unknown and fingerprints cannot be obtained, remove the 'glove' of the skin, if present. Save the fingers if no other means of obtaining fingerprints is possible. Save fingernail clippings and any under-nail tissue (nail scrapings). Nails can be removed by dissecting the lateral margins and proximal base, and then the undersurface of the nails can be inspected. If this is done, the hands must be photographed before and after the nails are removed. Carefully examine the soles of the feet, noting any evidence of beating. Incise the soles to delineate the extent of any injuries. Examine the palms and knees, looking especially for glass shards or lacerations;

(xvii) Examine the external genitalia and note the presence of any foreign material or semen. Note the size, location and number of any abrasions or contusions.

Note any injury to the inner thighs or peri-anal area; look for any peri-anal burns;

(xviii) In cases of suspected sexual assault, examine all potentially involved orifices. A speculum should be used to examine the vaginal walls. Collect foreign hair by combing the pubic hair. Pull and save at least 20 of the deceased's own pubic hairs, including roots. Aspirate fluid from the vagina and/or rectum for acid phosphatase, blood group and spermatozoa evaluation. Take swabs from the same areas for seminal fluid typing. Dry the swabs quickly with cool, blown air if possible, and preserve them in clean plain paper envelopes.

(xix) The length of the back, the buttocks and extremities including wrists and ankles must be systematically incised to look for deep injuries. The shoulders, elbows, hips and knee joints must also be incised to look for ligamentous injury;

(h) The internal examination for internal evidence of injury should clarify and augment the external examination:

(i) Be systematic in the internal examination. Perform the examination either by body regions or by systems, including the cardiovascular, respiratory, biliary, gastrointestinal, reticuloendothelial, genitourinary, endocrine, musculoskeletal, and central nervous systems. Record the weight, size, shape, colour and consistency of each organ, and note any inflammation, anomalies, haemorrhage, ischemia, infarcts, surgical procedures or injuries. Take sections or normal and any abnormal areas of each organ for microscopic examination. Take samples of any fractured bones for radiographic and microscopic estimation of the age of the fracture;

(ii) Examine the chest. Note any abnormalities of the breasts. Record any rib fractures, noting whether cardiopulmonary resuscitation was attempted. Before opening, check for pneumothoraces. Record the thickness of subcutaneous fat. Immediately after opening the chest, evaluate the pleural cavities and the pericardial sac for the presence of blood or other fluid, and describe the quantity of any fluid present. Save any fluid present until foreign objects are accounted for. Note the presence of air embolism, characterized by frothy blood within the right atrium and right ventricle. Trace any injuries before removing the organs. If blood is not available at other sites, collect a sample directly from the heart. Examine the heart, noting degree and location of coronary artery disease or other abnormalities. Examine the lungs, noting any abnormalities;

(iii) Examine the abdomen and record the amount of subcutaneous fat. Retain 50 grams of adipose tissue for toxicological evaluation. Note the interrelationships of the organs. Trace any injuries before removing the organs. Note any fluid or blood present in the peritoneal cavity, and save it until foreign objects are accounted for. Save all urine and bile for toxicological examination;

(iv) Remove, examine and record the quantitative information on the liver, spleen, pancreas, kidney and liver for toxicological evaluation. Remove the gastrointestinal tract and examine the contents. Note any food present and its degree of digestion. Save the contents of the stomach. If a more detailed toxicological evaluation is desired, the contents of other regions of the gastrointestinal tract may be saved. Examine the rectum and anus for burns, lacerations or other injuries. Locate and retain any foreign bodies present. Examine the aorta, inferior vena cava and iliac vessels;

(v) Examine the organs in the pelvis, including ovaries, fallopian tubes, uterus, testes, prostate gland, seminal vesicles, urethra and urinary bladder. Trace any injuries before removing organs. Remove these organs carefully so as not to injure them artifactually. Note any evidence of previous or current pregnancy, miscarriage or delivery. Save any foreign objects within the cervix, uterus, vagina, urethra or rectum;

(vi) Palpate the head and examine the external and internal surfaces of the scalp, noting any trauma or haemorrhage. Note any skull fractures. Remove the calvarium carefully and note epidural and subdural haematomas. Quantify, date and save any haematomas that are present. Remove the dura to examine the internal surface of the skull for fractures. Remove the brain and note any abnormalities. Dissect and describe any injuries. Cerebral cortical atrophy, whether focal or generalised, should be specifically commented upon;

(vii) Evaluate the cerebral vessels. Save at least 150 grams of cerebral tissue for toxicological evaluation. Submerge the brain in fixative prior to examination, if this is indicated;

(viii) Examine the neck after the heart and brain have been removed and the neck vessels have been drained. Remove the neck organs, taking care not to fracture the hyoid bone. Dissect and describe any injuries. Check the mucosa of the larynx, pyriform sinuses and oesophagus, and note any petechiae, oedema or burns caused by corrosive substances. Note any article or substances within the lumina of these structures. Examine the thyroid gland. Separate and examine the parathyroid glands, if they are readily identifiable;

(ix) Dissect the neck muscles, noting any haemorrhage. Remove all organs, including the tongue. Dissect the muscles from the bones and note any fractures of the hyoid bone or thyroid or cricoid cartilages;

(x) Examine the cervical, thoracic and lumbar spine. Examine the vertebrae from their anterior aspects and note any fracture, dislocations, compressions or haemorrhages. Examine the vertebral bodies. Cerebrospinal fluid may be obtained if additional toxicological evaluation is indicated;

(xi) In cases in which spinal injury is suspected, dissect and describe the spinal cord. Examine the cervical spine anteriorly and note any haemorrhage in the paravertebral muscles. The posterior approach is best for evaluating high cervical injuries. Open the spinal canal and remove the spinal cord. Make transverse sections every 0.5 cm and note any abnormalities;

(i) After the autopsy has been completed, record which specimens have been saved. Label all specimens with the name of the deceased, the autopsy identification number, the date and time of collection, the name of the prosector and the contents. Carefully preserve all evidence and record the chain of custody with appropriate release forms:

(i) Perform appropriate toxicological tests and retain portions of the tested samples to permit retesting;

(a) Tissues: 150 grams of liver and kidney should be saved routinely. Brain, hair and adipose tissue may be saved for additional studies in cases where drugs, poisons or other toxic substances are suspected;

(b) Fluids: 50 cc (if possible) of blood (spin and save serum in all or some of the tubes), all available urine, vitreous humor and stomach contents should be saved routinely. Bile, regional gastrointestinal tract contents and cerebrospinal fluid should be saved in cases where drugs, poisons or toxic substances are suspected. Oral, vaginal and rectal fluid should be saved in cases of suspected sexual assault;

(ii) Representative samples of all major organs, including areas of normal and any abnormal tissue, should be processed histologically and stained with hematoxylin and eosin (and other stains as indicated). The slides, wet tissue and paraffin blocks should be kept indefinitely;

(iii) Evidence that must be saved includes:

(a) All foreign objects, including projectiles, projectile fragments, pellets, knives and fibres. Projectiles must be subjected to ballistic analysis;

(b) All clothes and personal effects of the deceased, worn by or in the possession of the deceased at the time of death;

(c) Fingernails and under-nail scrapings;

(d) Hair, foreign and pubic, in cases of suspected sexual assault;

(e) Head hair, in cases where the place of death or location of the body prior to its discovery may be an issue;

(j) After the autopsy, all unretained organs should be replaced in the body, and the body should be well embalmed to facilitate a second autopsy in case one is desired at some future point;

(k) The written autopsy report should address those items that are emphasized in boldface type in the protocol. At the end of the autopsy reports should be a summary of the findings and the cause of death. This should include the prosector's comments attributing any injuries to external trauma, therapeutic effects, postmortem change, or other causes. A full report should be given to the appropriate authorities and to the deceased's family.

ANNEX II

POSTMORTEM DETECTION OF TORTURE

Torture technique	*Physical findings*
Beating	
1. General	Scars. Bruises, Lacerations. Multiple fractures at different stages of healing, especially in unusual locations, which have not been medically treated.
2. To the soles of the feet ('falanga', 'falaka', 'bastinado'), or fractures of the bones of the feet.	Haemorrhage in the soft tissues of the soles of the feet and ankles. Aseptic necrosis.
3. With the palms on both ears simultaneously ('el telefone').	Ruptured or scarred tympanic membranes. Injuries to external ear.
4. On the abdomen, while lying on a table with the upper half of the body unsupported ('operating table', 'el quirofano').	Bruises on the abdomen. Back injuries. Ruptures abdominal viscera.

5. To the head.	Cerebral cortical atrophy. Skull fractures. Bruises. Haematomas.

Suspension.

6. By the wrists ('la bandera').	Bruises or scars about the wrists. Joint injuries.
7. By the arms or neck.	Bruises or scars at the site of binding. Prominent lividity in the lower extremities.
8. By the ankles ('murcielago').	Bruises or scars about the ankles. Joint injuries.
9. Head down, from a horizontal pole placed under the knees with the wrists bound to the ankles ('parrot's perch', 'Jack', 'pau de arara').	Bruises or scars on the anterior forearms and backs of the knees. marks on the wrists and ankles.

Near suffocation.

10. Forced immersion of head in water, often contaminated ('wet submarine', 'pileta', 'Latina').	Faecal material or other debris in the mouth, pharynx, trachea, oesophagus or lungs. Intrathoracic petechiae.
11. Tying of a plastic bag over the head ('dry submarine').	

Sexual abuse.

12. Sexual abuse	Sexually transmitted diseases. Pregnancy. Injuries to breasts, external genitalia, vagina, anus or rectum.

Forced posture.

13. Prolonged standing ('el planton').	Dependent oedema. Petechiae in lower extremities.
14. Forced straddling of a bar ('saw horse', 'el cabellete').	Perianal or scrotal haematomas.

Electric shock.

15. Cattle prod ('la picana').	Burns: appearance depends on the age of the injury. Immediately: red spots, vesicles, and/or black exudate. Within a few weeks: circular, reddish, macular scars. At several months: small, white, reddish or brown spots resembling telaniectasias.
16. Wires connected to a source of electricity.	
17. Heated metal skewer inserted into the anus ('black slave').	Peri-anal or rectal burns.

Miscellaneous.

18. Dehydration
    Animal bites (spiders, insects, rats, mice, dogs).

Vitreous humor electrolyte abnormalities.
Bite marks.

MODEL PROTOCOL FOR DISINTERMENT AND ANALYSIS OF SKELETAL REMAINS

A Introduction

This proposed model protocol for the disinterment and analysis of skeletal remains includes a comprehensive checklist of the steps in a basic forensic examination. The objectives of an anthropological investigation are the same as those of a medicolegal investigation of a recently deceased person. The anthropologist must collect information that will establish the identity of the deceased, the time and place of death, the cause of death and the manner or mode of death (homicide, suicide, accident or natural). The approach of the anthropologist differs, however, because of the nature of the material to be examined. Typically, a prosector is required to examine a body, whereas an anthropologist is required to examine a skeleton. The prosector focuses on information obtained from soft tissues, whereas the anthropologist focuses on information from hard tissues. Since decomposition is a continuous process, the work of both specialists can overlap. An anthropologist may examine a fresh body when bone is exposed or when bone trauma is a factor. An experienced prosector may be required when mummified tissues are present. In some circumstances, use of both this protocol and the model autopsy protocol may be necessary to yield the maximum information. The degree of decomposition of the body will dictate the type of investigation and, therefore, the protocol(s) to be followed.

The questions addressed by the anthropologist differ from those pursued in a typical autopsy. The anthropological investigation invests more time and attention to basic questions such as the following:

(a) Are the remains human?
(b) Do they represent a single individual or several?
(c) What was the decedent's sex, race, stature, body weight, handedness and physique?
(d) Are there any skeletal traits or anomalies that could serve to positively identify the decedent?

The time, cause and manner of death are also addressed by the anthropologist, but the margin of error is usually greater than that which can be achieved by an autopsy shortly after death.

This model protocol may be of use in many diverse situations. Its application may be affected, however, by poor conditions, inadequate financial resources or lack of time. Variation from the protocol may be inevitable or even preferable in some cases. It is suggested, however, that any major deviations, with the supporting reasons, should be noted in the final report.

B Proposed model skeletal analysis protocol

1 Scene investigation

A burial recovery should be handled with the same exacting care given to a crime-scene search. Efforts should be co-ordinated between the principal investigator and the consulting physical anthropologist or archaeologist. Human remains are frequently exhumed by law enforcement officers or cemetery workers unskilled in the techniques of forensic anthropology. Valuable information may be lost in this manner and false information is sometimes generated. Disinterment by untrained persons should be prohibited. The consulting anthropologist should be present to conduct or supervise the disinterment. Specific problems and procedures accompany the excavation of each type of burial. The amount of information obtained from the excavation depends on knowledge of the burial situation and judgment based on experience. The final report should include a rationale for the excavation procedure.

The following procedure should be followed during disinterment:

(a) Record the date, location, starting and finishing times of the disinterment, and the names of all workers;

(b) Record the information in narrative form, supplemented by sketches and photographs;

(c) Photograph the work area from the same perspective before work begins and after it ends every day to document any disturbance not related to the official procedure;

(d) In some cases, it is necessary to first locate the grave within a given area. There are numerous methods of locating graves, depending on the age of the grave:

   (i) An experienced archaeologist may recognize clues such as changes in surface contour and variation in local vegetation;

   (ii) A metal probe can be used to locate the less compact soil characteristics of grave fill;

   (iii) The area to be explored can be cleared and the top soil scraped away with a flat shovel. Graves appear darker than the surrounding ground because the darker topsoil has mixed with the lighter subsoil in the grave fill. Sometimes a light spraying of the surface with water may enhance a grave's outline;

(e) Classify the burial as follows:

   (i) Individual or commingled. A grave may contain the remains of one person buried alone, or it may contain the commingled remains of two or more persons buried either at the same time or over a period of time;

   (ii) Isolated or adjacent. An isolated grave is separate from other graves and can be excavated without concern about encroaching upon another grave. Adjacent graves, such as in a crowded cemetery, require a different excavation technique because the wall of one grave is also the wall of another grave;

   (iii) Primary or secondary. A primary grave is the grave in which the deceased is first placed. If the remains are then removed and reburied, the grave is considered to be secondary;

   (iv) Undisturbed or disturbed. An undisturbed burial is unchanged (except by natural processes) since the time of primary burial. A disturbed burial is one that has been altered by human intervention after the time of primary burial. All secondary burials are considered to be disturbed; archaeological methods can be used to detect a disturbance in a primary burial;

(f) Assign an unambiguous number to the burial. If an adequate numbering system is not already in effect, the anthropologist should devise a system;

(g) Establish a datum point, then block and map the burial site using an appropriate-sized grid and standard archaeological techniques. In some cases, it may be adequate simply to measure the depth of the grave from the surface to the skull and from the surface to the feet. Associated material can then be recorded in terms of their position relative to the skeleton;

(h) Remove the overburden of earth, screening the dirt for associated materials. Record the level (depth) and relative co-ordinates of any such findings. The type of burial, especially whether primary or secondary, influences the care and attention that needs to be given to this step. Associated materials located at a secondary burial site are unlikely to reveal the circumstances of the primary burial but may provide information on events that have occurred after that burial;

(i) Search for items such as bullets or jewellery, for which a metal detector can be useful, particularly in the levels immediately above and below the level of the remains;

(j) Circumscribe the body, when the level of the burial is located, and, when possible, open the burial pit to a minimum of 30 cm on all sides of the body;

(k) Pedestal the burial by digging on all sides to the lowest level of the body (approximately 30 cm). Also pedestal any associated artefacts;

(l) Expose the remains with the use of a soft brush or whisk broom. Do not use a brush on fabric, as it may destroy fibre evidence. Examine the soil found around the skull for hair. Place this soil in a bag for laboratory study. Patience is invaluable at this time. The remains may be fragile, and interrelationships of elements are important and may be easily disrupted. Damage can seriously reduce the amount of information available for analysis;

(m) Photograph and map the remains *in situ*. All photographs should include an identification number, the date, a scale and an indication of magnetic north;

   (i) First photograph the entire burial, then focus on significant details so that their relation to the whole can be easily visualized;

   (ii) Anything that seems unusual or remarkable should be photographed at close range. Careful attention should be given to evidence of trauma or pathological change, either recent or healed;

   (iii) Photograph and map all associated materials (clothes, hair, coffin, artefacts, bullets, casings etc.). The map should include a rough sketch of the skeleton as well as any associated materials;

(n) Before displacing anything, measure the individual:

   (i) Measure the total length of the remains and record the terminal points of the measurement, eg apex to plantar surface of calcaneus (*Note:* This is not a stature measurement);

   (ii) If the skeleton is so fragile that it may break when lifted, measure as much as possible before removing it from the ground;

(o) Remove all elements and place them in bags or boxes, taking care to avoid damage. Number, date and initial every container;

(p) Excavate and screen the level of soil immediately under the burial. A level of 'sterile' (artefact-free) soil should be located before ceasing excavation and beginning to backfill.

2 Laboratory analysis of skeletal remains

The following protocol should be followed during the laboratory analysis of the skeletal remains:

(a) Record the date, location, starting and finishing times of the skeletal analysis, and the names of all workers;

(b) Radiograph all skeletal elements before any further cleaning:
  (i) Obtain bite-wing, apical and panoramic dental X-rays, if possible;
  (ii) The entire skeleton should be X-rayed. Special attention should be directed to fractures, developmental anomalies and the effects of surgical procedures. Frontal sinus films should be included for identification purposes;

(c) Retain some bones in their original state; two lumbar vertebrae should be adequate. Rinse the rest of the bones clean but do not soak or scrub them. Allow the bones to dry;

(d) Lay out the entire skeleton in a systematic way:
  (i) Distinguish left from right;
  (ii) Inventory every bone and record on a skeletal chart;
  (iii) Inventory the teeth and record on a dental chart. Note broken, carious, restored and missing teeth;
  (iv) Photograph the entire skeleton in one frame. All photographs should contain an identification number and scale;

(e) If more than one individual is to be analysed, and especially if there is any chance that comparisons will be made between individuals, number every element with indelible ink before any other work is begun;

(f) Record the condition of the remains, eg fully intact and solid, eroding and friable, charred or cremated;

(g) Preliminary identification:
  (i) Determine age, sex, race and stature;
  (ii) Record the reasons for each conclusion (eg sex identity based on skull and femoral head);
  (iii) Photograph all evidence supporting these conclusions;

(h) Individual identification:
  (i) Search for evidence of handedness, pathological change, trauma and developmental anomalies;
  (ii) Record the reasons for each conclusion;
  (iii) Photograph all evidence supporting these conclusions;

(i) Attempt to distinguish injuries resulting from therapeutic measures from those unrelated to medical treatment. Photograph all injuries:
  (i) Examine the hyoid bone for cracks or breaks;
  (ii) Examine the thyroid cartilage for damage;
  (iii) Each bone should be examined for evidence of contact with metal. The superior or inferior edges of the ribs require particular scrutiny. A dissecting microscope is useful;

(j) If the remains are to be reburied before obtaining an identification, retain the following samples for further analysis:
  (i) A mid-shaft cross-section from either femur, 2 cm or more in height;
  (ii) A mid-shaft cross-section from either fibula, 2 cm or more in height;
  (iii) A 4 cm section from the sternal end of a rib (sixth, if possible);
  (iv) A tooth (preferably a mandibular incisor) that was vital at the time of death;
  (v) Sever molar teeth or possible later deoxyribonucleic acid fingerprinting for identification;
  (vi) A cast of the skull for possible facial reconstruction;
  (vii) Record what samples have been saved, and label all samples with the identification number, date and name of the person who removed the sample.

3 Final report

The following steps should be taken in the preparation of a final report:

(a) Prepare a full report of all procedures and results;
(b) Include a short summary of the conclusions;
(c) Sign and date the report.

APPENDIX 7

THE STANDARD MINIMUM RULES FOR THE TREATMENT OF PRISONERS

[Adopted by the First United Nations Congress on the Prevention of Crime and the Treatment of Offenders, held at Geneva in 1955, and approved by the Economic and Social Council by its resolutions 663 C (XXIV) of 31 July 1957 and 2076 (LXII) of 13 May 1977]

1. The following rules are not intended to describe in detail a model system of penal institutions. They seek only, on the basis of the general consensus of contemporary thought and the essential elements of the most adequate systems of today, to set out what is generally accepted as being good principle and practice in the treatment of prisoners and the management of institutions.

2. In view of the great variety of legal, social, economic and geographical conditions of the world, it is evident that not all of the rules are capable of application in all places and at all times. They should, however, serve to stimulate a constant endeavour to overcome practical difficulties in the way of their application, in the knowledge that they represent, as a whole, the minimum conditions which are accepted as suitable by the United Nations.

3. On the other hand, the rules cover a field in which thought is constantly developing. They are not intended to preclude experiment and practices, provided these are in harmony with the principles and seek to further the purposes which derive from the text of the rules as a whole. It will always be justifiable for the central prison administration to authorize departures from the rules in this spirit.

4. (1) Part I of the rules covers the general management of institutions, and is applicable to all categories of prisoners, criminal or civil, untried or convicted, including prisoners subject to 'security measures' or corrective measures ordered by the judge.

(2) Part II contains rules applicable only to the special categories dealt with in each section. Nevertheless, the rules under section A, applicable to prisoners under sentence, shall be equally applicable to categories of prisoners dealt with in sections B, C and D, provided they do not conflict with the rules governing those categories and are for their benefit.

5. (1) The rules do not seek to regulate the management of institutions set aside for young persons such as Borstal institutions or correctional schools, but in general Part I would be equally applicable in such institutions.

(2) The category of young prisoners should include at least all young persons who come within the jurisdiction of juvenile courts. As a rule, such young persons should not be sentenced to imprisonment.

PART I: RULES OF GENERAL APPLICATION

Basic principle

6. (1) The following rules shall be applied impartially. There shall be no discrimination on grounds of race, colour, sex, language, religion, political or other opinion, national or social origin, property, birth or other status.

(2) On the other hand, it is necessary to respect the religious beliefs and moral precepts of the group to which a prisoner belongs.

Register

7. (1) In every place where persons are imprisoned there shall be kept a bound registration book with numbered pages in which shall be entered in respect of each prisoner received:
(a) Information concerning his identity;
(b) The reasons for his commitment and the authority therefor;
(c) The day and hour of his admission and release.
(2) No person shall be received in an institution without a valid commitment order of which the details shall have been previously entered in the register.

Separation of categories

8. The different categories of prisoners shall be kept in separate institutions or parts of institutions taking account of their sex, age, criminal record, the legal reason for their detention and the necessities of their treatment. Thus:
(a) Men and women shall so far as possible be detained in separate institutions; in an institution which receives both men and women the whole of the premises allocated to women shall be entirely separate;
(b) Untried prisoners shall be kept separate from convicted prisoners;
(c) Persons imprisoned for debt and other civil prisoners shall be kept separate from persons imprisoned by reason of a criminal offence;
(d) Young prisoners shall be kept separate from adults.

Accommodation

9. (1) Where sleeping accommodation is in individual cells or rooms, each prisoner shall occupy by night a cell or room by himself. If for special reasons, such as temporary overcrowding, it becomes necessary for the central prison administration to make an exception to this rule, it is not desirable to have two prisoners in a cell or room.
(2) Where dormitories are used, they shall be occupied by prisoners carefully selected as being suitable to associate with one another in those conditions. There shall be regular supervision by night, in keeping with the nature of the institution.

10. All accommodation provided for the use of prisoners and in particular all sleeping accommodation shall meet all requirements of health, due regard being paid to climatic conditions and particularly to cubic content of air, minimum floor space, lighting, heating and ventilation.

11. In all places where prisoners are required to live or work.
(a) The windows shall be large enough to enable the prisoners to read or work by natural light, and shall be so constructed that they can allow the entrance of fresh air whether or not there is artificial ventilation;
(b) Artificial light shall be provided sufficient for the prisoners to read or work without injury to eyesight.

12. The sanitary installations shall be adequate to enable every prisoner to comply with the needs of nature when necessary and in a clean and decent manner.

13. Adequate bathing and shower installations shall be provided so that every prisoner may be enabled and required to have a bath or shower, at a temperature suitable to the

climate, as frequently as necessary for general hygiene according to season and geographical region, but at least once a week in a temperate climate.

14. All parts of an institution regularly used by prisoners shall be properly maintained and kept scrupulously clean at all times.

Personal hygiene

15. Prisoners shall be required to keep their persons clean, and to this end they shall be provided with water and with such toilet articles as are necessary for health and cleanliness.

16. In order that prisoners may maintain a good appearance compatible with their self-respect, facilities shall be provided for the proper care of the hair and beard, and men shall be enabled to shave regularly.

Clothing and bedding

17. (1) Every prisoner who is not allowed to wear his own clothing shall be provided with an outfit of clothing suitable for the climate and adequate to keep him in good health. Such clothing shall in no manner be degrading or humiliating.

(2) All clothing shall be clean and kept in proper condition. Underclothing shall be changed and washed as often as necessary for the maintenance of hygiene.

(3) In exceptional circumstances, whenever a prisoner is removed outside the institution for an authorized purpose, he shall be allowed to wear his own clothing or other inconspicuous clothing.

18. If prisoners are allowed to wear their own clothing, arrangements shall be made on their admission to the institution to ensure that it shall be clean and fit for use.

19. Every prisoner shall, in accordance with local or national standards, be provided with a separate bed, and with separate and sufficient bedding which shall be clean when issued, kept in good order and changed often enough to ensure its cleanliness.

Food

20. (1) Every prisoner shall be provided by the administration at the usual hours with food of nutritional value adequate for health and strength, of wholesome quality and well prepared and served.

(2) Drinking water shall be available to prisoner whenever he needs it.

Exercise and sport

21. (1) Every prisoner who is not employed in outdoor work shall have at least one hour of suitable exercise in the open air daily if the weather permits.

(2) Young prisoners, and others of suitable age and physique, shall receive physical and recreational training during the period of exercise. To this end space, installations and equipment should be provided.

Medical services

22. (1) At every institution there shall be available the services of at least one qualified medical officer who should have some knowledge of psychiatry. The medical services should be organized in close relationship to the general health administration of the

community or nation. They shall include a psychiatric service for the diagnosis and, in proper cases, the treatment of states of mental abnormality.

(2) Sick prisoners who require specialist treatment shall be transferred to specialized institutions or to civil hospitals. Where hospital facilities are provided in an institution, their equipment, furnishings and pharmaceutical supplies shall be proper for the medical care and treatment of sick prisoners, and there shall be a staff of suitable trained officers.

(3) The services of a qualified dental officer shall be available to every prisoner.

23. (1) In women's institutions there shall be special accommodation for all necessary pre-natal and post-natal care and treatment. Arrangements shall be made wherever practicable for children to be born in a hospital outside the institution. If a child is born in prison, this fact shall not be mentioned in the birth certificate.

(2) Where nursing infants are allowed to remain in the institution with their mothers, provision shall be made for a nursery staffed by qualified persons, where the infants shall be placed when they are not in the care of their mothers.

24. The medical officer shall see and examine every prisoner as soon as possible after his admission and thereafter as necessary, with a view particularly to the discovery of physical or mental illness and the taking of all necessary measures; the segregation of prisoners suspected of infectious or contagious conditions; the noting of physical or mental defects which might hamper rehabilitation, and the determination of the physical capacity of every prisoner for work.

25. (1) The medical officer shall have the care of the physical and mental health of the prisoners and should daily see all sick prisoners, all who complain of illness, and any prisoner to whom his attention is specially directed.

(2) The medical officer shall report to the director whenever he considers that a prisoner's physical or mental health has been or will be injuriously affected by continued imprisonment or by any condition of imprisonment.

26. (1) The medical officer shall regularly inspect and advise the director upon:
(a) The quantity, quality, preparation and service of food;
(b) The hygiene and cleanliness of the institution and the prisoners;
(c) The sanitation, heating, lighting and ventilation of the institution;
(d) The suitability and cleanliness of the prisoners' clothing and bedding;
(e) The observance of the rules concerning physical education and sports, in cases where there is no technical personnel in charge of these activities.

(2) The director shall take into consideration the reports and advice that the medical officer submits according to rules 25(2) and 26 and, in case he concurs with the recommendations made, shall take immediate steps to give effect to those recommendations; if they are not within his competence or if he does not concur with them, he shall immediately submit his own report and the advice of the medical officer to higher authority.

Discipline and punishment

27. Discipline and order shall be maintained with firmness, but with no more restriction than is necessary for safe custody and well-ordered community life.

28. (1) No prisoner shall be employed, in the service of the institution, in any disciplinary capacity.

(2) This rule shall not, however, impede the proper functioning of systems based on self-government, under which specified social, educational or sports activities or

responsibilities are entrusted, under supervision, to prisoners who are formed into groups for the purposes of treatment.

29. The following shall always be determined by the law or by the regulation of the competent administrative authority:

(a) Conduct constituting a disciplinary offence;

(b) The types and duration of punishment which may be inflicted;

(c) The authority competent to impose such punishment.

30. (1) No prisoner shall be punished except in accordance with the terms of such law or regulation, and never twice for the same offence.

(2) No prisoner shall be punished unless he has been informed of the offence alleged against him and given a proper opportunity of presenting his defence. The competent authority shall conduct a thorough examination of the case.

(3) Where necessary and practicable the prisoner shall be allowed to make his defence through an interpreter.

31. Corporal punishment, punishment by placing in a dark cell, and all cruel, inhuman or degrading punishments shall be completely prohibited as punishments for disciplinary offences.

32. (1) Punishment by close confinement or reduction of diet shall never be inflicted unless the medical officer has examined the prisoner and certified in writing that he is fit to sustain it.

(2) The same shall apply to any other punishment that may be prejudicial to the physical or mental health of a prisoner. In no case may such punishment be contrary to or depart from the principle stated in rule 31.

(3) The medical officer shall visit daily prisoners undergoing such punishments and shall advise the director if he considers the termination or alteration of the punishment necessary on grounds of physical or mental health.

Instruments of restraint

33. Instruments of restraint, such as handcuffs, chains, irons and straitjackets, shall never be applied as a punishment. Furthermore, chains or irons shall not be used as restraints. Other instruments of restraint shall not be used except in the following circumstances:

(a) As a precaution against escape during a transfer, provided that they shall be removed when the prisoner appears before a judicial or administrative authority;

(b) On medical grounds by direction of the medical officer;

(c) By order of the director, if other methods of control fail, in order to prevent a prisoner from injuring himself or others or from damaging property; in such instances the director will at once consult the medical officer and report to the higher administrative authority.

34. The patterns and manner of use of instruments of restraint shall be decided by the central prison administration. Such instruments must not be applied for any longer time than is strictly necessary.

Information to and complaints by prisoners

35. (1) Every prisoner on admission shall be provided with written information about the regulations governing the treatment of prisoners of his category, the disciplinary requirements of the institution, the authorized methods of seeking information and

making complaints, and all such other matters as are necessary to enable him to understand both his rights and his obligations and to adapt himself to the life of the institution.

(2) If a prisoner is illiterate, the aforesaid information shall be conveyed to him orally.

36. (1) Every prisoner shall have the opportunity each week day of making requests or complaints to the director of the institution or the officer authorized to represent him.

(2) It shall be possible to make requests or complaints to the inspector of prisons during his inspection. The prisoner shall have the opportunity to talk to the inspector or to any other inspecting officer without the director or other members of the staff being present.

(3) Every prisoner shall be allowed to make a request or complaint, without censorship as to substance but in proper form, to the central prison administration, the judicial authority or other proper authorities through approved channels.

(4) Unless it is evidently frivolous or groundless, every request or complaint shall be promptly dealt with and replied to without undue delay.

Contact with the outside world

37. Prisoners shall be allowed under necessary supervision to communicate with their family and reputable friends at regular intervals both by correspondence and by receiving visits.

38. (1) Prisoners who are foreign nationals shall be allowed reasonable facilities to communicate with the diplomatic and consular representatives of the state to which they belong.

(2) Prisoners who are nationals of states without diplomatic or consular representation in the country and refugees or stateless persons shall be allowed similar facilities to communicate with the diplomatic representative of the state which takes charge of their interests or any national or international authority whose task it is to protect such persons.

39. Prisoners shall be kept informed regularly of the more important items of news by the reading of newspapers, periodicals or special institutional publications, by hearing wireless transmissions, by lectures or by any similar means as authorized or controlled by the administration.

Books

40. Every institution shall have a library for the use of all categories of prisoners adequately stocked with both recreational and instructional books, and prisoners shall be encouraged to make full use of it.

Religion

41. (1) If the institution contains a sufficient number of prisoners of the same religion, a qualified representative of that religion shall be appointed or approved. If the number of prisoners justifies it and conditions permit, the arrangement should be on a full-time basis.

(2) A qualified representative appointed or approved under paragraph (1) shall be allowed to hold regular services and to pay pastoral visits in private to prisoners of his religion at proper times.

(3) Access to a qualified representative of any religion shall not be refused to any

prisoner. On the other hand, if any prisoner should object to a visit of any religious representative, his attitude shall be fully respected.

42. So far as practicable, every prisoner shall be allowed to satisfy the needs of his religious life by attending the services provided in the institution and having in his possession the books of religious observance and instruction of his denomination.

Retention of prisoners' property

43. (1) All money, valuables, clothing and other effects belonging to a prisoner which under the regulations of the institution he is not allowed to retain shall on his admission to the institution be placed in safe custody. An inventory thereof shall be signed by the prisoner. Steps shall be taken to keep them in good condition.

(2) On the release of the prisoner all such articles and money shall be returned to him except in so far as he has been authorized to spend money or send any such property out of the institution, or it has been found necessary on hygienic grounds to destroy any article of clothing. The prisoner shall sign a receipt for the articles and money returned to him.

(3) Any money or effects received for a prisoner from outside shall be treated in the same way.

(4) If a prisoner brings in any drugs or medicine, the medical officer shall decide what use shall be made of them.

Notification of death, illness, transfer, etc.

44. (1) Upon the death or serious illness of, or serious injury to a prisoner, or his removal to an institution for the treatment of mental affections, the director shall at once inform the spouse, if the prisoner is married, or the nearest relative and shall in any event inform any other person previously designated by the prisoner.

(2) A prisoner shall be informed at once of the death or serious illness of any near relative. In case of the critical illness of a near relative, the prisoner should be authorized, whenever circumstances allow, to go to his bedside either under escort or alone.

(3) Every prisoner shall have the right to inform at once his family of his imprisonment or his transfer to another institution.

Removal of prisoners

45. (1) When the prisoners are being removed to or from an institution, they shall be exposed to public view as little as possible, and proper safeguards shall be adopted to protect them from insult, curiosity and publicity in any form.

(2) The transport of prisoners in conveyances with inadequate ventilation or light, or in any way which would subject them to unnecessary physical hardship, shall be prohibited.

(3) The transport of prisoners shall be carried out at the expense of the administration and equal conditions shall obtain for all of them.

Institutional personnel

46. (1) The prison administration shall provide for the careful selection of every grade of the personnel, since it is on their integrity, humanity, professional capacity and personal suitability for the work that the proper administration of the institutions depends.

(2) The prison administration shall constantly seek to awaken and maintain in the

minds both of the personnel and of the public the conviction that this work is a social service of great importance, and to this end all appropriate means of informing the public should be used.

(3) To secure the foregoing ends, personnel shall be appointed on a full-time basis as professional prison officers and have civil service status with security of tenure subject only to good conduct, efficiency and physical fitness. Salaries shall be adequate to attract and retain suitable men and women; employment benefits and conditions of service shall be favourable in view of the exacting nature of the work.

47. (1) The personnel shall possess an adequate standard of education and intelligence.

(2) Before entering on duty, the personnel shall be given a course of training in their general and specific duties and be required to pass theoretical and practical tests.

(3) After entering on duty and during their career, the personnel shall maintain and improve their knowledge and professional capacity by attending courses of in-service training to be organized at suitable intervals.

48. All members of the personnel shall at all times so conduct themselves and perform their duties as to influence the prisoners for good by their example and to command their respect.

49. (1) So far as possible, the personnel shall include a sufficient number of specialists such as psychiatrists, psychologists, social workers, teachers and trade instructors.

(2) The services of social workers, teachers and trade instructors shall be secured on a permanent basis, without thereby excluding part-time or voluntary workers.

50. (1) The director of an institution should be adequately qualified for his task by character, administrative ability, suitable training and experience.

(2) He shall devote his entire time to his official duties and shall not be appointed on a part-time basis.

(3) He shall reside on the premises of the institution or in its immediate vicinity.

(4) When two or more institutions are under the authority of one director, he shall visit each of them at frequent intervals. A responsible resident official shall be in charge of each of these institutions.

51. (1) The director, his deputy, and the majority of the other personnel of the institution shall be able to speak the language of the greatest number of prisoners, or a language understood by the greatest number of them.

(2) Whenever necessary, the services of an interpreter shall be used.

52. (1) In institutions which are large enough to require the services of one or more full-time medical officers, at least one of them shall reside on the premises of the institution or in its immediate vicinity.

(2) In other institutions the medical officer shall visit daily and shall reside near enough to be able to attend without delay in cases of urgency.

53. (1) In an institution for both men and women, the part of the institution set aside for women shall be under the authority of a responsible woman officer who shall have the custody of the keys of all that part of the institution.

(2) No male member of the staff shall enter the part of the institution set aside for women unless accompanied by a woman officer.

(3) Women prisoners shall be attended and supervised only by women officers. This does not, however, preclude male members of the staff, particularly doctors and teachers, from carrying out their professional duties in institutions or parts of institutions set aside for women.

54. (1) Officers of the institutions shall not, in their relations with the prisoners, use force except in self-defence or in cases of attempted escape, or active or passive physical resistance to an order based on law or regulations. Officers who have recourse to force must use no more than is strictly necessary and must report the incident immediately to the director of the institution.

(2) Prison officers shall be given special physical training to enable them to restrain aggressive prisoners.

(3) Except in special circumstances, staff performing duties which bring them into direct contact with prisoners should not be armed. Furthermore, staff should in no circumstances be provided with arms unless they have been trained in their use.

Inspection

55. There shall be a regular inspection of penal institutions and services by qualified and experienced inspectors appointed by a competent authority. Their task shall be in particular to ensure that these institutions are administered in accordance with existing laws and regulations and with a view to bringing about the objectives of penal and correctional services.

PART II: RULES APPLICABLE TO SPECIAL CATEGORIES

A Prisoners under sentence

Guiding principles

56. The guiding principles hereafter are intended to show the spirit in which penal institutions should be administered and the purposes at which they should aim, in accordance with the declaration made under Preliminary Observation 1 of the present text.

57. Imprisonment and other measures which result in cutting off an offender from the outside world are afflictive by the very fact of taking from the person the right of self-determination by depriving him of his liberty. Therefore the prison system shall not, except as incidental to justifiable segregation or the maintenance of discipline, aggravate the suffering inherent in such a situation.

58. The purpose and justification of a sentence of imprisonment or a similar measure deprivative of liberty is ultimately to protect society against crime. This end can only be achieved if the period of imprisonment is used to ensure, so far as possible, that upon his return to society the offender is not only willing but able to lead a law-abiding and self-supporting life.

59. To this end, the institution should utilize all the remedial, educational, moral, spiritual and other forces and forms of assistance which are appropriate and available, and should seek to apply them according to the individual treatment needs of the prisoners.

60. (1) The régime of the institution should seek to minimize any differences between prison life and life at liberty which tend to lessen the responsibility of the prisoners or the respect due to their dignity as human beings.

(2) Before the completion of the sentence, it is desirable that the necessary steps be taken to ensure for the prisoner a gradual return to life in society. This aim may be achieved, depending on the case, by a pre-release régime organized in the same

institution or in another appropriate institution, or by release on trial under some kind of supervision which must not be entrusted to the police but should be combined with effective social aid.

61. The treatment of prisoners should emphasize not their exclusion from the community, but their continuing part in it. Community agencies should, therefore, be enlisted wherever possible to assist the staff of the institution in the task of social rehabilitation of the prisoners. There should be in connection with every institution social workers charged with the duty of maintaining and improving all desirable relations of a prisoner with his family and with valuable social agencies. Steps should be taken to safeguard, to the maximum extent compatible with the law and the sentence, the rights relating to civil interests, social security rights and other social benefits of prisoners.

62. The medical services of the institution shall seek to detect and shall treat any physical or mental illnesses or defects which may hamper a prisoner's rehabilitation. All necessary medical, surgical and psychiatric services shall be provided to that end.

63. (1) The fulfilment of these principles requires individualization of treatment and for this purpose a flexible system of classifying prisoners in groups; it is therefore desirable that such groups should be distributed in separate institutions suitable for the treatment of each group.

(2) These institutions need not provide the same degree of security for every group. It is desirable to provide varying degrees of security according to the needs of different groups. Open institutions, by the very fact that they provide no physical security against escape but rely on the self-discipline of the inmates, provide the conditions most favourable to rehabilitation for carefully selected prisoners.

(3) It is desirable that the number of prisoners in closed institutions should not be so large that the individualization of treatment is hindered. In some countries it is considered that the population of such institutions should not exceed five hundred. In open institutions the population should be as small as possible.

(4) On the other hand, it is undesirable to maintain prisons which are so small that proper facilities cannot be provided.

64. The duty of society does not end with a prisoner's release. There should, therefore, be governmental or private agencies capable of lending the released prisoner efficient after-care directed towards the lessening of prejudice against him and towards his social rehabilitation.

Treatment

65. The treatment of persons sentenced to imprisonment or a similar measure shall have as its purpose, so far as the length of the sentence permits, to establish in them the will to lead law-abiding and self-supporting lives after their release and to fit them to do so. The treatment shall be such as will encourage their self-respect and develop their sense of responsibility.

66. (1) To these ends, all appropriate means shall be used, including religious care in the countries where this is possible, education, vocational guidance and training, social casework, employment counselling, physical development and strengthening of moral character, in accordance with the individual needs of each prisoner, taking account of his social and criminal history, his physical and mental capacities and aptitudes, his personal temperament, the length of his sentence and his prospects after release.

(2) For every prisoner with a sentence of suitable length, the director shall receive, as

soon as possible after his admission, full reports on all the matters referred to in the foregoing paragraph. Such reports shall always include a report by a medical officer, wherever possible qualified in psychiatry, on the physical and mental condition of the prisoner.

(3) The reports and other relevant documents shall be placed in an individual file. This file shall be kept up to date and classified in such a way that it can be consulted by the responsible personnel whenever the need arises.

Classification and individualization

67. The purposes of classification shall be:
(a) To separate from others those prisoners who, by reason of their criminal records or bad characters, are likely to exercise a bad influence;
(b) To divide the prisoners into classes in order to facilitate their treatment with a view to their social rehabilitation.

68. So far as possible separate institutions or separate sections of an institution shall be used for the treatment of the different classes of prisoners.

69. As soon as possible after admission and after a study of the personality of each prisoner with a sentence of suitable length, a programme of treatment shall be prepared for him in the light of the knowledge obtained about his individual needs, his capacities and dispositions.

Privileges

70. Systems of privileges appropriate for the different classes of prisoners and the different methods of treatment shall be established at every institution, in order to encourage good conduct, develop a sense of responsibility and secure the interest and co-operation of the prisoners in their treatment.

Work

71. (1) Prison labour must not be of an afflictive nature.
(2) All prisoners under sentence shall be required to work, subject to their physical and mental fitness as determined by the medical officer.
(3) Sufficient work of a useful nature shall be provided to keep prisoners actively employed for a normal working day.
(4) So far as possible the work provided shall be such as will maintain or increase the prisoners' ability to earn an honest living after release.
(5) Vocational training in useful trades shall be provided for prisoners able to profit thereby and especially for young prisoners.
(6) Within the limits compatible with proper vocational selection and with the requirements of institutional administration and discipline, the prisoners shall be able to choose the type of work they wish to perform.

72. (1) The organization and methods of work in the institutions shall resemble as closely as possible those of similar work outside institutions, so as to prepare prisoners for the conditions of normal occupational life.
(2) The interests of the prisoners and of their vocational training, however, must not be subordinated to the purpose of making a financial profit from an industry in the institution.

73. (1) Preferably institutional industries and farms should be operated directly by the administration and not by private contractors.

(2) Where prisoners are employed in work not controlled by the administration, they shall always be under the supervision of the institution's personnel. Unless the work is for other departments of the government the full normal wages for such work shall be paid to the administration by the persons to whom the labour is supplied, account being taken of the output of the prisoners.

74. (1) The precautions laid down to protect the safety and health of free workmen shall be equally observed in institutions.

(2) Provision shall be made to indemnify prisoners against industrial injury, including occupational disease, on terms not less favourable than those extended by law to free workmen.

75. (1) The maximum daily and weekly working hours of the prisoners shall be fixed by law or by administrative regulation, taking into account local rules or custom in regard to the employment of free workmen.

(2) The hours so fixed shall leave one rest day a week and sufficient time for education and other activities required as part of the treatment and rehabilitation of the prisoners.

76. (1) There shall be a system of equitable remuneration of the work of prisoners.

(2) Under the system prisoners shall be allowed to spend at least a part of their earnings on approved articles for their own use and to send a part of their earnings to their family.

(3) The system should also provide that a part of the earnings should be set aside by the administration so as to constitute a savings fund to be handed over to the prisoner on his release.

Education and recreation

77. (1) Provision shall be made for the further education of all prisoners capable of profiting thereby, including religious instruction in the countries where this is possible. The education of illiterates and young prisoners shall be compulsory and special attention shall be paid to it by the administration;

(2) So far as practicable, the education of prisoners shall be integrated with the educational system of the country so that after their release they may continue their education without difficulty.

78. Recreational and cultural activities shall be provided in all institutions for the benefit of the mental and physical health of prisoners.

Social relations and aftercare

79. Special attention shall be paid to the maintenance and improvement of such relations between a prisoner and his family as are desirable in the best interests of both.

80. From the beginning of a prisoner's sentence consideration shall be given to his future after release and he shall be encouraged and assisted to maintain or establish such relations with persons or agencies outside the institution as may promote the best interests of his family and his own social rehabilitation.

81. (1) Services and agencies, governmental or otherwise, which assist released prisoners to re-establish themselves in society shall ensure, so far as is possible and necessary, that released prisoners be provided with appropriate documents and identification papers, have suitable homes and work to go to, are suitably and adequately

clothed having regard to the climate and season, and have sufficient means to reach their destination and maintain themselves in the period immediately following their release.

(2) The approved representatives of such agencies shall have all necessary access to the institution and to prisoners and shall be taken into consultation as to the future of a prisoner from the beginning of his sentence.

(3) It is desirable that the activities of such agencies shall be centralized or co-ordinated as far as possible in order to secure the best use of their efforts.

B Insane and mentally abnormal prisoners

82. (1) Persons who are found to be insane shall not be detained in prisons and arrangements shall be made to remove them to mental institutions as soon as possible.

(2) Prisoners who suffer from other mental diseases or abnormalities shall be observed and treated in specialized institutions under medical management.

(3) During their stay in a prison, such prisoners shall be placed under the special supervision of a medical officer.

(4) The medical or psychiatric service of the penal institutions shall provide for the psychiatric treatment of all other prisoners who are in need of such treatment.

83. It is desirable that steps should be taken, by arrangement with the appropriate agencies, to ensure if necessary the continuation of psychiatric treatment after release and the provision of social-psychiatric after-care.

C Prisoners under arrest or awaiting trial

84. (1) Persons arrested or imprisoned by reason of a criminal charge against them, who are detained either in police custody or in prison custody (jail) but have not yet been tried and sentenced, will be referred to as 'untried prisoners' hereinafter in these rules.

(2) Unconvicted prisoners are presumed to be innocent and shall be treated as such.

(3) Without prejudice to legal rules for the protection of individual liberty or prescribing the procedure to be observed in respect of untried prisoners, these prisoners shall benefit by a special régime which is described in the following rules in its essential requirements only.

85. (1) Untried prisoners shall be kept separate from convicted prisoners.

(2) Young untried prisoners shall be kept separate from adults and shall in principle be detained in separate institutions.

86. Untried prisoners shall sleep singly in separate rooms, with the reservation of different local custom in respect of the climate.

87. Within the limits compatible with the good order of the institution, untried prisoners may, if they so desire, have their food procured at their own expense from the outside, either through the administration or through their family or friends. Otherwise, the administration shall provide their food.

88. (1) An untried prisoner shall be allowed to wear his own clothing if it is clean and suitable.

(2) If he wears prison dress, it shall be different from that supplied to convicted prisoners.

89. An untried prisoner shall always be offered opportunity to work, but shall not be required to work. If he chooses to work, he shall be paid for it.

90. An untried prisoner shall be allowed to procure at his own expense or at the

expense of a third party such books, newspapers, writing materials and other means of occupation as are compatible with the interests of the administration of justice and the security and good order of the institution.

91. An untried prisoner shall be allowed to be visited and treated by his own doctor or dentist if there is reasonable ground for his application and he is able to pay any expenses incurred.

92. An untried prisoner shall be allowed to inform immediately his family of his detention and shall be given all reasonable facilities for communicating with his family and friends, and for receiving visits from them, subject only to restrictions and supervision as are necessary in the interests of the administration of justice and of the security and good order of the institution.

93. For the purposes of his defence, an untried prisoner shall be allowed to apply for free legal aid where such aid is available, and to receive visits from his legal adviser with a view to his defence and to prepare and hand to him confidential instructions. For these purposes, he shall if he so desires be supplied with writing material. Interviews between the prisoner and his legal adviser may be within sight but not within the hearing of a police or institution official.

D Civil prisoners

94. In countries where the law permits imprisonment for debt, or by order of a court under any other non-criminal process, persons so imprisoned shall not be subjected to any greater restriction or severity than is necessary to ensure safe custody and good order. Their treatment shall be not less favourable than that of untried prisoners, with the reservation, however, that they may possibly be required to work.

E Persons arrested or detained without charge

95. Without prejudice to the provisions of article 9 of the International Covenant on Civil and Political Rights, persons arrested or imprisoned without charge shall be accorded the same protection as that accorded under Part I and Part II, section C. Relevant provisions of Part II, section A, shall likewise be applicable where their application may be conducive to the benefit of this special group of persons in custody, provided that no measures shall be taken implying that re-education or rehabilitation is in any way appropriate to persons not convicted of any criminal offence.

APPENDIX 8

CODE OF CONDUCT FOR LAW ENFORCEMENT OFFICIALS

[Adopted by General Assembly resolution 34/169 of 17 December 1979]

The General Assembly

Considering that the purposes proclaimed in the Charter of the United Nations include the achievement of international co-operation in promoting and encouraging respect for human rights and for fundamental freedoms for all without distinction as to race, sex, language or religion.

Recalling, in particular, the Universal Declaration of Human Rights and the International Covenants on Human Rights.

Recalling also the Declaration on the Protection of All Persons from Being Subjected to Torture and Other Cruel, Inhuman or Degrading Treatment or Punishment, adopted by the General Assembly in its resolution 3452(XXX) of 9 December 1975.

Mindful that the nature of the functions of law enforcement in the defence of public order and the manner in which those functions are exercised have a direct impact on the quality of life of individuals as well as of society as a whole.

Conscious of the important task which law enforcement officials are performing diligently and with dignity, in compliance with the principles of human rights.

Aware, nevertheless, of the potential for abuse which the exercise of such duties entails.

Recognizing that the establishment of a code of conduct for law enforcement officials is only one of several important measures for providing the citizenry served by law enforcement officials with protection of all their rights and interests.

Aware that there are additional important principles and prerequisites for the humane performance of law enforcement functions, namely:

(a) That, like all agencies of the criminal justice system, every law enforcement agency should be representative of and responsive and accountable to the community as a whole.

(b) That the effective maintenance of ethical standards among law enforcement officials depends on the existence of a well-conceived, popularly accepted and humane system of laws.

(c) That every law enforcement official is part of the criminal justice system, the aim of which is to prevent and control crime, and that the conduct of every functionary within the system has an impact on the entire system.

(d) That every law enforcement agency, in fulfilment of the first premise of every profession, should be held to the duty of disciplining itself in complete conformity with the principles and standards herein provided and that the actions of law enforcement officials should be responsible to public scrutiny, whether exercised by a review board, a ministry, a procuracy, the judiciary, an ombudsman, a citizens' committee or any combination thereof, or any other reviewing agency.

(e) That standards as such lack practical value unless their content and meaning, through education and training and through monitoring, become part of the creed of every law enforcement official.

Adopts the Code of Conduct for Law Enforcement Officials set forth in the annex to the present resolution and decides to transmit it to Governments with the recommendation that favourable consideration should be given to its use within the framework of national legislation or practice as a body of principles for observance by law enforcement officials.

ANNEXURE

Code of Conduct for Law Enforcement Officials

Article 1

Law enforcement officials shall at all times fulfil the duty imposed upon them by law, by serving the community and by protecting all persons against illegal acts, consistent with the high degree of responsibility required by their profession.

Commentary

(a) The term 'law enforcement officials' includes all officers of the law, whether appointed or elected, who exercise police powers, especially the powers of arrest or detention.

(b) In countries where police powers are exercised by military authorities, whether uniformed or not, or by state security forces, the definition of law enforcement officials shall be regarded as including officers of such services.

(c) Service to the community is intended to include particularly the rendition of services of assistance to those members of the community who by reason of personal, economic, social or other emergencies are in need of immediate aid.

(d) This provision is intended to cover not only all violent, predatory and harmful acts, but extends to the full range of prohibitions under penal statutes. It extends to conduct by persons not capable of incurring criminal liability.

Article 2

In the performance of their duty, law enforcement officials shall respect and protect human dignity and maintain and uphold the human rights of all persons.

Commentary

(a) The human rights in question are identified and protected by national and international law. Among the relevant international instruments are the Universal Declaration of Human Rights, the International Covenant on Civil and Political Rights, the Declaration on the Protection of All Persons from Being Subjected to Torture and Other Cruel, Inhuman or Degrading Treatment or Punishment, the United Nations Declaration on the Elimination of All Forms of Racial Discrimination, the International Convention on the Elimination of All Forms of Racial Discrimination, the International Convention on the Suppression and Punishment of the Crime of Apartheid, the Convention on the Prevention and Punishment of the Crime of Genocide, the Standard Minimum Rules for the Treatment of Prisoners and the Vienna Convention on Consular Relations.

(b) National commentaries to this provision should indicate regional or national provisions identifying and protecting these rights.

Article 3

Law enforcement officials may use force only when strictly necessary and to the extent required for the performance of their duty.

Commentary

(a) This provision emphasizes that the use of force by law enforcement officials should be exceptional; while it implies that law enforcement officials may be authorized to use force as is reasonably necessary under the circumstances for the prevention of crime or in effecting or assisting in the lawful arrest of offenders or suspected offenders, no force going beyond that may be used.

(b) National law ordinarily restricts the use of force by law enforcement officials in accordance with a principle of proportionality. It is to be understood that such national principles of proportionality are to be respected in the interpretation of this provision. In no case should this provision be interpreted to authorize the use of force which is disproportionate to the legitimate objective to be achieved.

(c) The use of firearms is considered an extreme measure. Every effort should be made to exclude the use of firearms, especially against children. In general, firearms should not be used except when a suspected offender offers armed resistance or otherwise jeopardizes the lives of others and less extreme measures are not sufficient to restrain or apprehend the suspected offender. In every instance in which a firearm is discharged, a report should be made promptly to the competent authorities.

Article 4

Matters of a confidential nature in the possession of law enforcement officials shall be kept confidential, unless the performance of duty or the needs of justice strictly require otherwise.

Commentary

By the nature of their duties, law enforcement officials obtain information which may relate to private lives or be potentially harmful to the interests, and especially the reputation, of others. Great care should be exercised in safeguarding and using such information, which should be disclosed only in the performance of duty or to serve the needs of justice. Any disclosure of such information for other purposes is wholly improper.

Article 5

No law enforcement official may inflict, instigate or tolerate any act of torture or other cruel, inhuman or degrading treatment or punishment, nor may any law enforcement official invoke superior orders or exceptional circumstances such as a state of war or a threat of war, a threat to national security, internal political instability or any other public emergency as a justification of torture or other cruel, inhuman or degrading treatment or punishment.

Commentary

(a) This prohibition derives from the Declaration on the Protection of All Persons from

Being Subjected to Torture and Other Cruel, Inhuman or Degrading Treatment or Punishment, adopted by the General Assembly, according to which:

'[Such an act is] an offence to human dignity and shall be condemned as a denial of the purposes of the Charter of the United Nations and as a violation of the human rights and fundamental freedoms proclaimed in the Universal Declaration of Human Rights [and other international human rights instruments].'

(b) The Declaration defines torture as follows:

'. . . torture means any act by which severe pain or suffering, whether physical or mental, is intentionally inflicted by or at the instigation of a public official on a person for such purposes as obtaining from him or a third person information or confession, punishing him for an act he has committed or is suspected of having committed, or intimidating him or other persons. It did not include pain or suffering arising only from inherent in or incidental to, lawful sanctions to the extent consistent with the Standard Minimum Rules for the Treatment of Prisoners.'

(c) The term 'cruel, inhuman or degrading treatment or punishment' has not been defined by the General Assembly but should be interpreted so as to extend the widest possible protection against abuses, whether physical or mental.

Article 6

Law enforcement officials shall ensure the full protection of the health of persons in their custody and, in particular, shall take immediate action to secure medical attention whenever required.

Commentary

(a) 'Medical attention', which refers to services rendered by any medical personnel, including certified medical practitioners and paramedics, shall be secured when needed or requested.

(b) While the medical personnel are likely to be attached to the law enforcement operation, law enforcement officials must take into account the judgment of such personnel when they recommend providing the person in custody with appropriate treatment through, or in consultation with, medical personnel from outside the law enforcement operation.

(c) It is understood that law enforcement officials shall also secure medical attention for victims of violations of law or of accidents occurring in the course of violations of law.

Article 7

Law enforcement officials shall not commit any act of corruption. They shall also rigorously oppose and combat all such acts.

Commentary

(a) Any act of corruption, in the same way as any other abuse of authority, is incompatible with the profession of law enforcement officials. The law must be enforced fully with respect to any law enforcement official who commits an act of corruption, as Governments cannot expect to enforce the law among their citizens if they cannot, or will not, enforce the law against their own agents and within their agencies.

(b) While the definition of corruption must be subject to national law, it should be understood to encompass the commission or omission of an act in the performance of or in connection with one's duties, in response to gifts, promises or incentives demanded or accepted, or the wrongful receipt of these once the act has been committed or omitted.

(c) The expression 'act of corruption' referred to above should be understood to encompass attempted corruption.

Article 8

Law enforcement officials shall respect the law and the present Code. They shall also, to the best of their capability, prevent and rigorously oppose any violations of them.

Law enforcement officials who have reason to believe that a violation of the present Code has occurred or is about to occur shall report the matter to their superior authorities and, where necessary, to other appropriate authorities or organs vested with reviewing or remedial power.

Commentary

(a) This Code shall be observed whenever it has been incorporated into national legislation or practice. If legislation or practice contains stricter provisions than those of the present Code, those stricter provisions shall be observed.

(b) The article seeks to preserve the balance between the need for internal discipline of the agency on which public safety is largely dependent, on the one hand, and the need for dealing with violations of basic human rights, on the other. Law enforcement officials shall report violations within the chain of command and take other lawful action outside the chain of command only when no other remedies are available or effective. It is understood that law enforcement officials shall not suffer administrative or other penalties because they have reported that a violation of this Code has occurred or is about to occur.

(c) The term 'appropriate authorities or organs vested with reviewing or remedial power' refers to any authority or organ existing under national law, whether internal to the law enforcement agency or independent thereof, with statutory, customary or other power to review grievances and complaints arising out of violations within the purview of this Code.

(d) In some countries, the mass media may be regarded as performing complaint review functions similar to those described in subparagraph (c) above. Law enforcement officials may, therefore, be justified if, as a last resort and in accordance with the laws and customs of their own countries and with the provisions of Article 4 of the present Code, they bring violations to the attention of public opinion through the mass media.

(e) Law enforcement officials who comply with the provisions of this Code deserve the respect, the full support and the co-operation of the community and of the law enforcement agency in which they serve, as well as the law enforcement profession.

BASIC PRINCIPLES ON THE USE OF FORCE AND FIREARMS BY LAW ENFORCEMENT OFFICIALS

[Adopted by the Eighth United Nations Congress on the Prevention of Crime and the Treatment of Offenders, Havana, Cuba, 27 August–7 September 1990]

The Eighth United Nations Congress on the Prevention of Crime and the Treatment of Offenders

Recalling the Milan Plan of Action, adopted by the Seventh United Nations Congress on the Prevention of Crime and the Treatment of Offenders and endorsed by the General Assembly in its Resolution 40/32 of 29 November 1985.

Recalling also Resolution 14 of the Seventh Congress, in which the Committee on Crime Prevention and Control was called upon to consider measures for the more effective implementation of the Code of Conduct for Law Enforcement Officials.

Taking note with appreciation of the work accomplished, in pursuance of Resolution 14 of the Seventh Congress, by the Committee, by the interregional preparatory meeting for the Eighth United Nations Congress on the Prevention of Crime and the Treatment of Offenders on United Nations norms and guidelines in crime prevention and criminal justice and implementation and priorities for further standard-setting and by the regional preparatory meetings for the Eighth Congress.

1. Adopts the Basic Principles on the Use of Force and Firearms by Law Enforcement Officials contained in the annex to the present resolution;

2. Recommends the Basic Principles for national, regional and interregional action and implementation, taking into account the political, economic, social and cultural circumstances and traditions of each country;

3. Invites Member states to take into account and to respect the Basic Principles within the framework of their national legislation and practice;

4. Also invites Member states to bring the Basic Principles to the attention of law enforcement officials and other members of the executive branch of government, judges, lawyers, the legislature and the public in general;

5. Further invites Member states to inform the Secretary-General every five years, beginning in 1992, of the progress achieved in the implementation of the Basic Principles, including their dissemination, their incorporation into domestic legislation, practice, procedures and policies, the problems faced in their implementation at the national level and assistance that might be needed from the international community, and requests the Secretary-General to report thereon to the Ninth United Nations Congress on the Prevention of Crime and the Treatment of Offenders;

6. Appeals to all Governments to promote seminars and training courses at the national and regional levels on the role of law enforcement and the need for restraints on the use of force and firearms by law enforcement officials;

7. Urges the regional commissions, the regional and interregional institutes on crime

prevention and criminal justice, the specialized agencies and other entities within the United Nations system, other intergovernmental organizations concerned and non-governmental organizations in consultative status with the Economic and Social Council to become actively involved in the implementation of the Basic Principles and to inform the Secretary-General of the efforts made to disseminate and implement the Basic Principles and the extent of their implementation, and requests the Secretary-General to include this information in his report to the Ninth Congress;

8. Calls upon the Committee on Crime Prevention and Control to consider, as a matter of priority, ways and means of ensuring the effective implementation of the present resolution;

9. Requests the Secretary-General:

(a) To take steps, as appropriate, to bring this resolution to the attention of Governments and all United Nations bodies concerned, and to provide for the widest possible dissemination of the Basic Principles;

(b) To include the Basic Principles in the next edition of the United Nations publication entitled Human Rights: A Compilation of International Instruments;

(c) To provide Governments, at their request, with the services of experts and regional and interregional advisers to assist in implementing the Basic Principles and to report to the Ninth Congress on the technical assistance and training actually provided;

(d) To report to the Committee, at its twelfth session, on the steps taken to implement the Basic Principles;

10. Requests the Ninth Congress and its preparatory meetings to consider the progress achieved in the implementation of the Basic Principles.

ANNEXURE

Basic Principles on the Use of Force and Firearms by Law Enforcement Officials

Whereas the work of law enforcement officials is a social service of great importance and there is, therefore, a need to maintain and, whenever necessary, to improve the working conditions and status of these officials.

Whereas a threat to the life and safety of law enforcement officials must be seen as a threat to the stability of society as a whole.

Whereas law enforcement officials have a vital role in the protection of the right to life, liberty and security of the person, as guaranteed in the Universal Declaration of Human Rights and reaffirmed in the International Covenant on Civil and Political Rights.

Whereas the Standard Minimum Rules for the Treatment of Prisoners provide for the circumstances in which prison officials may use force in the course of their duties.

Whereas Article 3 of the Code of Conduct for Law Enforcement Officials provides that law enforcement officials may use force only when strictly necessary and to the extent required for the performance of their duty.

Whereas the preparatory meeting for the Seventh United Nations Congress on the Prevention of Crime and the Treatment of Offenders, held at Varenna, Italy, agreed on elements to be considered in the course of further work on restraints on the use of force and firearms by law enforcement officials.

Whereas the Seventh Congress, in its Resolution 14, inter alia, emphasizes that the use of force and firearms by law enforcement officials should be commensurate with due respect for human rights.

Whereas the Economic and Social Council, in its Resolution 1986/10, section IX, of 21 May 1986, invited Member states to pay particular attention in the implementation of the Code to the use of force and firearms by law enforcement officials, and the General Assembly, in its Resolution 41/149 of 4 December 1986, inter alia, welcomed this recommendation made by the Council.

Whereas it is appropriate that, with due regard to their personal safety, consideration be given to the role of law enforcement officials in relation to the administration of justice, to the protection of the right to life, liberty and security of the person, to their responsibility to maintain public safety and social peace and to the importance of their qualifications, training and conduct.

The basic principles set forth below, which have been formulated to assist Member states in their task of ensuring and promoting the proper role of law enforcement officials, should be taken into account and respected by Governments within the framework of their national legislation and practice, and be brought to the attention of law enforcement officials as well as other persons, such as judges, prosecutors, lawyers, members of the executive branch and the legislature, and the public.

General provisions

1. Governments and law enforcement agencies shall adopt and implement rules and regulations on the use of force and firearms against persons by law enforcement officials. In developing such rules and regulations, Governments and law enforcement agencies shall keep the ethical issues associated with the use of force and firearms constantly under review.

2. Governments and law enforcement agencies should develop a range of means as broad as possible and equip law enforcement officials with various types of weapons and ammunition that would allow for a differentiated use of force and firearms. These should include the development of non-lethal incapacitating weapons for use in appropriate situations, with a view to increasingly restraining the application of means capable of causing death or injury to persons. For the same purpose, it should also be possible for law enforcement officials to be equipped with self-defensive equipment such as shields, helmets, bullet-proof vests and bullet-proof means of transportation, in order to decrease the need to use weapons of any kind.

3. The development and deployment of non-lethal incapacitating weapons should be carefully evaluated in order to minimize the risk of endangering uninvolved persons, and the use of such weapons should be carefully controlled.

4. Law enforcement officials, in carrying out their duty, shall, as far as possible, apply non-violent means before resorting to the use of force and firearms. They may use force and firearms only if other means remain ineffective or without any promise of achieving the intended result.

5. Whenever the lawful use of force and firearms is unavoidable, law enforcement officials shall:
(a) Exercise restraint in such use and act in proportion to the seriousness of the offence and the legitimate objective to be achieved;
(b) Minimize damage and injury, and respect and preserve human life;

(c) Ensure that assistance and medical aid are rendered to any injured or affected persons at the earliest possible moment;

(d) Ensure that relatives or close friends of the injured or affected person are notified at the earliest possible moment.

6. Where injury or death is caused by the use of force and firearms by law enforcement officials, they shall report the incident promptly to their superiors, in accordance with Principle 22.

7. Governments shall ensure that arbitrary or abusive use of force and firearms by law enforcement officials is punished as a criminal offence under their law.

8. Exceptional circumstances such as internal political instability or any other public emergency may not be invoked to justify any departure from these basic principles.

Special provisions

9. Law enforcement officials shall not use firearms against persons except in self-defence or defence of others against the imminent threat of death or serious injury, to prevent the perpetration of a particularly serious crime involving grave threat to life, to arrest a person presenting such a danger and resisting their authority, or to prevent his or her escape, and only when less extreme means are insufficient to achieve these objectives. In any event, intentional lethal use of firearms may only be made when strictly unavoidable in order to protect life.

10. In the circumstances provided for under Principle 9, law enforcement officials shall identify themselves as such and give a clear warning of their intent to use firearms, with sufficient time for the warning to be observed, unless to do so would unduly place the law enforcement officials at risk or would create a risk of death or serious harm to other persons, or would be clearly inappropriate or pointless in the circumstances of the incident.

11. Rules and regulations on the use of firearms by law enforcement officials should include guidelines that:

(a) Specify the circumstances under which law enforcement officials are authorized to carry firearms and prescribe the types of firearms and ammunition permitted;

(b) Ensure that firearms are used only in appropriate circumstances and in a manner likely to decrease the risk of unnecessary harm;

(c) Prohibit the use of those firearms and ammunition that cause unwarranted injury or present an unwarranted risk;

(d) Regulate the control, storage and issuing of firearms, including procedures for ensuring that law enforcement officials are accountable for the firearms and ammunition issued to them;

(e) Provide for warnings to be given, if appropriate, when firearms are to be discharged;

(f) Provide for a system of reporting whenever law enforcement officials use firearms in the performance of their duty.

Policing unlawful assemblies

12. As everyone is allowed to participate in lawful and peaceful assemblies, in accordance with the principles embodied in the Universal Declaration of Human Rights and the International Covenant on Civil and Political Rights, Governments and law enforcement agencies and officials shall recognize that force and firearms may be used only in accordance with Principles 13 and 14.

13. In the dispersal of assemblies that are unlawful but non-violent, law enforcement officials shall avoid the use of force or, where that is not practicable, shall restrict such force to the minimum extent necessary.

14. In the dispersal of violent assemblies, law enforcement officials may use firearms only when less dangerous means are not practicable and only to the minimum extent necessary. Law enforcement officials shall not use firearms in such cases, except under the conditions stipulated in Principle 9.

Policing persons in custody or detention

15. Law enforcement officials, in their relations with persons in custody or detention, shall not use force, except when strictly necessary for the maintenance of security and order within the institution, or when personal safety is threatened.

16. Law enforcement officials, in their relations with persons in custody or detention, shall not use firearms, except in self-defence or in the defence of others against the immediate threat of death or serious injury, or when strictly necessary to prevent the escape of a person in custody or detention presenting the danger referred to in Principle 9.

17. The preceding principles are without prejudice to the rights, duties and responsibilities of prison officials, as set out in the Standard Minimum Rules for the Treatment of Prisoners, particularly Rules 33, 34 and 54.

Qualifications, training and counselling

18. Governments and law enforcement agencies shall ensure that all law enforcement officials are selected by proper screening procedures, have appropriate moral, psychological and physical qualities for the effective exercise of their functions and receive continuous and thorough professional training. Their continued fitness to perform these functions should be subject to periodic review.

19. Governments and law enforcement agencies shall ensure that all law enforcement officials are provided with training and are tested in accordance with appropriate proficiency standards in the use of force. Those law enforcement officials who are required to carry firearms should be authorized to do so only upon completion of special training in their use.

20. In the training of law enforcement officials, Governments and law enforcement agencies shall give special attention to issues of police ethics and human rights, especially in the investigative process, to alternatives to the use of force and firearms, including the peaceful settlement of conflicts, the understanding of crowd behaviour, and the methods of persuasion, negotiation and mediation, as well as to technical means, with a view to limiting the use of force and firearms. Law enforcement agencies should review their training programmes and operational procedures in the light of particular incidents.

21. Governments and law enforcement agencies shall make stress counselling available to law enforcement officials who are involved in situations where force and firearms are used.

Reporting and review procedures

22. Governments and law enforcement agencies shall establish effective reporting and review procedures for all incidents referred to in Principles 6 and 11 (f). For incidents

reported pursuant to these principles, Governments and law enforcement agencies shall ensure that an effective review process is available and that independent administrative or prosecutorial authorities are in a position to exercise jurisdiction in appropriate circumstances. In cases of death and serious injury or other grave consequences, a detailed report shall be sent promptly to the competent authorities responsible for administrative review and judicial control.

23. Persons affected by the use of force and firearms or their legal representatives shall have access to an independent process, including a judicial process. In the event of the death of such persons, this provision shall apply to their dependants accordingly.

24. Governments and law enforcement agencies shall ensure that superior officers are held responsible if they know, or should have known, that law enforcement officials under their command are resorting, or have resorted, to the unlawful use of force and firearms, and they did not take all measures in their power to prevent, suppress or report such use.

25. Governments and law enforcement agencies shall ensure that no criminal or disciplinary sanction is imposed on law enforcement officials who, in compliance with the Code of Conduct for Law Enforcement Officials and these basic principles, refuse to carry out an order to use force and firearms, or who report such use by other officials.

26. Obedience to superior orders shall be no defence if law enforcement officials knew that an order to use force and firearms resulting in the death or serious injury of a person was manifestly unlawful and had a reasonable opportunity to refuse to follow it. In any case, responsibility also rests on the superiors who gave the unlawful orders.

BASIC PRINCIPLES ON THE INDEPENDENCE OF THE JUDICIARY

[Adopted by the Seventh United Nations Congress on the Prevention of Crime and the Treatment of Offenders held at Milan from 26 August to 6 September 1985 and endorsed by General Assembly resolutions 40/32 of 29 November 1985 and 40/146 of 13 December 1985]

The Seventh United Nations Congress on the Prevention of Crime and the Treatment of Offenders

Recalling the Caracas Declaration unanimously adopted by the Sixth United Nations Congress on the Prevention of Crime and the Treatment of Offenders and endorsed by the General Assembly in its Resolution 35/171 of 15 December 1980.

Recalling also Resolution 16 adopted by the Sixth United Nations Congress on the Prevention of Crime and the Treatment of Offenders, in which the Congress called upon the Committee on Crime Prevention and Control to include among its priorities the elaboration of guidelines relating to the independence of judges.

Taking note with appreciation of the work accomplished in pursuance of the mandate cited above by the Committee on Crime Prevention and Control and by the Interregional Preparatory Meeting for the Seventh United Nations Congress on the Prevention of Crime and the Treatment of Offenders, held at Varenna, Italy, from 24–28 September 1984.

Further taking note with appreciation of the extensive discussions during the Seventh United Nations Congress on the Prevention of Crime and the Treatment of Offenders with respect to the draft guidelines on the independence of the judiciary, which led to the formulation of the Basic Principles on the Independence of the Judiciary.

1. Adopts the Basic Principles on the Independence of the Judiciary contained in the Annex to the present resolution;

2. Recommends the Basic Principles for national, regional and interregional action and implementation, taking into account the political, economic, social and cultural circumstances and traditions of each country;

3. Invites Governments to take into account within the framework of their national legislation and practice and to respect the Basic Principles;

4. Also invites Member states to bring the Basic Principles to the attention of judges, lawyers, members of the executive and the legislature and the public in general;

5. Urges the regional commissions, the regional and interregional institutes in the field of the prevention of crime and the treatment of offenders, the specialized agencies and other entities within the United Nations system, other intergovernmental organizations concerned and non-governmental organization having consultative status with the Economic and Social Council to become actively involved in the implementation of the Basic Principles;

6. Calls upon the Committee on Crime Prevention and Control to consider, as a matter of priority, the effective implementation of the present resolution;

7. Requests the Secretary-General to take steps, as appropriate, to ensure the widest possible dissemination of the Basic Principles;

8. Also requests the Secretary-General to prepare a report on the implementation of the Basic Principles;

9. Further requests the Secretary-General to assist Member states, at their request, in the implementation of the Basic Principles and to report thereon regularly to the Committee on Crime Prevention and Control;

10. Requests that the present resolution be brought to the attention of all United Nations bodies concerned.

ANNEXURE

Whereas in the Charter of the United Nations the peoples of the world affirm, inter alia, their determination to establish conditions under which justice can be maintained to achieve international co-operation in promoting and encouraging respect for human rights and fundamental freedoms without any discrimination.

Whereas the Universal Declaration of Human Rights enshrines in particular the principles of equality before the law, of the presumption of innocence and of the right to a fair and public hearing by a competent, independent and impartial tribunal established by law.

Whereas the International Covenants on Economic, Social and Cultural Rights and on Civil and Political Rights both guarantee the exercise of those rights, and in addition, the Covenant on Civil and Political Rights further guarantees the right to be tried without undue delay.

Whereas frequently there still exists a gap between the vision underlying those principles and the actual situation.

Whereas the organization and administration of justice in every country should be inspired by those principles, and efforts should be undertaken to translate them fully into reality.

Whereas rules concerning the exercise of judicial office should aim at enabling judges to act in accordance with those principles.

Whereas judges are charged with the ultimate decision over life, freedoms, rights, duties and property of citizens.

Whereas the Sixth United Nations Congress on the Prevention of Crime and the Treatment of Offenders, by its Resolution 16, called upon the Committee on Crime Prevention and Control to include among its priorities the elaboration of guidelines relating to the independence of judges and the selection, professional training and status of judges and prosecutors.

Whereas it is, therefore, appropriate that consideration be first given to the role of judges in relation to the system of justice and to the importance of their selection, training and conduct.

The following basic principles, formulated to assist member states in their task of securing and promoting the independence of the judiciary should be taken into account and respected by Governments within the framework of their national legislation and practice and be brought to the attention of judges, lawyers, members of the executive and the legislature and the public in general. The principles have been formulated principally with professional judges in mind, but they apply equally, as appropriate, to lay judges, where they exist.

Independence of the judiciary

1. The independence of the judiciary shall be guaranteed by the state and enshrined in the Constitution or the law of the country. It is the duty of all governmental and other institutions to respect and observe the independence of the judiciary.

2. The judiciary shall decide matters before them impartially, on the basis of facts and in accordance with the law, without any restrictions, improper influences, inducements, pressures, threats or interferences, direct or indirect, from any quarter or for any reason.

3. The judiciary shall have jurisdiction over all issues of a judicial nature and shall have exclusive authority to decide whether an issue submitted for its decision is within its competence as defined by law.

4. There shall not be any inappropriate or unwarranted interference with the judicial process, nor shall judicial decisions by the courts be subject to revision. This principle is without prejudice to judicial review or to mitigation or commutation by competent authorities of sentences imposed by the judiciary, in accordance with the law.

5. Everyone shall have the right to be tried by ordinary courts or tribunals using established legal procedures. Tribunals that do not use the duly established procedures of the legal process shall not be created to displace the jurisdiction belonging to the ordinary courts or judicial tribunals.

6. The principle of the independence of the judiciary entitles and requires the judiciary to ensure that judicial proceedings are conducted fairly and that the rights of the parties are respected.

7. It is the duty of each member state to provide adequate resources to enable the judiciary to properly perform its functions.

Freedom of expression and association

8. In accordance with the Universal Declaration of Human Rights, members of the judiciary are like other citizens entitled to freedom of expression, belief, association and assembly; provided, however, that in exercising such rights, judges shall always conduct themselves in such a manner as to preserve the dignity of their office and the impartiality and independence of the judiciary.

9. Judges shall be free to form and join associations of judges or other organizations to represent their interests, to promote their professional training and to protect their judicial independence.

Qualifications, selection and training

10. Persons selected for judicial office shall be individuals of integrity and ability with appropriate training or qualifications in law. Any method of judicial selection shall safeguard against judicial appointments for improper motives. In the selection of judges, there shall be no discrimination against a person on the grounds of race, colour, sex, religion, political or other opinion, national or social origin, property, birth or status, except that a requirement, that a candidate for judicial office must be a national of the country concerned, shall not be considered discriminatory.

Conditions of service and tenure

11. The term of office of judges, their independence, security, adequate remuneration,

conditions of service, pensions and the age of retirement shall be adequately secured by law.

12. Judges, whether appointed or elected, shall have guaranteed tenure until a mandatory retirement age or the expiry of their term of office, where such exists.

13. Promotion of judges, wherever such a system exists, should be based on objective factors, in particular ability, integrity and experience.

14. The assignment of cases to judges within the court to which they belong is an internal matter of judicial administration.

Professional secrecy and immunity

15. The judiciary shall be bound by professional secrecy with regard to their deliberations and to confidential information acquired in the course of their duties other than in public proceedings, and shall not be compelled to testify on such matters.

16. Without prejudice to any disciplinary procedure or to any right of appeal or to compensation from the state, in accordance with national law, judges should enjoy personal immunity from civil suits for monetary damages for improper acts or omissions in the exercise of their judicial functions.

Discipline, suspension and removal

17. A charge or complaint made against a judge in his/her judicial and professional capacity shall be processed expeditiously and fairly under an appropriate procedure. The judge shall have the right to a fair hearing. The examination of the matter at its initial stage shall be kept confidential, unless otherwise requested by the judge.

18. Judges shall be subject to suspension or removal only for reasons of incapacity or behaviour that renders them unfit to discharge their duties.

19. All disciplinary, suspension or removal proceedings shall be determined in accordance with established standards of judicial conduct.

20. Decisions in disciplinary, suspension or removal proceedings should be subject to an independent review. This principle may not apply to the decisions of the highest court and those of the legislature in impeachment or similar proceedings.

APPENDIX 11

BASIC PRINCIPLES ON THE ROLE OF LAWYERS

[Adopted by the Eighth United Nations Congress on the Prevention of Crime and the Treatment of Offenders, Havana, Cuba, 27 August–7 September 1990]

The Eighth United Nations Congress on the Prevention of Crime and the Treatment of Offenders

Recalling the Milan Plan of Action, adopted by the Seventh United Nations Congress on the Prevention of Crime and the Treatment of Offenders and endorsed by the General Assembly in its Resolution 40/32 of 29 November 1985.

Recalling also Resolution 18 of the Seventh Congress, in which the Congress recommended that Member states provide for the protection of practising lawyers against undue restrictions and pressures in the exercise of their functions.

Taking note with appreciation of the work accomplished, in pursuance of Seventh Congress Resolution 18, by the Committee on Crime Prevention and Control, by the interregional preparatory meeting for the Eighth United Nations Congress on the Prevention of Crime and the Treatment of Offenders on United Nations norms and guidelines in crime prevention and criminal justice and implementation and priorities for further standard settling, and by the regional preparatory meetings for the Eighth Congress.

1. Adopts the Basic Principles on the Role of Lawyers contained in the annex to the present resolution;

2. Recommends the Basic Principles for national, regional and interregional action and implementation, taking into account the political, economic, social and cultural circumstances and traditions of each country;

3. Invites member states to take into account and to respect the Basic Principles within the framework of their national legislation and practice;

4. Also invites member states to bring the Basic Principles to the attention of lawyers, judges, members of the executive branch of government and the legislature, and the public in general;

5. Further invites member states to inform the Secretary-General every five years, beginning in 1992, of the progress achieved in the implementation of the Basic Principles, including their dissemination, their incorporation into domestic legislation, practice, procedures and policies, the problems faced in their implementation at the national level and assistance that might be needed from the international community, and requests the Secretary-General to report thereon to the Ninth United Nations Congress on the Prevention of Crime and the Treatment of Offenders;

6. Appeals to all Governments to promote seminars and training courses at the national and regional levels on the role of lawyers and on respect for equality of conditions of access to the legal profession;

7. Urges the regional commissions, the regional and interregional institutes on crime

prevention and criminal justice, the specialized agencies and other entities within the United Nations system, other intergovernmental organizations concerned and non-governmental organizations in consultative status with the Economic and Social Council to become actively involved in the implementation of the Basic Principles and to inform the Secretary-General of the efforts made to disseminate and implement the Basic Principles and the extent of their implementation, and requests the Secretary-General to include this information in his report to the Ninth Congress;

8. Calls upon the Committee on Crime Prevention and Control to consider, as a matter of priority, ways and means of ensuring the effective implementation of this resolution;

9. Requests the Secretary-General:

(a) To take steps, as appropriate, to bring this resolution to the attention of Governments and all the United Nations bodies concerned and to provide for the widest possible dissemination of the Basic Principles;

(b) To include the Basic Principles in the next edition of the United Nations publication entitled Human Rights: A Compilation of International Instruments;

(c) To provide Governments, at their request, with the services of experts and regional and interregional advisers to assist in implementing the Basic Principles and to report to the Ninth Congress on the technical assistance and training actually provided;

(d) To report to the Committee on Crime Prevention and Control, at its twelfth session, on the steps taken to implement the Basic Principles.

ANNEXURE

Basic Principles on the Role of Lawyers

Whereas in the Charter of the United Nations the peoples of the world affirm, inter alia, their determination to establish conditions under which justice can be maintained, and proclaim as one of their purposes the achievement of international co-operation in promoting and encouraging respect for human rights and fundamental freedoms without distinction as to race, sex, language or religion.

Whereas the Universal Declaration of Human Rights enshrines the principles of equality before the law, the presumption of innocence, the right to a fair and public hearing by an independent and impartial tribunal, and all the guarantees necessary for the defence of everyone charged with a penal offence.

Whereas the International Covenant on Civil and Political Rights proclaims, in addition, the right to be tried without undue delay and the right to a fair and public hearing by a competent, independent and impartial tribunal established by law.

Whereas the International Covenant on Economic, Social and Cultural Rights recalls the obligation of states under the Charter to promote universal respect for, and observance of, human rights and freedoms.

Whereas the Body of Principles for the Protection of All Persons under Any Form of Detention or Imprisonment provides that a detained person shall be entitled to have the assistance of, and to communicate and consult with, legal counsel.

Whereas the Standard Minimum Rules for the Treatment of Prisoners recommend, in particular, that legal assistance and confidential communication with counsel should be ensured to untried prisoners.

Whereas the Safeguards guaranteeing protection of those facing the death penalty reaffirm the right of everyone suspected or charged with a crime for which capital punishment may be imposed to adequate legal assistance at all stages of the proceedings, in accordance with Article 14 of the International Covenant on Civil and Political Rights.

Whereas the Declaration of Basic Principles of Justice for Victims of Crime and Abuse of Power recommends measures to be taken at the international and national levels to improve access to justice and fair treatment, restitution, compensation and assistance for victims of crime.

Whereas adequate protection of the human rights and fundamental freedoms to which all persons are entitled, be they economic, social and cultural, or civil and political, requires that all persons have effective access to legal services provided by an independent legal profession.

Whereas professional associations of lawyers have a vital role to play in upholding professional standards and ethics, protecting their members from persecution and improper restrictions and infringements, providing legal services to all in need of them, and co-operating with governmental and other institutions in furthering the ends of justice and public interest.

The Basic Principles on the Role of Lawyers, set forth below, which have been formulated to assist member states in their task of promoting and ensuring the proper role of lawyers, should be respected and taken into account by Governments within the framework of their national legislation and practice and should be brought to the attention of lawyers as well as other persons, such as judges, prosecutors, members of the executive and the legislature, and the public in general. These principles shall also apply, as appropriate, to persons who exercise the functions of lawyers without having the formal status of lawyers.

Access to lawyers and legal services

1. All persons are entitled to call upon the assistance of a lawyer of their choice to protect and establish their rights and to defend them in all stages of criminal proceedings.

2. Governments shall ensure that efficient procedures and responsive mechanisms for effective and equal access to lawyers are provided for all persons within their territory and subject to their jurisdiction, without distinction of any kind, such as discrimination based on race, colour, ethnic origin, sex, language, religion, political or other opinion, national or social origin, property, birth, economic or other status.

3. Governments shall ensure the provision of sufficient funding and other resources for legal services to the poor and, as necessary, to other disadvantaged persons. Professional associations of lawyers shall co-operate in the organization and provision of services, facilities and other resources.

4. Governments and professional associations of lawyers shall promote programmes to inform the public about their rights and duties under the law and the important role of lawyers in protecting their fundamental freedoms. Special attention should be given to assisting the poor and other disadvantaged persons so as to enable them to assert their rights and where necessary call upon the assistance of lawyers.

Special safeguards in criminal justice matters

5. Governments shall ensure that all persons are immediately informed by the competent authority of their right to be assisted by a lawyer of their own choice upon arrest or detention or when charged with a criminal offence.

6. Any such persons who do not have a lawyer shall, in all cases in which the interests of justice so require, be entitled to have a lawyer of experience and competence commensurate with the nature of the offence assigned to them in order to provide effective legal assistance, without payment by them if they lack sufficient means to pay for such services.

7. Governments shall further ensure that all persons arrested or detained, with or without criminal charge, shall have prompt access to a lawyer, and in any case not later than forty-eight hours from the time of arrest or detention.

8. All arrested, detained or imprisoned persons shall be provided with adequate opportunities, time and facilities to be visited by and to communicate and consult with a lawyer, without delay, interception or censorship and in full confidentiality. Such consultations may be within sight, but not within the hearing, of law enforcement officials.

Qualifications and training

9. Governments, professional associations of lawyers and educational institutions shall ensure that lawyers have appropriate education and training and be made aware of the ideals and ethical duties of the lawyer and of human rights and fundamental freedoms recognized by national and international law.

10. Governments, professional associations of lawyers and educational institutions shall ensure that there is no discrimination against a person with respect to entry into or continued practice within the legal profession on the grounds of race, colour, sex, ethnic origin, religion, political or other opinion, national or social origin, property, birth, economic or other status, except that a requirement, that a lawyer must be a national of the country concerned, shall not be considered discriminatory.

11. In countries where there exist groups, communities or regions whose needs for legal services are not met, particularly where such groups have distinct cultures, traditions or languages or have been the victims of past discrimination, Governments, professional associations of lawyers and educational institutions should take special measures to provide opportunities for candidates from these groups to enter the legal profession and should ensure that they receive training appropriate to the needs of their groups.

Duties and responsibilities

12. Lawyers shall at all times maintain the honour and dignity of their profession as essential agents of the administration of justice.

13. The duties of lawyers towards their clients shall include:
(a) Advising clients as to their legal rights and obligations, and as to the working of the legal system in so far as it is relevant to the legal rights and obligations of the clients;
(b) Assisting clients in every appropriate way, and taking legal action to protect their interests;
(c) Assisting clients before courts, tribunals or administrative authorities, where appropriate.

14. Lawyers, in protecting the rights of their clients and in promoting the cause of justice, shall seek to uphold human rights and fundamental freedoms recognized by

national and international law and shall at all times act freely and diligently in accordance with the law and recognized standards and ethics of the legal profession.

15. Lawyers shall always loyally respect the interests of their clients.

Guarantees for the functioning of lawyers

16. Governments shall ensure that lawyers *(a)* are able to perform all of their professional functions without intimidation, hindrance, harassment or improper interference; *(b)* are able to travel and to consult with their clients freely both within their own country and abroad; and *(c)* shall not suffer, or be threatened with, prosecution or administrative, economic or other sanctions for any action taken in accordance with recognized professional duties, standards and ethics.

17. Where the security of lawyers is threatened as a result of discharging their functions, they shall be adequately safeguarded by the authorities.

18. Lawyers shall not be identified with their clients or their clients' causes as a result of discharging their functions.

19. No court or administrative authority before whom the right to counsel is recognized shall refuse to recognize the right of a lawyer to appear before it for his or her client unless that lawyer has been disqualified in accordance with national law and practice and in conformity with these principles.

20. Lawyers shall enjoy civil and penal immunity for relevant statements made in good faith in written or oral pleadings or in their professional appearances before a court, tribunal or other legal or administrative authority.

21. It is the duty of the competent authorities to ensure lawyers access to appropriate information, files and documents in their possession or control in sufficient time to enable lawyers to provide effective legal assistance to their clients. Such access should be provided at the earliest appropriate time.

22. Governments shall recognize and respect that all communications and consultations between lawyers and their clients within their professional relationship are confidential.

Freedom of expression and association

23. Lawyers like other citizens are entitled to freedom of expression, belief, association and assembly. In particular, they shall have the right to take part in public discussion of matters concerning the law, the administration of justice and the promotion and protection of human rights and to join or form local, national or international organizations and attend their meetings, without suffering professional restrictions by reason of their lawful action or their membership in a lawful organization. In exercising these rights, lawyers shall always conduct themselves in accordance with the law and the recognized standards and ethics of the legal profession.

Professional associations of lawyers

24. Lawyers shall be entitled to form and join self-governing professional associations to represent their interests, promote their continuing education and training and protect their professional integrity. The executive body of the professional associations shall be elected by its members and shall exercise its functions without external interference.

25. Professional associations of lawyers shall co-operate with Governments to ensure

that everyone has effective and equal access to legal services and that lawyers are able, without improper interference, to counsel and assist their clients in accordance with the law and recognized professional standards and ethics.

Disciplinary proceedings

26. Codes of professional conduct for lawyers shall be established by the legal profession through its appropriate organs, or by legislation, in accordance with national law and custom and recognized international standards and norms.

27. Charges or complaints made against lawyers in their professional capacity shall be processed expeditiously and fairly under appropriate procedures. Lawyers shall have the right to a fair hearing, including the right to be assisted by a lawyer of their choice.

28. Disciplinary proceedings against lawyers shall be brought before an impartial disciplinary committee established by the legal profession, before an independent statutory authority, or before a court, and shall be subject to an independent judicial review.

29. All disciplinary proceedings shall be determined in accordance with the code of professional conduct and other recognized standards and ethics of the legal profession and in the light of these principles.

GUIDELINES ON THE ROLE OF PROSECUTORS

[Adopted by the Eighth United Nations Congress on the Prevention of Crime and the Treatment of Offenders, Havana, Cuba, 27 August–September 1990.]

The Eighth United Nations Congress on the Prevention of Crime and the Treatment of Offenders

Recalling the Milan Plan of Action, adopted by the Seventh United Nations Congress on the Prevention of Crime and the Treatment of Offenders and endorsed by the General Assembly in its Resolution 40/32 of 29 November 1985.

Recalling also Resolution 7 of the Seventh Congress, in which the Committee on Crime Prevention and Control was called upon to consider the need for guidelines relating to prosecutors.

Taking note with appreciation of the work accomplished, in pursuance of that resolution, by the Committee and the regional preparatory meetings for the Eighth United Nations Congress on the Prevention of Crime and the Treatment of Offenders.

1. Adopts the Guidelines on the Role of Prosecutors contained in the annex to the present resolution;

2. Recommends the Guidelines for national, regional and interregional action and implementation, taking into account the political, economic, social and cultural circumstances and traditions of each country;

3. Invites Member states to take into account and to respect the Guidelines within the framework of their national legislation and practice;

4. Also invites Member states to bring the Guidelines to the attention of prosecutors as well as others, including judges, lawyers, members of the executive branch of government and the legislature, and the public in general;

5. Urges the regional commissions, the regional and interregional institutes on crime prevention and the treatment of offenders, the specialized agencies and other entities within the United Nations system, other intergovernmental organizations concerned and non-governmental organizations in consultative status with the Economic and Social Council to become actively involved in the implementation of the Guidelines;

6. Calls upon the Committee on Crime Prevention and Control to consider, as a matter of priority, the implementation of the present resolution;

7. Requests the Secretary-General to take steps, as appropriate, to ensure the widest possible dissemination of the Guidelines, including their transmission to Governments, intergovernmental and non-governmental organizations and other parties concerned;

8. Also requests the Secretary-General to prepare every five years, beginning in 1993, a report on the implementation of the Guidelines;

9. Further requests the Secretary-General to assist Member states, at their request, in the implementation of the Guidelines and to report regularly thereon to the Committee;

10. Requests that the present resolution be brought to the attention of all the United Nations bodies concerned.

ANNEXURE

Guidelines on the role of prosecutors

Whereas in the Charter of the United Nations the peoples of the world affirm, inter alia, their determination to establish conditions under which justice can be maintained, and proclaim as one of their purposes the achievement of international co-operation in promoting and encouraging respect for human rights and fundamental freedoms without distinction as to race, sex, language or religion.

Whereas the Universal Declaration of Human Rights enshrines the principles of equality before the law, the presumption of innocence and the right to a fair and public hearing by an independent and impartial tribunal.

Whereas frequently there still exists a gap between the vision underlying those principles and the actual situation.

Whereas the organization and administration of justice in every country should be inspired by those principles, and efforts undertaken to translate them fully into reality.

Whereas prosecutors play a crucial role in the administration of justice, and rules concerning the performance of their important responsibilities should promote their respect for and compliance with the above-mentioned principles, thus contributing to fair and equitable criminal justice and the effective protection of citizens against crime.

Whereas it is essential to ensure that prosecutors possess the professional qualifications required for the accomplishment of their functions, through improved methods of recruitment and legal and professional training, and through the provision of all necessary means for the proper performance of their role in combating criminality, particularly in its new forms and dimensions.

Whereas the General Assembly, by its Resolution 34/169 of 17 December 1979, adopted the Code of Conduct for Law Enforcement Officials, on the recommendation of the Fifth United Nations Congress on the Prevention of Crime and the Treatment of Offenders.

Whereas in Resolution 16 of the Sixth United Nations Congress on the Prevention of Crime and the Treatment of Offenders, the Committee on Crime Prevention and Control was called upon to include among its priorities the elaboration of guidelines relating to the independence of judges and the selection, professional training and status of judges and prosecutors.

Whereas the Seventh United Nations Congress on the Prevention of Crime and the Treatment of Offenders adopted the Basic Principles on the Independence of the Judiciary, subsequently endorsed by the General Assembly in its Resolutions 40/32 of 29 November 1985 and 40/146 of 13 December 1985.

Whereas the Declaration of Basic Principles of Justice for Victims of Crime and Abuse of Power, recommends measures to be taken at the international and national levels to improve access to justice and fair treatment, restitution, compensation and assistance for victims of crime.

Whereas, in Resolution 7 of the Seventh Congress, the Committee was called upon to consider the need for guidelines relating, inter alia, to the selection, professional training and status of prosecutors, their expected tasks and conduct, means to enhance their contribution to the smooth functioning of the criminal justice system and their co-operation with the police, the scope of their discretionary powers, and their role in criminal proceedings, and to report thereon to future United Nations congresses.

The Guidelines set forth below, which have been formulated to assist member states in their tasks of securing and promoting the effectiveness, impartiality and fairness of prosecutors in criminal proceedings, should be respected and taken into account by Governments within the framework of their national legislation and practice, and should be brought to the attention of prosecutors, as well as other persons, such as judges, lawyers, members of the executive and the legislature and the public in general. The present Guidelines have been formulated principally with public prosecutors in mind, but they apply equally, as appropriate, to prosecutors appointed on an ad hoc basis.

Qualifications, selection and training

1. Persons selected as prosecutors shall be individuals of integrity and ability, with appropriate training and qualifications.

2. States shall ensure that:

(a) Selection criteria for prosecutors embody safeguards against appointments based on partiality or prejudice, excluding any discrimination against a person on the grounds of race, colour, sex, language, religion, political or other opinion, national, social or ethnic origin, property, birth, economic or other status, except that it shall not be considered discriminatory to require a candidate for prosecutorial office to be a national of the country concerned;

(b) Prosecutors have appropriate education and training and should be made aware of the ideals and ethical duties of their office, of the constitutional and statutory protections for the rights of the suspect and the victim, and of human rights and fundamental freedoms recognized by national and international law.

Status and conditions of service

3. Prosecutors, as essential agents of the administration of justice, shall at all times maintain the honour and dignity of their profession.

4. States shall ensure that prosecutors are able to perform their professional functions without intimidation, hindrance, harassment, improper interference or unjustified exposure to civil, penal or other liability.

5. Prosecutors and their families shall be physically protected by the authorities when their personal safety is threatened as a result of the discharge of prosecutorial functions.

6. Reasonable conditions of service of prosecutors, adequate remuneration and, where applicable, tenure, pension and age of retirement shall be set out by law or published rules or regulations.

7. Promotion of prosecutors, wherever such a system exists, shall be based on objective factors, in particular professional qualifications, ability, integrity and experience, and decided upon in accordance with fair and impartial procedures.

Freedom of expression and association

8. Prosecutors like other citizens are entitled to freedom of expression, belief, association and assembly. In particular, they shall have the right to take part in public

discussion of matters concerning the law, the administration of justice and the promotion and protection of human rights and to join or form local, national or international organizations and attend their meetings, without suffering professional disadvantage by reason of their lawful action or their membership in a lawful organization. In exercising these rights, prosecutors shall always conduct themselves in accordance with the law and the recognized standards and ethics of their profession.

9. Prosecutors shall be free to form and join professional associations or other organizations to represent their interests, to promote their professional training and to protect their status.

Role in criminal proceedings

10. The office of prosecutors shall be strictly separated from judicial functions.

11. Prosecutors shall perform an active role in criminal proceedings, including institution of prosecution and, where authorized by law or consistent with local practice, in the investigation of crime, supervision over the legality of these investigations, supervision of the execution of court decisions and the exercise of other functions as representatives of the public interest.

12. Prosecutors shall, in accordance with the law, perform their duties fairly, consistently and expeditiously, and respect and protect human dignity and uphold human rights, thus contributing to ensuring due process and the smooth functioning of the criminal justice system.

13. In the performance of their duties, prosecutors shall:
(a) Carry out their functions impartially and avoid all political, social, religious, racial, cultural, sexual or any other kind of discrimination;
(b) Protect the public interest, act with objectivity, take proper account of the position of the suspect and the victim, and pay attention to all relevant circumstances, irrespective of whether they are to the advantage or disadvantage of the suspect;
(c) Keep matters in their possession confidential, unless the performance of duty or the needs of justice require otherwise;
(d) Consider the views and concerns of victims when their personal interests are affected and ensure that victims are informed of their rights in accordance with the Declaration of Basic Principles of Justice for Victims of Crime and Abuse of Power.

14. Prosecutors shall not initiate or continue prosecution, or shall make every effort to stay proceedings, when an impartial investigation shows the charge to be unfounded.

15. Prosecutors shall give due attention to the prosecution of crimes committed by public officials, particularly corruption, abuse of power, grave violations of human rights and other crimes recognized by international law and, where authorized by law or consistent with local practice, the investigation of such offences.

16. When prosecutors come into possession of evidence against suspects that they know or believe on reasonable grounds was obtained through recourse to unlawful methods, which constitute a grave violation of the suspect's human rights, especially involving torture or cruel, inhuman or degrading treatment or punishment, or other abuses of human rights, they shall refuse to use such evidence against anyone other than those who used such methods, or inform the Court accordingly, and shall take all necessary steps to ensure that those responsible for using such methods are brought to justice.

Discretionary functions

17. In countries where prosecutors are vested with discretionary functions, the law or published rules or regulations shall provide guidelines to enhance fairness and consistency of approach in taking decisions in the prosecution process, including institution or waiver of prosecution.

Alternatives to prosecution

18. In accordance with national law, prosecutors shall give due consideration to waiving prosecution, discontinuing proceedings conditionally or unconditionally, or diverting criminal cases from the formal justice system, with full respect for the rights of suspect(s) and the victim(s). For this purpose, states should fully explore the possibility of adopting diversion schemes not only to alleviate excessive court loads, but also to avoid the stigmatization of pretrial detention, indictment and conviction, as well as the possible adverse effects of imprisonment.

19. In countries where prosecutors are vested with discretionary functions as to the decision whether or not to prosecute a juvenile, special considerations shall be given to the nature and gravity of the offence, protection of society and the personality and background of the juvenile. In making that decision, prosecutors shall particularly consider available alternatives to prosecution under the relevant juvenile justice laws and procedures. Prosecutors shall use their best efforts to take prosecutory action against juveniles only to the extent strictly necessary.

Relations with other government agencies or institutions

20. In order to ensure the fairness and effectiveness of prosecution, prosecutors shall strive to co-operate with the police, the courts, the legal profession, public defenders and other government agencies or institutions.

Disciplinary proceedings

21. Disciplinary offences of prosecutors shall be based on law or lawful regulations. Complaints against prosecutors which allege that they acted in a manner clearly out of the range of professional standards shall be processed expeditiously and fairly under appropriate procedures. Prosecutors shall have the right to a fair hearing. The decision shall be subject to independent review.

22. Disciplinary proceedings against prosecutors shall guarantee an objective evaluation and decision. They shall be determined in accordance with the law, the code of professional conduct and other established standards and ethics and in the light of the present Guidelines.

Observance of the Guidelines

23. Prosecutors shall respect the present Guidelines. They shall also, to the best of their capability, prevent and actively oppose any violations thereof.

24. Prosecutors who have reason to believe that a violation of the present Guidelines has occurred or is about to occur shall report the matter to their superior authorities and, where necessary, to other appropriate authorities or organs vested with reviewing or remedial power.

INTERNATIONAL LABOUR CONFERENCE

Convention 169

CONVENTION CONCERNING INDIGENOUS AND TRIBAL PEOPLES IN INDEPENDENT COUNTRIES

The General Conference of the International Labour Organization

Having been convened at Geneva by the governing Body of the International Labour Office, and having met in its 76th Session on 7 June 1989, and

Noting the international standards contained in the Indigenous and Tribal Populations Convention and Recommendation, 1957, and

Recalling the terms of the Universal Declaration of Human Rights, the International Covenant on Economic, Social and Cultural Rights, the International Covenant on Civil and Political Rights, and the many international instruments on the prevention of discrimination, and

Considering that the developments which have taken place in international law since 1957, as well as developments in the situation of indigenous and tribal peoples in all regions of the world, have made it appropriate to adopt new international standards on the subject with a view to removing the assimilationist orientation of the earlier standards, and

Recognizing the aspirations of these peoples to exercise control over their own institutions, ways of life and economic development and to maintain and develop their identities, languages and religions, within the framework of the states in which they live, and

Noting that in many parts of the world these people are unable to enjoy their fundamental human rights to the same degree as the rest of the population of the states within which they live, and that their laws, values, customs and perspectives have often been eroded, and

Calling attention to the distinctive contributions of indigenous and tribal peoples to the cultural diversity and social and ecological harmony of humankind and to international co-operation and understanding, and

Noting that the following provisions have been framed with the co-operation of the United Nations, the Food and Agriculture Organization of the United Nations, the United Nations Educational, Scientific and Cultural Organization and the World Health Organization, as well as of the Inter-American Indian Institute, at appropriate levels and in their respective fields, and that it is proposed to continue this co-operation in promoting and securing the application of these provisions, and

Having decided upon the adoption of certain proposals with regard to the partial revision of the Indigenous and Tribal Populations Convention, 1957 (No 107), which is the fourth item on the agenda of the session, and

Having determined that these proposals shall take the form of an international Convention revising the Indigenous and Tribal Populations Convention, 1957; adopts this twenty-seventh day of June of the year one thousand nine hundred and eighty-nine the following Convention, which may be cited as the Indigenous and Tribal Peoples Convention, 1989:

PART I GENERAL POLICY

Article 1

1. This Convention applies to:
(a) tribal people in independent countries whose social, cultural and economic conditions distinguish them from other sections of the national community, and whose status is regulated wholly or partially by their own customs or traditions or by special laws or regulations;
(b) peoples in independent countries who are regarded as indigenous on account of their descent from the populations which inhabited the country, or a geographical region to which the country belongs, at the time of conquest or colonization or the establishment of present state boundaries and who, irrespective of their legal status, retain some or all of their own social, economic, cultural and political institutions.

2. Self-identification as indigenous or tribal shall be regarded as a fundamental criterion for determining the groups to which the provisions of this Convention apply.

3. The use of the term 'peoples' in this Convention shall not be construed as having any implications as regards the rights which may attach to the term under international law.

Article 2

1. Governments shall have the responsibility for developing, with the participation of the peoples concerned, co-ordinated and systematic action to protect the rights of these peoples and to guarantee respect for their integrity.

2. Such action shall include measures for:
(a) ensuring that members of these peoples benefit on an equal footing from the rights and opportunities which national laws and regulations grant to other members of the population;
(b) promoting the full realization of the social, economic and cultural rights of these peoples with respect for their social and cultural identity, their customs and traditions and their institutions;
(c) assisting the members of the peoples concerned to eliminate socio-economic gaps that may exist between indigenous and other members of the national community, in a manner compatible with their aspirations and ways of life.

Article 3

1. Indigenous and tribal peoples shall enjoy the full measure of human rights and fundamental freedoms without hindrance or discrimination. The provisions of the Convention shall be applied without discrimination to male and female members of these peoples.

2. No form of force or coercion shall be used in violation of the human rights and fundamental freedoms of the peoples concerned, including the rights contained in this Convention.

Article 4

1. Special measures shall be adopted as appropriate for safeguarding the persons, institutions, property, labour, cultures and environment of the peoples concerned.

2. Such special measures shall not be contrary to the freely expressed wishes of the peoples concerned.

3. Enjoyment of the general rights of citizenship, without discrimination, shall not be prejudiced in any way by such special measures.

Article 5

In applying the provisions of this Convention:
(a) the social, cultural, religious and spiritual values and practices of these peoples shall be recognized and protected, and due account shall be taken of the nature of the problems which face them both as groups and as individuals;
(b) the integrity of the values, practices and institutions of these peoples shall be respected;
(c) policies aimed at mitigating the difficulties experienced by these peoples in facing new conditions of life and work shall be adopted, with the participation and co-operation of the peoples affected.

Article 6

1. In applying the provisions of this Convention, governments shall:
(a) consult the peoples concerned, through appropriate procedures and in particular through their representative institutions, whenever consideration is being given to legislative or administrative measures which may affect them directly;
(b) establish means by which these peoples can freely participate, to at least the same extent as other sectors of the population, at all levels of decision-making in elective institutions and administrative and other bodies responsible for policies and programmes which concern them;
(c) establish means for the full development of these peoples' own institutions and initiatives, and in appropriate cases provide the resources necessary for this purpose.

2. The consultations carried out in application of this Convention shall be undertaken, in good faith and in a form appropriate to the circumstances, with the objective of achieving agreement or consent to the proposed measures.

Article 7

1. The peoples concerned shall have the right to decide their own priorities for the process of development as it affects their lives, beliefs, institutions and spiritual well-being and the lands they occupy or otherwise use, and to exercise control, to the extent possible, over their own economic, social and cultural development. In addition, they shall participate in the formulation of, implementation and evaluation of plans and programmes for national and regional development which may affect them directly.

2. The improvement of the conditions of life and work and levels of health and education of the peoples concerned, with their participation and co-operation, shall be a matter of priority in plans for the overall economic development of areas they inhabit. Special projects for development of the areas in question shall also be so designed as to promote such improvement.

3. Governments shall ensure that, whenever appropriate, studies are carried out, in co-operation with the peoples concerned, to assess the social, spiritual, cultural and environmental impact on them of planned development activities. The results of these studies shall be considered as fundamental criteria for the implementation of these activities.

4. Governments shall take measures, in co-operation with the peoples concerned, to protect and preserve the environment of the territories they inhabit.

Article 8

1. In applying national laws and regulations to the peoples concerned, due regard shall be had to their customs or customary laws.

2. These peoples shall have the right to retain their own customs and institutions, where these are not incompatible with fundamental rights defined by the national legal system and with internationally recognized human rights. Procedures shall be established, whenever necessary, to resolve conflicts which may arise in the application of this principle.

3. The application of paragraphs 1 and 2 of this Article shall not prevent members of these peoples from exercising the rights granted to all citizens and from assuming the corresponding duties.

Article 9

1. To the extent compatible with the national legal system and internationally recognized human rights, the methods customarily practised by the peoples concerned for dealing with offences committed by their members shall be respected.

2. The customs of these peoples in regard to penal matters shall be taken into consideration by the authorities and courts dealing with such cases.

Article 10

1. In imposing penalties laid down by general law on members of these peoples account shall be taken of their economic, social and cultural characteristics.

2. Preference shall be given to methods of punishment other than confinement in prison.

Article 11

The exaction from members of the peoples concerned of compulsory personal services in any form, whether paid or unpaid, shall be prohibited and punishable by law, except in cases prescribed by law for all citizens.

Article 12

The peoples concerned shall be safeguarded against the abuse of their rights and shall be able to take legal proceedings, either individually or through their representative bodies, for the effective protection of these rights. Measures shall be taken to ensure that members of these peoples can understand and be understood in legal proceedings, where necessary through the provision of interpretation or by other effective means.

Article 13

1. In applying the provisions of this Part of the Convention governments shall respect the special importance for the cultures and spiritual values of the peoples concerned of their relationship with the lands or territories, or both as applicable, which they occupy or otherwise use, and in particular the collective aspects of this relationship.

2. The use of the term 'lands' in Articles 15 and 16 shall include the concept of territories, which covers the total environment of the areas which the peoples concerned occupy or otherwise use.

Article 14

1. The rights of ownership and possession of the peoples concerned over the lands which they traditionally occupy shall be recognized. In addition, measures shall be taken in appropriate cases to safeguard the right of the peoples concerned to use lands not exclusively occupied by them, but to which they have traditionally had access for their subsistence and traditional activities. Particular attention shall be paid to the situation of nomadic peoples and shifting cultivators in this respect.

2. Governments shall take steps as necessary to identify the lands which the peoples concerned traditionally occupy, and to guarantee effective protection of their rights of ownership and possession.

3. Adequate procedures shall be established within the national legal system to resolve land claims by the peoples concerned.

Article 15

1. The rights of the peoples concerned to the natural resources pertaining to their lands shall be specially safeguarded. These rights include the right of these peoples to participate in the use, management and conservation of these resources.

2. In cases in which the state retains the ownership of mineral or sub-surface resources or rights to other resources pertaining to lands, governments shall establish or maintain procedures through which they shall consult these peoples, with a view to ascertaining whether and to what degree their interests would be prejudiced, before undertaking or permitting any programmes for the exploration or exploitation of such resources pertaining to their lands. The peoples concerned shall wherever possible participate in the benefits of such activities, and shall receive fair compensation for any damages which they may sustain as a result of such activities.

Article 16

1. Subject to the following paragraphs of this Article, the peoples concerned shall not be removed from the land which they occupy.

2. Where the relocation of these peoples is considered necessary as an exceptional measure, such relocation shall take place only with their free and informed consent. Where their consent cannot be obtained, such relocation shall take place only following appropriate procedures established by national laws and regulations, including public inquiries where appropriate, which provide the opportunity for effective representation of the peoples concerned.

3. Whenever possible, these peoples shall have the right to return to their traditional lands, as soon as the grounds for relocation cease to exist.

4. When such return is not possible, as determined by agreement or, in the absence of such agreement, through appropriate procedures these peoples shall be provided in all possible cases with lands of quality and legal status at least equal to that of the lands previously occupied by them, suitable to provide for their present needs and future development. Where the peoples concerned express a preference for compensation in money or in kind, they shall be so compensated under appropriate guarantees.

5. Persons thus relocated shall be fully compensated for any resulting loss or injury.

Article 17

1. Procedures established by the peoples concerned for the transmission of land rights among members of these peoples shall be respected.

2. The peoples concerned shall be consulted whenever consideration is being given to their capacity to alienate their lands or otherwise transmit their rights outside their own community.

3. Persons not belonging to these peoples shall be prevented from taking advantage of their customs or of lack of understanding of the laws on the part of their members to secure the ownership, possession or use of land belonging to them.

Article 18

Adequate penalties shall be established by law for unauthorized intrusion upon, or use of, the lands of the peoples concerned, and governments shall take measures to prevent such offences.

Article 19

National agrarian programmes shall secure to the peoples concerned treatment equivalent to that accorded to other sectors of the population with regard to:
(a) the provision of more land for these peoples when they have not the area necessary for providing the essentials of a normal existence, or for any possible increase in their numbers;
(b) the provision of the means required to promote the development of the lands which these peoples already possess.

PART III RECRUITMENT AND CONDITIONS OF EMPLOYMENT

Article 20

1. Governments shall, within the framework of national laws and regulations, and in co-operation with the peoples concerned, adopt special measures to ensure the effective protection with regard to recruitment and conditions of employment of workers belonging to these peoples, to the extent that they are not effectively protected by laws applicable to workers in general.

2. Governments shall do everything possible to prevent any discrimination between workers belonging to the peoples concerned and other workers, in particular as regards:
(a) admission to employment, including skilled employment, as well as measures for promotion and advancement;

(b) equal remuneration for work of equal value;

(c) medical and social assistance, occupational safety and health, all social security benefits and any other occupationally related benefits, and housing;

(d) the right of association and freedom for all lawful trade union activities, and the right to conclude collective agreements with employers or employers' organizations.

3. The measures taken shall include measures to ensure:

(a) that workers belonging to the peoples concerned, including seasonal, casual and migrant workers in agricultural and other employment, as well as those employed by labour contractors, enjoy the protection afforded by national law and practice to other such workers in the same sectors, and that they are fully informed of their rights under labour legislation and of the means of redress available to them;

(b) that workers belonging to these peoples are not subjected to working conditions hazardous to their health, in particular through exposure to pesticides or other toxic substances;

(c) that workers belonging to these peoples are not subjected to coercive recruitment systems, including bonded labour and other forms of debt servitude;

(d) that workers belonging to these peoples enjoy equal opportunities and equal treatment in employment for men and women, and protection from sexual harassment.

4. Particular attention shall be paid to the establishment of adequate labour inspection services in areas where workers belonging to the peoples concerned undertake wage employment, in order to ensure compliance with the provisions of this Part of this Convention.

PART IV VOCATIONAL TRAINING, HANDICRAFTS AND RURAL INDUSTRIES

Article 21

Members of the peoples concerned shall enjoy opportunities at least equal to those of other citizens in respect of vocational training measures.

Article 22

1. Measures shall be taken to promote the voluntary participation of members of the peoples concerned in vocational training programmes of general applications.

2. Whenever existing programmes of vocational training of general application do not meet the special needs of the peoples concerned, governments shall, with the participation of these peoples, ensure the provision of special training programmes and facilities.

3. Any special training programmes shall be based on the economic environment, social and cultural conditions and practical needs of the peoples concerned. Any studies made in this connection shall be carried out in co-operation with these peoples, who shall be consulted on the organization and operation of such programmes. Where feasible, these peoples shall progressively assume responsibility for the organization and operation of such special training programmes, if they so decide.

Article 23

1. Handicrafts, rural and community-based industries, and subsistence economy and traditional activities of the peoples concerned, such as hunting, fishing, trapping and gathering, shall be recognized as important factors in the maintenance of their cultures and in their economic self-reliance and developments. Governments shall, with the participation of these peoples and whenever appropriate, ensure that these activities are strengthened and promoted.

2. Upon the request of the peoples concerned, appropriate technical and financial assistance shall be provided wherever possible, taking into account the traditional technologies and cultural characteristics of these peoples, as well as the importance of sustainable and equitable development.

PART V SOCIAL SECURITY AND HEALTH

Article 24

Social security schemes shall be extended progressively to cover the peoples concerned, and applied without discrimination against them.

Article 25

1. Governments shall ensure that adequate health services are made available to the peoples concerned, or shall provide them with resources to allow them to design and deliver such services under their own responsibility and control, so that they may enjoy the highest attainable standard of physical and mental health.

2. Health services shall, to the extent possible, be community-based. These services shall be planned and administered in co-operation with the peoples concerned and take into account their economic, geographic, social and cultural conditions as well as their traditional preventive care, healing practices and medicines.

3. The health care system shall give preference to the training and employment of local community health workers, and focus on primary health care while maintaining strong links with other levels of health care services.

4. The provision of such health services shall be co-ordinated with other social, economic and cultural measures in the country.

PART VI EDUCATION AND MEANS OF COMMUNICATION

Article 26

Measures shall be taken to ensure that members of the peoples concerned have the opportunity to acquire education at all levels on at least an equal footing with the rest of the national community.

Article 27

1. Education programmes and services for the peoples concerned shall be developed and implemented in co-operation with them to address their special needs, and shall incorporate their histories, their knowledge and technologies, their value systems and their further social, economic and cultural aspirations.

2. The competent authority shall ensure the training of members of these peoples and their involvement in the formulation and implementation of education programmes, with a view to the progressive transfer of responsibility for the conduct of these programmes to these peoples as appropriate.

3. In addition, governments shall recognize the right of these peoples to establish their own educational institutions and facilities, provided that such institutions meet minimum standards established by the competent authority in consultation with these peoples. Appropriate resources shall be provided for this purpose.

Article 28

1. Children belonging to the peoples concerned shall, wherever practicable, be taught to read and write in their own indigenous language or in the language most commonly used by the group to which they belong. When this is not practicable, the competent authorities shall undertake consultations with these peoples with a view to the adoption of measures to achieve this objective.

2. Adequate measures shall be taken to ensure that these peoples have the opportunity to attain fluency in the national language or in one of the official languages of the country.

3. Measures shall be taken to preserve and promote the development and practice of the indigenous languages of the peoples concerned.

Article 29

The imparting of general knowledge and skills that will help children belonging to the peoples concerned to participate fully and on an equal footing in their own community and in the national community shall be an aim of education for these peoples.

Article 30

1. Governments shall adopt measures appropriate to the traditions and cultures of the peoples concerned, to make known to them their rights and duties, especially in regard to labour, economic opportunities, education and health matters, social welfare and their rights deriving from this Convention.

2. If necessary, this shall be done by means of written translations and through the use of mass communications in the languages of these peoples.

Article 31

Educational measures shall be taken among all sections of the national community, and particularly among those that are in most direct contact with the peoples concerned, with the object of eliminating prejudices that they may harbour in respect of these peoples. To this end, efforts shall be made to ensure that history textbooks and other educational materials provide a fair, accurate and informative portrayal of the societies and cultures of these peoples.

PART VII CONTACTS AND CO-OPERATION ACROSS BORDERS

Article 32

Governments shall take appropriate measures, including by means of international agreements, to facilitate contacts and co-operation between indigenous and tribal peoples across borders, including activities in the economic, social, cultural, spiritual and environmental fields.

PART VIII ADMINISTRATION

Article 33

1. The governmental authority responsible for the matters covered in this Convention shall ensure that agencies or other appropriate mechanisms exist to administer the programme affecting the peoples concerned, and shall ensure that they have the means necessary for the proper fulfilment of the functions assigned to them.

2. These programmes shall include:

(a) the planning, co-ordination, execution and evaluation, in co-operation with the peoples concerned, of the measures provided for in this Convention;

(b) the proposing of legislative and other measures to the competent authorities and supervision of the application of the measures taken, in co-operation with the peoples concerned.

PART IX GENERAL PROVISIONS

Article 34

The nature and scope of the measures to be taken to give effect to this Convention shall be determined in a flexible manner, having regard to the conditions characteristic of each country.

Article 35

The application of the provisions of this Convention shall not adversely affect rights and benefits of the peoples concerned pursuant to other Conventions and Recommendations, international instruments, treaties, or national laws, awards, customs or agreements.

PART X FINAL PROVISIONS

Article 36

This Convention revises the Indigenous and Tribal Populations Convention, 1957.

Article 37

The formal ratification of this Convention shall be communicated to the Director-General of the International Labour Office for registration.

Article 38

1. This Convention shall be binding only upon those members of the International Labour Organization whose ratifications have been registered with the Director-General.

2. It shall come into force twelve months after the date on which the ratifications of two Members have been registered with the Director-General.

3. Thereafter, this Convention shall come into force for any Member twelve months after the date on which its ratification has been registered.

Article 39

1. A Member which has ratified this Convention may denounce it after the expiration of ten years from the date on which the Convention first comes into force, by an act communicated to the Director-General of the International Labour Office for registration. Such denunciation shall not take effect until one year after the date on which it is registered.

2. Each Member which has ratified this Convention and which does not, within the year following the expiration of the period of ten years mentioned in the preceding paragraph, exercise the right of denunciation provided for in this Article, will be bound for another period of ten years and, thereafter, may denounce this Convention at the expiration of each period of ten years under the terms provided for in this Article.

Article 40

1. The Director-General of the International Labour Office shall notify all the Members of the International Labour Organization of the registration of all ratifications and denunciations communicated to him by the Members of the Organization.

2. When notifying the Members of the Organization of the registration of the second ratification communicated to him, the Director-General shall draw the attention of the Members of the Organization to the date upon which the Convention will come into force.

Article 41

The Director-General of the International Labour Office shall communicate to the Secretary-General of the United Nations for registration in accordance with Article 102 of the Charter of the United Nations full particulars of all ratifications and acts of denunciation registered by him in accordance with the provisions of the preceding Articles.

Article 42

At such times as it may consider necessary the Governing Body of the International Labour Office shall present to the General Conference a report on the working of this Convention and shall examine the desirability of placing on the agenda of the Conference the question of its revision in whole or in part.

Article 43

1. Should the Conference adopt a new Convention revising this Convention in whole or in part, then, unless the new Convention otherwise provides –
(a) the ratification of a Member of the new revising Convention shall ipso jure involve the immediate denunciation of this Convention, notwithstanding the provisions of Article 39 above, if and when the new revising Convention shall have come into force;
(b) as from the date when the new revising Convention comes into force this Convention shall cease to be open to ratification by the Members.

2. This Convention shall in any case remain in force in its actual form and content for those Members which have ratified it but have not ratified the revising Convention.

Article 44

The English and French versions of the text of this Convention are equally authoritative.

In accordance with the commentary to Article 1 of the Code of Conduct for Law Enforcement Officials, the term 'law enforcement officials' includes all officers of the law, whether appointed or elected, who exercise police powers, especially the powers of arrest or detention. In countries where police powers are exercised by military authorities, whether uniformed or not, or by state security forces, the definition of law enforcement officials shall be regarded as including officers of such services.

APPENDIX 14

NGOS

(Characters in bold after the organization's title indicate its consultative status)

GENERAL

Amnesty International (II),
1 Easton Street, London WC1X 8DJ, UK
Tel: (44) 171 413 5500; Fax: (44) 171 956 1157
15, route des Morillons, 1218 Grand-Saconnex, Geneva, SWITZERLAND
Tel: (41) 22 798 2500   Fax: (41) 22 791 0390

International Federation of Human Rights
(Fédération des Droits de L'Homme – FIDH) (II)
14 Passage Dubail, 75010 Paris, FRANCE
Tel: (33) 1 40 37 54 26   Fax: (33) 1 44 72 05 86

Human Rights Internet (II)
8 York St., Suite 202, Ottawa, Ontario K1N 6N5 CANADA
Tel: (1-613) 789 7407   Fax: (1-613) 789 7414

Lawyers for Human Rights
730 Van Erkom Building, 217 Pretorius St., Pretoria 0002
Republic of South Africa
Tel: (27-12) 21 2135   Fax: (27-12) 32 56318

Human Rights Watch
485 Fifth Avenue – 3rd Floor, New York NY 10017, USA
Tel: (1) 212 972 8400   Fax: (1) 212 972 0905

LABOUR

International Labour Organization (ILO)
Application of Standards Branch, CH-1211, Geneva 22, SWITZERLAND
Tel: (41) 22 799 7154   Fax: (41) 22 798 8685

International Confederation of Free Trade Unions (I)
37-41 rue Montagne-aux-Herbes-Potagäres, B-1000 Bruxelles, BELGIUM
Tel: (32) 217 80 85   Fax: (32) 218 84 15

WAR

International Committee of the Red Cross (ICRC) (II)
17 Avenue de la Paix, 1211 Geneva, SWITZERLAND
Tel: (41) 22 734 6001   Fax: (41) 22 734 8280
9 Downie Ave., PO Box 3970, Harare, Zimbabwe
Tel: (263) 79 0268/9   Fax: (263) 79 0260

MINES

Mines Advisory Group
54A Main Street, Cockermouth, Cumbria CA13 9LU, UK
Tel: (44) 1900 828580   Fax: (44) 1900 827088

CHILDREN

Radda Barnen
Torsgaten 4, S-107 88, Stockholm, SWEDEN
Tel: (46-8) 698 9000   Fax: (46-8) 698 9010

Save The Children (SCF)
Mary Datchelor House, 17 Grove Lane, Camberwell,
London SE5 8RD, UK
Tel: (44) 171 703 5400   Fax: (44) 171 703 2278

Street Kids International
56 The Esplanade, Suite 202, Toronto, Ontario M5E 1A7 CANADA
Tel: (1-416) 861 1816   Fax: (1-416) 861 9386

DISAPPEARANCE AND PRISONERS OF CONSCIENCE

Amnesty International (see above)

PRESS AND FREEDOM OF EXPRESSION

Article 19
33 Islington High St., London N1 9LH UK
Tel: (44) 171 278 9292   Fax: (44) 171 713 1356

Index on Censorship
32 Queen Victoria St., London EC4N 4SS, UK
Tel: (44) 171 329 6434   Fax: (44) 171 329 6461

International P.E.N. (In consultative status with UNESCO)
9/10 Charterhouse Buildings, Goswell Road, London EC1 M7AT
Tel: (44) 171 253 4308   Fax: (44) 171 253 5711

Reporters Sans Frontiéres
17, rue Abbé de l'Epée, 34000 Montpellier, FRANCE
Tel: (33) 67 79 81 82   Fax: (33) 67 79 60 80

International Federation of Journalists – IFJ – (II)
266 rue Royale, 1210 Brussels, BELGIUM
Tel: (32-2) 223 2265   Fax: (32-2) 219 2976

MEDICAL

World Medical Association (WMA)
BP 63-01212, Feley-Voltaire, Cedex, FRANCE

Physicians for Human Rights (PHR)
100 Boylston St., Suite 702, Boston, MA 02116, USA
Tel: (1-617) 695 0041   Fax: (1-617) 695 0307

RULE OF LAW

International Commission of Jurists – ICJ – (II)
PO Box 160, 26 Chemin de Joinville, 1216 Cointrin, Geneva, SWITZERLAND
Tel: (41) 22 788 4747   Fax: (41) 22 788 4880

International Bar Association (II)
2 Harewood Place, Hannover Square, London W1R 9HB UK
Tel: (44) 171 629 1206   Fax: (44) 171 409 0456

Interights
Lancaster House, 33 Islington High St., London N1 9LH, UK
Tel: (44) 171 278 3230   Fax: (44) 171 278 4334

MINORITIES

International Work Group for Indigenous Affairs (II)
Fiolstraede 10, 1171 Copenhagen K, DENMARK
Tel (45) 33 12 4724   Fax: (45) 33 14 7749

Minority Rights Group (Ros)
379 Brixton Road, London SW9 7DE, UK
Tel: (44) 171 978 9498   Fax: (44) 171 738 6265

Survival International (Ros)
310 Edgware Road, London W2 1DY
Tel: (44) 171 723 5535   Fax: (44) 171 723 4059

PARLIAMENT

Inter-Parliamentary Union (IPU)
Place du Petit-Saconnex, CP 438, CH-1211 Geneva 19, SWITZERLAND
Tel: (41) 22 734 4150   Fax: (41) 22 733 3141

Parliamentary Human Rights Group
House of Lords, London SW1A OAA, UK
Fax: (44) 171 738 7864

PRISONS

International Committee of the Red Cross (see above)
Henry Dunant Institute
114, Ave de Lausanne, 1202 Geneva, SWITZERLAND
Tel: (41-22) 731 5310   Fax: (41-22) 732 0233

Penal Reform International (PRI)
169 Clapham Road, London SW9 OPU, UK
Tel: (44) 171 582 6500   Fax: (44) 171 735 4666

International Prison Watch
5, rue Victor Hugo, BP21258, Dakar-Ponty, SENEGAL
Tel: (221) 21 2060   Fax: (221) 21 2055

SLAVERY

Anti-Slavery International for the Protection of Human Rights (II)
180 Brixton Road, London SW9 6AT, UK
Tel: (44) 171 582 4040; Fax: (44) 171 956 1157

TORTURE

Amnesty International (see above)
Organization Mondiale Contre la Torture – SOS Torture (OMCT)
PO Box 119, CH-1211 Geneva 20, SWITZERLAND
Tel: (41) 22 733 3140   Fax: (41) 22 733 1051

Association for the Prevention of Torture (APT)
Rue de Ferney 10, CP2267, CH-1211 Geneva, SWITZERLAND
Tel: (41-22) 734 20 88   Fax: (41-22) 734 56 49

UNITED NATIONS

Raymonde Martineau
NGO Liaison Office, Room 176-2, Palais des Nations, CH-1211 Geneva 10, SWITZERLAND
Tel: (41) 22 917 2127   Fax: (41) 22 917 0001

Beatrice Murebwayire,
NGO Liaison Office in the Centre for Human Rights, Room A-505, Palais des Nations (as above)
Tel: (41) 22 917 1143

International Service for Human Rights (II)
1 rue de Varembé, PO Box 16, 1211 Geneva, SWITZERLAND
Tel: (41) 22 733 5123   Fax: (41) 22 733 0826

UN Centre for Human Rights
Special Rapporteur/Working Group on . . .
United Nations Office at Geneva, 8-14 Avenue de la Paix, 1211
Geneva 10, SWITZERLAND
Tel: (41) 22 917 4211   Fax: (41) 22 917 0123
Human Rights Fax Hotline: (41) 22 917 0092

REGIONAL

Inter-American Commission on Human Rights
1889 F Street, NW, Washington, DC 20006 USA
Tel: (1-202) 428 3967

European Commission of Human Rights,
Conseil de l'Europe, BP 431 R6, 67006 Strasbourg Cedex, FRANCE
Tel: (33) 88 61 49 61   Fax: (33) 88 36 70 57 or 35 19 61

African Commission on Human and Peoples' Rights
Kairaba Ave., PO Box 673, Banjul, THE GAMBIA
Tel: (220) 392 962   Fax: (220) 390 764

REFUGEES

United Nations High Commissioner for Refugees (UNHCR)
CP-2500, CH 1211 Geneva, SWITZERLAND
Tel: (41) 22 739 8111   Fax: (41) 22 731 9546

APPENDIX 15

APC E-MAIL NETWORK

The APC International Secretariat
Rua Vincente de Souza, 29
fax: +55(21)286 0541
22251-070 Rio de Janeiro
BRAZIL
tel: +55(21)286 4467
Email:apcadmin@apc.org

AlterNex – IBASE
as above
Email:support@ax.apc.org

APC North American Regional Office
18 De Boom Street,
San Francisco, CA 94107
USA
tel: +1(415)442 0220
fax: +1(415)546 1794

Chasque
Casilla Correo 1539,
Montevideo 11000
URUGUAY
tel:+598(2)496192
fax: +598(2)419222
Email:apoyo@chasque.apc.org

ComLink e. V
Emil-Meyer-Str. 20,
D-30165 Hannover, GERMANY
tel: +49(511)350 1573
Email:support@oln.comlink.apc.org

Ecuanex
12 de Octubre 622, Of. 504
Casilla 1712566,
Quito, ECUADOR
tel: +593(2)528 716
fax: +593(2)505 073
Email:intercom@ecuanex.apc.org

GlasNet
ulitsa Sadovaya-Chernogriazskaya
dom 4, Komnata 16, third floor, 107078
Moscow, RUSSIA
tel:+7(095)207 0704
fax:+7(095)2070889
Email:support@glas.apc.org

GreenNet
23 Bevenden Street,
London N1 6BH ENGLAND
tel: +44(71)608 3040
fax: +44(71)253 0801
Email:support@gn.apc.org

**Institute for Global Communications
(IGC)**
same as above
Email:support@igc.apc.org

Nicarao – CRIES
Apartado 3516
Iglesia Carmen 1 cuadra al lago
Managua, NICARAGUA
tel: +505(2)621 312
fax: +505(2)621 244
Email:ayuda@nicarao.apc.org

NordNet
HuvudskÑrsvÑgen 13 nb
S-12154 Johanneshov, SWEDEN
tel: +46(8) 6000 331
fax:+46(8)6000443
Email:support@pns.apc.org

Pegasus
PO Box 284
Broadway 4006
Queensland, AUSTRALIA
tel: +61(7) 257 1111
fax: +61(7) 257 1087
Email:support@peg.apc.org

Web – NirvCentre
401 Richmond Street West
Suite 104
Toronto, Ontario, M5V 3A8
CANADA
tel: +1(416) 596 0212
fax: +1(416) 596 1374
Email:support@web.apc.org

The networks cover the various regions of the globe in the following way:

AlterNex	– Brazil, South America
Chasque	– Uruguay, Argentina, Paraguay
ComLink	– Germany, Austria, Switzerland, Zagreb, Beograd, Northern Italy
EcuaNex	– Ecuador
GlasNet	– Russia, Commonwealth of Independent States' countries
GreenNet	– Great Britain, Europe, Africa, Asia
IGC	– USA, Mexico, China, Japan, Middle East
Nicarao	– Nicaragua, Central America, Panama
NordNet	– The Nordic, Baltic, St Petersburg region
Pegasus	– Australia, Pacific Islands
SE Asia Web	– Canada, Cuba

Other members of the network are listed below. To get started contact any of these. If you are unsure contact the APC Secretariat for advice either in Rio or in San Francisco.

Europe:

GLUK – GlasNet-Ukraine,
14b Metrologicheskaya Str
Kiev, 252143 Ukraine
tel: +7(044) 266 9481
fax: +7(044) 266 9475
Email: support@gluk.apc.org

Antenna Netherlands
Box 1513
NL-6501 BM Nijmegen
NETHERLANDS
tel: +31(80) 235372
fax: +31(80) 236798
Email:support@antenna.nl

Histria (ABM-BBS)
Ziherlova 43
61 Ljubljana,
SLOVENIA
tel: +386(61) 211533
fax: +386(61) 152 107
Email:support@histria.apc.org

Africa:

SangoNet
13 Floor Longsbank Building
PO Box 31, Johannesburg 2000,
SOUTH AFRICA
tel: +27-11-838 6944
fax: +27-11-838 6310
Email:support@wn.apc.org

Asia/Pacific:

Email Centre
108 V.Luna Road,
Sikatuna Village,
Quezon City
PHILIPPINES
tel: +632 921 9976
Email:sysop@phil.gn.apc.org

IndiaLink Bombay
YUVA, 33/8L Mughbat X Lane,
Thakurdwar, Charni Road,
Bombay 400004, INDIA
tel: +91(22) 388 9811
Email:yuva@inbb.gn.apc.org

IndiaLink New Delhi
Leo Fernandez,
Indian Social Institute,
10 Lodi Road,
Institutional Road,
New Delhi, INDIA
tel: +91 11 462 2379
fax: +91 11 469 0660
Email:leo@unv.ernet.in

Latin America:

Wamani
CCI Talcahuano 325-3F
1013 Buenos Aires,
ARGENTINA
tel: +54(1) 35 68 42
Email:apoyo@wamani.apc.org

CHART OF RATIFICATIONS

States	International Covenant on Economic, Social and Cultural Rights (1)	International Covenant on Civil and Political Rights (2)	Optional Protocol to the International Covenant on Civil and Political Rights (3)	Second Optional Protocol to the International Covenant on Civil and Political Rights aiming at the abolition of the death penalty (4)	International Convention on the Elimination of All Forms of Racial Discrimination (5)	International Convention on the Suppression and Punishment of the Crime of Apartheid (6)	International Convention against Apartheid in Sports (7)	Convention on the Prevention and Punishment of the Crime of Genocide (8)	Convention on the Non-Applicability of Statutory Limitations to War Crimes and Crimes against Humanity (9)	Convention on the Rights of the Child (10)	Convention on the Elimination of All Forms of Discrimination against Women (11)	Convention on the Political Rights of Women (12)	Convention on the Nationality of Married Women (13)	Convention on Consent to Marriage, Minimum Age for Marriage and Registration of Marriages (14)
Afghanistan	X	X			X	X		X	X	X	s	X		
Albania	X	X			X			X	X	X	X	X	X	
Algeria	X	X^a	X		X^b	X	X	X		X	X			
Angola	X	X	X				X	X		X	X	X		
Antigua and Barbuda					X	X	X	X		X	X	X	X	X
Argentina	X	X^a	X		X	X		X		X	X	X	X	X
Armenia	X	X	X		X	X		X	X	X	X	X		
Australia	X	X^a	X	X	X^b			X		X	X	X	X	
Austria	X	X^a	X	X	X			X		X	X	X	X	X
Azerbaijan	X	X								X				
Bahamas					X	X	X	X		X	X	X	X	
Bahrain					X	X		X		X				
Bangladesh					X					X	X			
Barbados	X	X	X		X	X	X	X		X	X	X	X	X
Belarus	X	X^a	X		X	X	X	X	X	X	X	X	X	
Belgium	X	X^a	X	s	X			X		X	X	X	s	
Belize										X	X			
Benin	X	X	X		s	X	s			X	X			X
Bhutan					s					X	X			
Bolivia	X	X	X		X	X	X	s	X	X	s	X		
Bosnia Herzegovina	X	X^a			X	X	X	X	X	X	X	X	X	X
Botswana					X					X				
Brazil	X	X			X			X		X	X			X
Brunei Darussalam														
Bulgaria	X	X^a	X		X^b	X	X	X	X	X	X	X	X	
Burkina Faso					X	X	X	X		X	X			X
Burma, *see* Myanmar														
Burundi	X	X			X	X	s			X	X	X		
Cambodia	X	X			X	X		X		X	X			
Cameroon	X	X	X		X	X	s		X	X	X			
Canada	X	X^a	X		X			X		X	X	X	X	
Cape Verde	X	X			X	X	s			X	X			
Central African Republic	X	X	X		X	X	s			X		X		
Chad					X	X				X				
Chile	X	X^a	X		X			X		X	X	X	s	s
China					X	X	s	X		X	X			
Colombia	X	X	X		X	X	s	X		X	X	X	s	
Comoros										X	X			
Congo	X	X^a	X		X	X				X	X			
Costa Rica	X	X	X	s	X^b	X		X		X	X	X		
Côte d'Ivoire	X	X			X					X	s			
Croatia	X	X			X	X	X	X	X	X	X	X	X	X
Cuba					X	X	X	X	X	X	X	X	X	
Cyprus	X	X	X		X^b		s			X	X	X	X	
Czech Republic	X	X	X		X	X	X	X	X	X	X	X	X	X

Convention against Torture and other Cruel, Inhuman or Degrading Treatment or Punishment	Slavery Convention of 1926	1953 Protocol amending the 1926 Convention	Slavery Convention of 1926 as amended	Supplementary Convention on the Abolition of Slavery, the Slave Trade, and Institutions and Practices Similar to Slavery	Convention for the Suppression of the Traffic in Persons and of the Exploitation of the Prostitution of others	Convention on the Reduction of Statelessness	Convention relating to the Status of Stateless Persons	Convention relating to the Status of Refugees	Protocol relating to the Status of Refugees	Convention on the rights of migrant workers and the members of their families				States
(15)	(16)	(17)	(18)	(19)	(20)	(21)	(22)	(23)	(24)	(25)	(26)	(27)	(28)	States
X	X	X	X	X	X									Afghanistan
X	s		X	X	X			X	X					Albania
X^c			X	X	X		X	X	X					Algeria
								X	X					Angola
X^c	X	X	X	X			X							Antigua and Barbuda
X^c					X		X	X	X					Argentina
X							X	X	X					Armenia
X^c	X	X	X	X		X	X	X	X					Australia
X^c	X	X	X	X			X	X	X					Austria
								X	X					Azerbaijan
	X	X	X	X				X	X					Bahamas
			X	X										Bahrain
	X	X	X	X	X									Bangladesh
	X	X	X	X			X							Barbados
X			X	X	X									Belarus
s	X	X	X	X	X		X	X	X					Belgium
X	X							X	X					Belize
X								X	X					Benin
														Bhutan
s	X	X	X	X	X	X	X	X	X					Bolivia
X		X	X	X	X		X	X	X					Bosnia Herzegovina
							X	X	X					Botswana
X			X	X	X		s	X	X					Brazil
														Brunei Darussalam
X^c	X			X	X			X	X					Bulgaria
					X			X	X					Burkina Faso
														Burma, *see* Myanmar
X								X	X					Burundi
X				X				X	X					Cambodia
X	X	X	X	X	X	X		X	X					Cameroon
X^c	X	X	X	X		X		X	X					Canada
X	X								X					Cape Verde
	X			X	X			X	X					Central African Republic
								X	X					Chad
X	X	X		X				X	X	s				Chile
X	s							X	X					China
X							s	X	X					Colombia
														Comoros
	X			X	X			X	X					Congo
X	X			X	X	X	X	X	X					Costa Rica
	X			X			X	X	X					Côte d'Ivoire
X^c	X	X	X	X	X		X	X	X					Croatia
s	X	X	X	X	X									Cuba
X			X	X	X			X	X					Cyprus
X	X			X	X			X	X					Czech Republic

States	International Covenant on Economic, Social and Cultural Rights (1)	International Covenant on Civil and Political Rights (2)	Optional Protocol to the International Covenant on Civil and Political Rights (3)	Second Optional Protocol to the International Covenant on Civil and Political Rights aiming at the abolition of the death penalty (4)	International Convention on the Elimination of All Forms of Racial Discrimination (5)	International Convention on the Suppression and Punishment of the Crime of Apartheid (6)	International Convention against Apartheid in Sports (7)	Convention on the Prevention and Punishment of the Crime of Genocide (8)	Convention on the Non-Applicability of Statutory Limitations to War Crimes and Crimes against Humanity (9)	Convention on the Rights of the Child (10)	Convention on the Elimination of All Forms of Discrimination against Women (11)	Convention on the Political Rights of Women (12)	Convention on the Nationality of Married Women (13)	Convention on Consent to Marriage, Minimum Age for Marriage and Registration of Marriages (14)
Dem. People's Rep of Korea	X	X						X	X	X				
Denmark	X	X^a	X	X	X^b			X		X	X	X	X	X
Djibouti										X				
Dominica	X	X								X				
Dominican Republic	X	X	X		X			s		X	X	X	X	X
Ecuador	X	X^a	X	X	X^b	X	X	X		X	X	X	X	
Egypt	X	X			X	X	X	X		X	X	X		
El Salvador	X	X	s		X	X		X		X	X	s		
Equatorial Guinea	X	X	X				X			X	X			
Eritrea										X				
Estonia	X	X	X		X	X	X	X	X	X	X			
Ethiopia	X	X			X	X	X	X		X	X	X		
Fed. States of Micronesia										X				
Fiji					X			X		X		X	X	X
Finland	X	X^a	X	X	X			X		X	X	X	X	X
France	X	X	X		X^b			X		X	X	X		s
Gabon	X	X			X	X	s	X		X	X	X		
Gambia	X	X^a	X		X	X		X	X	X	X			
Georgia	X	X	X					X		X	X			
Germany	X	X^a	X	X	X	X*	X*	X	X*	X	X	X	X	
Ghana					X	X	X	X		X	X	X	X	
Greece	X				X			X		X	X	X		s
Grenada	X	X			s					X	X			
Guatemala	X	X			X			X		X	X	X	X	X
Guinea	X	X	X		X	X	X	X	X	X	X	X	s	X
Guinea-Bissau	X						s			X	X			
Guyana	X	X^a	X		X	X	X			X	X			
Haiti		X			X	X	s	X		s	X	X		
Holy See					X					X				
Honduras	X	s	s	s				X		X	X			
Hungary	X	X^a	X	X	X^b	X	s	X	X	X	X	X	X	X
Iceland	X	X^a	X	X	X^b			X		X	X	X	X	X
India	X	X			X	X	X	X	X	X	X	X	s	
Indonesia							X			X	X	X		
Iran (Islamic Rep.)	X	X			X	X	X	X		X				
Iraq	X	X			X	X	X	X		X	X			
Ireland	X		X	X	s			X		X	X	X	X	
Israel	X	X^a	X		X			X		X	X	X	X	s
Italy	X	X^a	X	s	X^b			X		X	X	X		s

Convention against Torture and other Cruel, Inhuman or Degrading Treatment or Punishment	Slavery Convention of 1926	1953 Protocol amending the 1926 Convention	Slavery Convention of 1926 as amended	Supplementary Convention on the Abolition of Slavery, the Slave Trade, and Institutions and Practices Similar to Slavery	Convention for the Suppression of the Traffic in Persons and of the Exploitation of the Prostitution of others	Convention on the Reduction of Statelessness	Convention relating to the Status of Stateless Persons	Convention relating to the Status of Refugees	Protocol relating to the Status of Refugees	Convention on the rights of migrant workers and the members of their families			States
(15)	(16)	(17)	(18)	(19)	(20)	(21)	(22)	(23)	(24)	(25)	(26)	(27)	(28)
													Dem. People's Rep of Korea
X	X	X	X	X	s	X	X	X	X				Denmark
	X		X	X	X			X	X				Dijbouti
	X	X	X	X				X	X				Dominica
s	s			X		s		X	X				Dominican Republic
X[c]	X	X	X	X	X		X	X	X				Ecuador
X	X	X	X	X	X			X	X	X			Egypt
			s		s	s	X	X	X				El Salvador
							X	X	X				Equatorial Guinea
													Eritrea
X													Estonia
X			X	X	X			X	X				Ethiopia
													Fed. States of Micronesia
	X	X	X	X			X	X	X				Fiji
X[c]	X	X	X	X	X		X	X	X				Finland
X[c]	X	X	X	X	X	s	X	X	X				France
s								X	X				Gabon
s								X	X				Gambia
X													Georgia
X	X	X	X	X	X*	X	X	X	X				Germany
	X			X				X	X				Ghana
X[c]	X	X	X	X				X	X				Greece
													Grenada
X	X	X	X	X			s	X	X				Guatemala
X	X	X	X	X	X		X	X	X				Guinea
								X	X				Guinea-Bissau
X													Guyana
	X			X	X			X	X				Haiti
							s	X	X				Holy See
				X	X		s	X	X				Honduras
X[c]	X	X	X	X	X			X	X				Hungary
s				X				X	X				Iceland
	X	X	X	X	X								India
s													Indonesia
		s		X	s			X	X				Iran (Islamic Rep.)
	X	X	X	X									Iraq
s	X	X	X	X		X	X	X	X				Ireland
X	X	X	X	X	X	s		X	X				Israel
X[c]	X	X	X	X	X		X	X	X				Italy

States	(1)	(2)	(3)	(4)	(5)	(6)	(7)	(8)	(9)	(10)	(11)	(12)	(13)	(14)
International Covenant on Economic, Social and Cultural Rights	International Covenant on Civil and Political Rights	Optional Protocol to the International Covenant on Civil and Political Rights	Second Optional Protocol to the International Covenant on Civil and Political Rights aiming at the abolition of the death penalty	International Convention on the Elimination of All Forms of Racial Discrimination	International Convention on the Suppression and Punishment of the Crime of Apartheid	International Convention against Apartheid in Sports	Convention on the Prevention and Punishment of the Crime of Genocide	Convention on the Non-Applicability of Statutory Limitations to War Crimes and Crimes against Humanity	Convention on the Rights of the Child	Convention on the Elimination of All Forms of Discrimination against Women	Convention on the Political Rights of Women	Convention on the Nationality of Married Women	Convention on Consent to Marriage, Minimum Age for Marriage and Registration of Marriages	
Jamaica	X	X	X		X	X	X	X		X	X	X	X	
Japan	X	X								X	X	X	X	
Jordan	X	X			X	X	X	X		X	X	X	X	X
Kazakhstan										X				
Kenya	X	X					s	s	X	X	X			
Kiribati														
Kuwait					X	X				X	X			
Kyrgyzstan	X	X	X							X	X			
Lao People's Dem. Rep.					X	X		X	X	X	X	X		
Latvia	X	X	X		X	X	X	X	X	X	X	X	X	
Lebanon	X	X			X		s	X		X		X		
Lesotho	X	X			X	X		X		X	s	X	X	
Liberia	s	s			X	X	s	X		X	X	s		
Libyan Arab Jamahiriya	X	X	X		X	X	X	X	X	X	X	X	X	
Liechtenstein								X		s				
Lithuania	X	X	X							X	X			
Luxembourg	X	X^a	X	X	X			X		X	X	X	X	
Macedonia (The former Yugoslav Republic of)	X	X			X					X	X		X	
Madagascar	X	X	X		X	X	s			X	X	X		X
Malawi	X	X								X	X	X		X
Malaysia							s	X		X				X
Maldives					X	X	s	X		X	X			
Mali	X	X			X	X	X	X		X	X	X	X	X
Malta	X	X^a	X	X	X					X				
Marshall Islands										X				
Mauritania					X	X	X			X		X		
Mauritius	X	X	X		X	X				X	X	X	X	
Mexico	X	X			X	X	X	X	s	X		X	X	X
Monaco								X		X				
Mongolia	X	X	X		X	X	X	X	X	X	X	X		X
Morocco	X	X			X		s	X		X	X	X		
Mozambique		X		X	X	X		X		X				
Myanmar								X		X		s		
Namibia	X	X	X	X	X	X		X		X	X			
Nauru										X				
Nepal	X	X	X		X	X	X	X		X	X	X		
Netherlands	X	X^a	X	X	X	X^b		X		X	s	X	X	X
New Zealand	X	X^a	X	X	X			X		X	X	X	X	X
Nicaragua	X	X	X	s	X	X	s	X	X	X	X	X		X
Niger	X	X	X		X	X	X	X		X	X	X		X
Nigeria	X	X			X	X		X	X	X	X	X		
Norway	X	X^a	X	X	X^b	X		X	X	X	X	X	X	X

Convention against Torture and other Cruel, Inhuman or Degrading Treatment or Punishment	Slavery Convention of 1926	1953 Protocol amending the 1926 Convention	Slavery Convention of 1926 as amended	Supplementary Convention on the Abolition of Slavery, the Slave Trade, and Institutions and Practices Similar to Slavery	Convention for the Suppression of the Traffic in Persons and of the Exploitation of the Prostitution of others	Convention on the Reduction of Statelessness	Convention relating to the Status of Stateless Persons	Convention relating to the Status of Refugees	Protocol relating to the Status of Refugees	Convention on the rights of migrant workers and the members of their families				States
(15)	(16)	(17)	(18)	(19)	(20)	(21)	(22)	(23)	(24)	(25)	(26)	(27)	(28)	
			X	X				X	X					Jamaica
					X			X	X					Japan
X			X	X	X									Jordan
														Kazakhstan
								X	X					Kenya
				X			X							Kiribati
			X	X	X									Kuwait
														Kyrgyzstan
														Lao People's Dem. Rep.
X				X	X	X								Latvia
	X													Lebanon
			X	X			X	X	X					Lesotho
	X		X	s	s		X	X	X					Liberia
X[c]			X	X	X	X	X							Libyan Arab Jamahiriya
			X				s	X	X					Liechtenstein
X[c]				X	X		X	X	X					Lithuania
X[c]			X	X	X		X	X	X					Luxembourg
								X	X					Macedonia (The former Yugoslav Republic of)
			X	X	X			X						Madagascar
			X	X	X			X	X					Malawi
				X										Malaysia
														Maldives
	X	X	X	X	X			X	X					Mali
X[c]	X	X	X	X				X	X					Malta
														Marshall Islands
	X	X	X	X	X			X	X					Mauritania
			X	X										Mauritius
X	X	X	X	X	X					s				Mexico
X[c]	X	X	X					X		s				Monaco
			X	X										Mongolia
X	X	X	X	X				X	X	X				Morocco
								X	X					Mozambique
	X	X	X		s									Myanmar
X														Namibia
														Nauru
X			X	X										Nepal
X[c]	X	X	X	X		X	X	X	X					Netherlands
X[c]	X	X	X	X		X	X	X	X					New Zealand
s	X	X	X	X				X	X					Nicaragua
	X	X	X	X		X	X	X	X					Niger
	X		X	X	X	X		X	X					Nigeria
X[c]	X	X	X	X	X	X	X	X	X					Norway

States	(1)	(2)	(3)	(4)	(5)	(6)	(7)	(8)	(9)	(10)	(11)	(12)	(13)	(14)
Oman							X							
Pakistan					X	X		X		X		X	s	
Panama	X	X	X	X	X	X	s	X		X	X	X		
Papua New Guinea					X			X		X		X		
Paraguay	X	X						s		X	X	X		
Peru	X	X[a]	X		X[b]	X	X			X	X	X		
Philippines	X	X[a]	X		X	X	X	X	X	X	X	X		
Poland	X	X[a]	X		X	X	X	X	X	X	X	X	X	X
Portugal	X	X	X	X	X					X	X		s	
Qatar						X	X	X		s				
Republic of Korea	X	X[a]	X		X			X		X	X	X		
Republic of Moldova	X	X			X			X	X	X	X	X		
Romania	X	X	X	X	X	X		X	X	X	X	X	X	X
Russian Federation	X	X	X		X[b]	X	X	X	X	X	X	X	X	
Rwanda	X	X			X	X	s	X	X	X				
Saint Kitts and Nevis							X			X	X			
Saint Lucia					X		s			X	X		X	
Saint Vincent & Grenadines	X	X	X		X	X		X	X	X	X			
Samoa										X	X			X
San Marino	X	X	X							X				
Sao Tome and Principe							X			X				
Saudi Arabia								X						
Senegal	X	X[a]	X		X[b]	X	X	X		X	X	X		
Seychelles	X	X	X		X	X		X		X	X	X	X	
Sierra Leone					X		s			X	X	X	X	
Singapore										X	X			
Slovakia	X	X	X		X	X		X	X	X	X	X		
Slovenia	X	X[a]	X	X	X	X		X	X	X	X	X	X	
Solomon Islands	X				X					X		X		
Somalia	X	X	X		X	X	s			s				
South Africa	s	s			s					s	s	s	s	X
Spain	X	X[a]	X	X	X			X		X	X	X		X
Sri Lanka	X	X[a]			X	X		X		X	X		X	s
Sudan	X	X	X		X	X	X			X				
Suriname	X	X	X		X	X				X	X			
Swaziland					X					s		X	X	
Sweden	X	X[a]	X	X	X[b]			X		X	X	X	X	X
Switzerland	X	X[a]		X	X					X		s		
Syrian Arab Rep.	X	X			X	X	X	X		X				
Tajikistan										X	X			
Thailand										X	X	X		
Togo	X	X	X		X	X	X	X		X	X			

Column legend:

- (15) *Convention against Torture and other Cruel, Inhuman or Degrading Treatment or Punishment*
- (16) *Slavery Convention of 1926*
- (17) *1953 Protocol amending the 1926 Convention*
- (18) *Slavery Convention of 1926 as amended*
- (19) *Supplementary Convention on the Abolition of Slavery, the Slave Trade, and Institutions and Practices Similar to Slavery*
- (20) *Convention for the Suppression of the Traffic in Persons and of the Exploitation of the Prostitution of others*
- (21) *Convention on the Reduction of Statelessness*
- (22) *Convention relating to the Status of Stateless Persons*
- (23) *Convention relating to the Status of Refugees*
- (24) *Protocol relating to the Status of Refugees*
- (25) *Convention on the rights of migrant workers and the members of their families*

(15)	(16)	(17)	(18)	(19)	(20)	(21)	(22)	(23)	(24)	(25)	(26)	(27)	(28)	States
														Oman
			X	X	X									Pakistan
X	s							X	X					Panama
			X					X	X					Papua New Guinea
X								X	X					Paraguay
X				s				X	X					Peru
X			X	X	X		s	X	X	s				Philippines
X[c]	X			X	X			X	X					Poland
X[c]	X			X	X			X	X					Portugal
														Qatar
					X		X	X	X					Republic of Korea
														Republic of Moldova
X	X	X	X	X	X			X	X					Romania
X[c]			X	X	X			X	X					Russian Federation
								X	X					Rwanda
														Saint Kitts and Nevis
	X	X	X	X										Saint Lucia
	X	X	X	X										Saint Vincent & Grenadines
								X	X					Samoa
					X									San Marino
							X	X						Sao Tome and Principe
			X	X										Saudi Arabia
X	X		X	X	X			X	X					Senegal
X	X			X	X			X	X	X				Seychelles
s			X	X				X	X					Sierra Leone
				X	X									Singapore
X	X			X	X			X	X					Slovakia
X[c]	X			X	X			X	X					Slovenia
	X	X	X	X										Solomon Islands
X								X	X					Somalia
s	X	X	X		X									South Africa
X[c]	X	X	X	X	X			X	X					Spain
X			X	X	X									Sri Lanka
s	X		X	X				X	X					Sudan
	X			X				X	X					Suriname
	X								X					Swaziland
X[c]	X	X	X	X		X	X	X	X					Sweden
X[c]	X	X	X	X			X	X	X					Switzerland
	X	X	X	X	X									Syrian Arab Rep.
								X	X					Tajikistan
														Thailand
X[c]	X	X	X	X	X			X	X					Togo

States	International Covenant on Economic, Social and Cultural Rights (1)	International Covenant on Civil and Political Rights (2)	Optional Protocol to the International Covenant on Civil and Political Rights (3)	Second Optional Protocol to the International Covenant on Civil and Political Rights aiming at the abolition of the death penalty (4)	International Convention on the Elimination of All Forms of Racial Discrimination (5)	International Convention on the Suppression and Punishment of the Crime of Apartheid (6)	International Convention against Apartheid in Sports (7)	Convention on the Prevention and Punishment of the Crime of Genocide (8)	Convention on the Non-Applicability of Statutory Limitations to War Crimes and Crimes against Humanity (9)	Convention on the Rights of the Child (10)	Convention on the Elimination of All Forms of Discrimination against Women (11)	Convention on the Political Rights of Women (12)	Convention on the Nationality of Married Women (13)	Convention on Consent to Marriage, Minimum Age for Marriage and Registration of Marriages (14)
Tonga					X			X						
Trinidad and Tobago	X	X	X		X	X	X			X	X	X	X	X
Tunisia	X	X^a			X	X	X	X	X	X	X	X	X	X
Turkey					s			X		X	X	X		
Turkmenistan					X					X				
Tuvalu														
Uganda	X				X		X			X	X		X	
Ukraine	X	X^a	X		X^b	X	X	X	X	X	X	X		X
United Arab Emirates					X	X								
United Kingdom of Great Britain and Northern Ireland	X	X^a			X			X		X	X	X		X
United Republic of Tanzania	X	X			X	X	X	X		X	X	X	X	
United States of America	s	X^a			X			X			s	X		s
Uruguay	X	X	X	X	X^b		X	X		X	X	s	s	
Uzbekistan										X				
Vanuatu										X				
Venezuela	X	X	X	X	X	X	X	X		X	X	X	X	X
Viet Nam	X	X			X	X		X	X	X	X			
Yemen	X	X			X	X**	s	X	X	X	X	X		X
Yugoslavia (Serbia and Montenegro)	X	X	s		X	X	X	X	X	X	X	X	X	X
Zaire	X	X	X		X	X	s	X		X	X	X		
Zambia	X	X	X		X	X	X			X	X	X	X	
Zimbabwe	X	X^a			X	X	X	X		X	X			
TOTAL NUMBER OF STATES PARTIES	131	128	80	24	141	99	58	115	39	174	135	104	64	43
Signatures not followed by ratification	3	3	4	5	7	1	28	3	1	11	8	5	9	7

X Ratification, accession, approval, notification or succession, acceptance or definitive signature.
s Signature not yet followed by ratification.
*Ratification, accession, approval, notification or succession, acceptance or definitive signature which have been given only by the former German Democratic Republic before the reunification.
**Ratification, accession, approval, notification or succession, acceptance or definitive signature which have been given only by the former Republic of Yemen.

(15) Convention against Torture and other Cruel, Inhuman or Degrading Treatment or Punishment	(16) Slavery Convention of 1926	(17) 1953 Protocol amending the 1926 Convention	(18) Slavery Convention of 1926 as amended	(19) Supplementary Convention on the Abolition of Slavery, the Slave Trade, and Institutions and Practices Similar to Slavery	(20) Convention for the Suppression of the Traffic in Persons and of the Exploitation of the Prostitution of others	(21) Convention on the Reduction of Statelessness	(22) Convention relating to the Status of Stateless Persons	(23) Convention relating to the Status of Refugees	(24) Protocol relating to the Status of Refugees	(25) Convention on the rights of migrant workers and the members of their families	(26)	(27)	(28)	States
														Tonga
X[c]			X	X			X							Trinidad and Tobago
X[c]	X	X	X	X			X							Tunisia
								X	X					Turkey
														Turkmenistan
								X	X					Tuvalu
X			X	X			X	X	X					Uganda
X			X	X	X									Ukraine
														United Arab Emirates
X[d]	X	X	X	X		X	X	X	X					United Kingdom of Great Britain and Northern Ireland
			X	X				X	X					United Republic of Tanzania
X	X	X	X	X					X					United States of America
X[c]	s								X					Uruguay
														Uzbekistan
														Vanuatu
X[c]					X				X					Venezuela
														Viëtnam
X			X		X**			X**	X**					Yemen
X[c]	X	X	X	X	X		X	X	X					Yugoslavia (Serbia and Montenegro)
				X				X	X					Zaire
	X		X	X			X	X	X					Zambia
								X	X					Zimbabwe
85	75	56	91	114	70	18	42	122	120	3				TOTAL NUMBER OF STATES PARTIES
15	6	0	1	3	4	4	7	0	0	4				Signatures not followed by ratification

[a]Declaration recognizing the competence of the Human Rights Committee under Article 41 of the International Covenant on Civil and Political Rights.

[b]Declaration recognizing the competence of the Committee on the Elimination of Racial Discrimination under Article 14 of the International Convention on the Elimination of All Forms of Racial Discrimination.

[c]Declarations recognizing the competence of the Committee against Torture under Articles 21 and 22 of the Convention against Torture and Other Cruel, Inhuman or Degrading Treatment or Punishment.

[d]Declaration under Article 21 only.

INDEX

CONVENTION, 11
  See also TREATY
CORROBORATION, 94
COURT
  Equality before, 44
  Competent, independent, impartial ICCPR
    14(1), 4, 45–46, 88
  Special/military, 45
  Right to appear in person before, ICCPR
    14(3) *(d)* 48
COVENANT ICCPR, 13
  Articles 1–27,16–66, 187–194
  Articles 28–53, 195–202
  ICESCR, 13, 58, 178–186
CRUEL PUNISHMENT
  ICCPR 7, 28
  definition of, 29

D

DEATH PENALTY
  ICCPR 6, 24
  State sanctioned killings, 25–26
  UN Safeguards guaranteeing protection
    of the rights of those facing the death
    penalty, 26
  Abolitionist countries, 26
  See also EXECUTION, ARBITRARY ARREST AND
    DISAPPEARANCE
  Optional Protocol 2, 26
DEATH SQUADS, 28
DEBT
  No imprisonment for, ICCPR 11, 40
DEBT BONDAGE, 33
DECLARATION, 11
  UDHR, 13, 62, 129, 173–177
DEGRADING TREATMENT
  ICCPR 7, 29–30
DEMOCRACY
  UDHR 21 & ICCPR 25, 61–62
DENUNCIATION, 12
DEROGATION, 12
  Non-derogable rights, 23, 25, 29, 32, 40, 50
DETENTION
  arbitrary ICCPR 9, 34
  secret places/ghost houses, 37, 86
  detained persons, rights of ICCPR 10, 39
  Standard Minimum Rules on the
    Treatment of Prisoners, 78, 222–235
  Juveniles, *see* Beijing Rules
  Disabled 20
DISAPPEARANCE, 33–39
  ICCPR 9, 33–34
  UN Declaration on the Protection of All
    Persons from Enforced Disappearance,
    36

  14 point programme for the Prevention of
    Disappearances, 36–38
  Habeas corpus, 35
  Vienna II.62, 167
DISCRIMINATION
  ICCPR 2, 17–20
  Racial, definition of, 19
  CERD, 19–20
  ICCPR 3, 20–22
  CEDAW, 21–22
  Convention against Discrimination in
    Education, 64
  ICCPR 24, 60
  ICCPR 26, 62
  Declaration on Race and Racial Prejudice,
    62–63
  Declaration on the Elimination of All Forms
    of Intolerance and of Discrimination
    based on Religion or Belief, 52

E

E-MAIL, 126–127, 279–281
ECONOMIC AND SOCIAL COUNCIL (ECOSOC), 8–9,
  123, 128, 132
EDUCATION
  Convention against Discrimination in, 64
  in promoting human rights, 109, 114
  Vienna II.78–82, 169–170
ELECTIONS
  Action plan for monitoring human rights
    during, 118–120
EMERGENCY
  State of, ICCPR 4, 5, 12, 22–23
ENQUIRY
  Commission of, 74, 116–117, 154–155
EQUALITY
  Definition of, 3
  Women and men, ICCPR 3, 20–22
  See also WOMEN
  before the courts/of arms, 45
  before the law, 62
  in marriage, 59
EUROPEAN
  Convention for the Protection of Human
    Rights and Fundamental Freedoms,
    142–144
  Court of Human Rights, 143
  Commission of Human Rights, 143
EVIDENCE
  what is, 93–98
  how to gather, 95
  Corroboration of, 94, 99
EXECUTION
  Arbitrary/Summary, Definition of, 26–27
  Judicial, *see* DEATH PENALTY

Principles on the effective prevention and
investigations of extra-legal, arbitrary
and summary executions, 27
Superior orders, no defence, 28
EXHIBITS
definition, 107
how to keep, 107
EXPERT
Statements of, 106–107
ILO Committee of, 140–141
EXPRESSION
Freedom of, ICCPR 19, 19, 53–54
restrictions on, 54
EXPULSION, 42
EXTRADITION, 42

F

FAIR HEARING
ICCPR 14, 44–45
Minimum guarantees for, 45
FAMILY
Right to found, ICCPR 23, 58–59
FIREARMS
Basic Principles on the use of, 25, 77,
243–246
FOLLOW-UP
Importance of, 86, 93
FORCE
Proportionate use of, 79
Code of conduct for LEOS, 77, 236–242
Basic Principles on the use of, 25, 77,
243–246
FORCED LABOUR
Definition of, 33
ICCPR 8, 31–33
FORENSIC ANTHROPOLOGY, 74

G

GENDER *See also* WOMEN
Gender-based violence, 21
Traditional attitudes, 21
Vienna I.18, 153
GENEVA
Declaration of, 70
Conventions, Common Article 3, 78–79
GENOCIDE
Definition of, 64
Convention on, 64
ICCPR 27, 63–66
GOOD OFFICES, 125–126
Judicial, *see* DEATH PENALTY
Principles on the effective prevention and
investigation of extra-legal, arbitrary
and summary executions, 27–28

H

HABEAS CORPUS
Definition of, 35–36
ICCPR 9(4), 34
HOSPITALS
Monitoring, 90
HUMAN RIGHT
definition, 1
inalienable, 2
universal, 2, 18
indivisible, 6, 23
HUMAN RIGHTS COMMITTEE (ICCPR)
General comments, 14
HUMAN RIGHTS NETWORK
Setting up, 68–69
Networking, 68, 90–91, 274–278
HUMAN RIGHTS MONITORING
Inherent danger in a repressive State, 84
Why monitor, 85
What to monitor, 85–91
HUMAN RIGHTS PROMOTION, *see* CHAPTER 5,
108–121
HUMAN RIGHTS VIOLATION
Definition, 4
How to manage, 91–93

I

INDIGENOUS PEOPLES
Definition of, 65
ICCPR 27, 63
ILO 169: Convention concerning Indigenous
and Tribal Peoples in Independent
Countries, 65, 262–273
Vulnerability of, 91
Vienna: I.20, 154
II.28–32, 162–163
INHUMAN TREATMENT OR PUNISHMENT
Definition of, 29
ICCPR 7, 28–31
INNOCENCE
Presumption of, ICCPR 14(2), 46–47
INQUEST, 28
INTER-AMERICAN COURT, 144–146
Commission, 144
American Convention on Human Rights,
144
American Declaration on the Rights and
Duties of Man, 144
INTERNATIONAL COMMUNITY, 4, 120
INTERNATIONAL COURT OF JUSTICE, 9
INTERNATIONAL LABOUR ORGANISATION, 10,
139–141
INTERNATIONAL REPORTING AND COMPLAINTS
PROCEDURES, 122–147
INVESTIGATION